Mosley: The Facts

by

Oswald Mosley

Mosley: The Facts

Oswald Mosley

Copyright © 2019 Sanctuary Press Ltd

ISBN-13: 978-1-913176-13-6

Sanctuary Press Ltd
71-75 Shelton Street
Covent Garden
London
WC2H 9JQ

www.sanctuarypress.com
Email: info@sanctuarypress.com

Contents

Oswald Mosley - Leader of British Union 1935.

Foreword

This is a book about Oswald Mosley, one of the most controversial figures of his age. It gives facts which the reader may verify for himself, and so form his own judgement.

What is the point of studying Mosley at all? Have not the rulers of the present system - the Establishment as they have come to be called - managed to exclude him for good? The answer to that question is found in another question; whether you believe the present system can last? If the answer is no, Mosley will be needed in the future because in that event he will be the only man who has been consistently right and who has proved his reliability and strength of character in the storms he has withstood. History shows that at such a moment of crisis the British people turn quickly and decisively to the man who has shown himself wise enough and strong enough to do what has to be done.

Mosley long ago came to the deliberate conclusion that the system could not last. He believed that the economic system was obsolete because it dated from the days when Britain had the industrial monopoly of the world, and he believed that the present political system was incapable of the rapid action required to put through the great changes that were necessary. This opinion was not reached hastily, or with the impatience sometimes ascribed to him. He worked within the old parties steadily and loyally through eleven years of parliamentary life; he tried his utmost to get anything effective done within both the Conservative and Labour parties. He became a minister, and did not resign until not only his own plan for dealing with the pre-war unemployment problem was rejected, but it also became clear that both great parties refused to lift a finger to deal with this cruel problem which, he was convinced, was easily soluble. Then, and not before, when all means of ordinary action were excluded, he launched a new movement in fundamental challenge to the old parties and the old system. He came to that decision not as a crank or an impossibilist with no practical achievement to his credit; he certainly could not be called a disappointed man. Until that moment he was the political success story of the age. His electoral record (Chapter 12) is unique in modern politics for its extraordinary sequence of successes. Has any man in modern times succeeded so often, or in such diverse circumstances, in converting a British electorate to his opinion? - so long as he remained within the limits of the possible, which are, of course, the boundaries of the present system until that system fails. From his second election fight at Harrow, when he turned a ten thousand Conservative majority into a seven and a half thousand majority for his candidature as an Independent in the face of the whole of the Conservative machine, to his triumphant fight against Neville Chamberlain in Birmingham and the subsequent rout of the Conservative Party in that long established stronghold of the Chamberlain family, no man in modern politics has reached anything approaching his record of success in winning the favour of the electorate.[1]

Nor was he disappointed in his parliamentary career; he was not only universally acclaimed as an orator by parliament and press (Chapters 2 and 5) but was given the most important post in a government that any man of his age had held for about half a century. No one, therefore, can suggest that Mosley was either disappointed, or without a well proved record of success to his credit, when he pulled out from the old world and challenged the old system. He then turned his back on the seats of power and went to the streets and homes of the people to find new men and new measures, because he was convinced, after a close experience of the existing order, that a new movement was necessary to save Britain in a crisis which he regarded as sooner or later inevitable.

---

1   That record is printed in Chapter 13 of this volume together with the remarkable results gained by the new movement not only before, but also since the war in tests of its electoral strength by the inexpensive method of municipal contests; most of our people have been kept in entire ignorance of these events by the press boycott.

Foreword

That name was fascist in name and in character, and he never for a moment denies it. But he may be permitted his own definition of fascism and not that of his enemies. He saw in fascism the revolution of the European spirit against both money power and communism. Above all he saw in it the urge to action; the sole means available in the pre-war period to do what he believed was necessary to be done. The principles for the fascism he created in Britain were different in certain vital respects from those of the fascist and national socialist movements on the continent. The attitude on racial questions was naturally different, because the British Empire consisted of many diverse races.

His movement was not totalitarian and did not aim at dictatorship. But certain vital principles of his creed had enough in common with the movements of men who had, long previously, founded fascist and national socialist parties on the continent, to make it in his view dishonest not to accept the name fascist. These principles, in crude summary, were: sufficient power of action to put through the great changes which the age of science made necessary, and the creation from the mass of the people of a popular but dedicated movement to challenge effectively both the exploitation of the money power and the corruption of communism; finally to establish a system which could carry out the people's will in an ordered and persistent movement to higher forms of living. Mosley was also impelled in a practical sphere to employ fascist methods against the red violence which had stopped public meetings and brought free speech to an end in many areas of Britain, as it had done previously in various countries on the continent (see Chapter 5, *Violence and the origin of the Blackshirt Movement*).

Impartial observers admitted that Mosley's fight against that squalid and brutal tyranny, as well as the passionate conviction which his creed inspired, evoked from English youth an enthusiasm which has not otherwise been seen in time of peace. Mosley's resolution, capacity to lead men and power of organisation restored free speech to Britain, with the result that no disorder of any kind occurred at his great indoor meetings for three years before the war (Chapter 5).

Since the war he has admitted that certain errors were made; as he put it "a man who has lived a life-time without learning anything is simply a fool." He ascribes the mistakes to a desire for action at all costs, and says it is possible to purchase too dearly even the rapid action which is now so vitally necessary. That is why, in his thinking since the war - which has "passed beyond both fascism and the old democracy to meet the new facts of a new age" - he has introduced careful safeguards to preserve individual liberty and the basic freedoms (his study of this question is entitled *The Problem of Power*). He sees the origin of fascist faults in the right and natural desire of all dynamic men to do in a hurry what urgently needs to be done. But the disaster to which this can lead, when certain basic decencies are ignored, leaves deeply engrained in his post-war consciousness the lesson that the structure of the state must contain impregnable safeguards for liberty as well as the principle of continuing dynamism. As he put it in his *European Situation* (1950): "We reconcile the old conflicts and begin to achieve, today in thought and tomorrow in deed, the union of authority with liberty, action with thought, decision with discussion, power with responsibility, vigour with duty, strength with kindness, and service of the people with the attainment of ever higher forms of life."

It was always something of a paradox that a "fascist" who was clearly pledged long before the war never to imprison anyone without trial, should himself have been imprisoned for some five years without trial during the war by a "democratic" government.

Chapter 6 of this book exposes once and for all and with detailed evidence the preposterous lie that Mosley could ever have contemplated any form of disloyalty to his country. His position in the war was, in fact identical with that of a long line of distinguished English statesmen in similar circumstances, ranging from Lord Chatham to Lloyd George. Those who believe

Foreword

that an English statesman can be excluded forever through the
transient unpopularity caused by opposition to an unnecessary
war, would find their error quickly corrected by a brief reading of
history. But, admittedly, Mosley has so far been excluded by the
combination of old party leaders and can probably be excluded
indefinitely by the old party machines and the money power on
which they rest, unless enough happens to convince the British
people that a great change is necessary.

Much has occurred already; many of the Mosley prophecies
have already been fulfilled. Few will now deny that the result of
the war has been the loss of the British Empire in any terms of
reality, and the establishment of Russian power together with
the clear menace of world communism. Mosley's belief that the
war of 1939 must result in these two disasters was, of course, the
persistently repeated reason of his opposition to that war. In that
matter his view has already been proved right with a weight of
evidence that overwhelms all contradiction. A long series of his
other published opinions have, also, already been proved right, as
many quotations in this book will show.

For instance, he read correctly the strategic and political effect
of the H-Bomb some four years before the reaching of the same
conclusion by the established favourite of the present system,
which was hailed as a stroke of "genius" by the world's leading
commentators (see Chapter 9). It was characteristic of the
present English situation that Mosley's *European Situation* - in
which recent events were forecast with an almost mathematical
precision - was inhibited from any very wide circulation among
the English people by the closely organised boycott of press,
radio, television and other vested interests which owe their power
to the influence of money. It is wrong when, in practical effect,
opinions are prevented from being heard in a democracy which
is supposed to rest on the principles of free speech; it is also, a
considerable loss when the democracy is thereby prevented for
several years from hearing a correct appraisal of a situation in
which time is invaluable. We are reaching a point when nothing

can be heard in Britain except the conventional errors of a slow thinking and slower moving establishment of vested interests. Britain is thus in danger of getting the worst of both worlds; the rigidity of tyranny's closed system, without dictatorship's capacity for rapid decision when action is clearly necessary.

The greatest danger will arise if Mosley's central theme should prove correct without the British people being made aware of it in good time. For this is a matter in which timely action can greatly reduce the suffering which catastrophe brings, and can preserve resources for the building of a new system which delay can lose. Mosley has staked his whole political life, from the time of his resignation from the government, on his conviction that sooner or later an economic crisis in Britain was inevitable, and that only a change of system can meet it. If he is wrong in this he will be proved wrong throughout in his main thesis, and he has always recognised that he will not be saved from the consequences of that error even by the fact that his friends can already claim that he has been proved so consistently right in so many things. But the fact that in other matters he has so often been right provides some additional warning that his view of the economic situation may also prove to be correct. Already many symptoms suggest that the events he envisaged in his resignation speech, and in innumerable other speeches and writings, are now slowly gathering momentum, after delays which were caused by a war and two armament booms. He has always refused to name any date because so many accidents can affect the chronology, but in the next few years we should know whether in this last and gravest matter he is right or wrong.

The chief development in his thinking since the war - apart from his suggested changes in the structure of the state to reconcile action with liberty, already mentioned - is to be found in his decisive movement from a solution within the Empire, which he advocated before the war, to a solution within a completely united Europe; this he believes to be the only possibility since the war so adversely affected the Imperial situation. He was always a European; in fact, he appears to be the first modern statesman who advocated a united Europe (see Chapter 9, *Pre-war Speeches*). But he believed before the war a solution of Britain's economic difficulties could be found within the Empire. Directly after the war he came to the conclusion that the Union of Europe was not only a political and strategic necessity if the culture of three thousand years was to survive, but also an absolute economic necessity for Great Britain. The result of this thinking was the birth of his concepts: Europe a Nation, and European Socialism.

This book cannot begin to present a complete, ordered and consistent account of his doctrine. For that the reader must turn to Mosley's post-war writings: *The Alternative, Mosley Policy and Debate, The Problem of Power European Socialism*, etc., etc.[2] The object of the present volume is not to analyse his philosophy of life or political programme, but to present some picture of this man; extracts from his writings and speeches are printed to give some idea of his mind and spirit as a complement to his record of action, achievement and sacrifice for his beliefs. Quite incidentally, also, this book provides some picture of Mosley's opponents, although his more astringent references to them have deliberately been omitted. For it is difficult to reconcile the extremes of their eulogies in his youth, when they thought he was on their side, with the extremes of disparagement which he has suffered from the lesser spirits among them. The contrast becomes the more glaring to anyone who studies closely the writings and speeches of Mosley in the earlier period, and compares them with his analytical thought and creative ideas in recent years. He obviously has a much abler mind, and more developed character, in his maturity than in his youth; this is usually the case in men who work hard, even without the paradoxical advantages which his career afforded. Perhaps the intensive reading and reflection of prison years made their contribution; he has since said that all statesmen would do well to retire for a period of intensive re-education in the forties, as Plato suggested in *The Republic*.

---

2   Chief pre-war writings were "*The Greater Britain*", "*100 Questions Answered*", "*Tomorrow We Live*", also immediately after the war "*My Answer*".

He has thus emerged from an extreme diversity of life's vicissitudes not only with a character proved by the tests of action, achievement and adversity but with an intellectual equipment which covers the whole range of politics, and enters spheres which are usually beyond the range of politicians, the reader will find some brief extracts from his ideas on these subjects in Chapter 10.

After early experience of administration and admitted success in that sphere, followed by a record of will, energy and endurance in a longer struggle and harder personal ordeal than any living statesman has had to face, he came to the new problem of Europe with a fresh and continually creative mind, a complete command of the main European languages and a very wide knowledge of the leading personalities and intimate character of the European peoples.

This man now emerges with experience behind him, and creative energy within him, to face a future of boundless possibilities if England should again feel the necessity for a great decision. He was born on November 16th, 1896, and is thus at the present time nearly six years younger than Sir Winston Churchill when he became Prime minister for the first time, some fourteen years younger than Dr. Adenauer when he took high political office for the first time at the nadir of Germany's fortunes, and some sixteen years younger than Clemenceau when he formed the government which saved France. Mosley has more than time enough to perform his service to England and to Europe if destiny should so decide.

One thing is certain is that his war-time unpopularity will be no impediment to his capacity for future achievement. In fact it may be said almost dogmatically that no man has ever attained the heights of popularity in England if he has not previously experienced the depths of unpopularity. In a strange instinctive fashion this seems to be one of the tests which the English people apply to their ultimate favourites. Mosley's electoral record at least proves his natural popularity among them, except on the one occasion when a prescience of disaster placed him in an impossible position. And already Mosley's packed and enthusiastic meetings in the spring and autumn of 1956 (Chapter 9) at a time when other politicians could draw no audiences at all, indicate a tendency much more definite than a turn of the tide. Those who think and feel in the mass of the people are beginning to ask questions concerning him which continually increase in interest and persistence as the situation gathers menace.

As the results of this disastrous war become clearer, more and more people ask: "Was he not right about the war?" - "Did not the destruction of Germany lead to the triumph of Russia and the menace of communism?" Even Sir Winston Churchill stated that the Russians would have conquered all Europe after the war if American scientists had not happened to invent the H bomb. Was not Mosley right to oppose the war which would have destroyed all Europe and Great Britain, except for this accident which no-one could foresee? Was he not right to stand for proper armament before the war, when most of his opponents stood for disarmament, and to oppose a war without arms to fight? Was he not right when he said that even a victorious war would weaken Britain and greatly injure the Empire? Did we not then throw away the resources which we needed to house our people and raise our standard of life? Was he not right to stand for the development of the Empire instead of entanglements in foreign war? Was Mosley so wrong to stand for peace in 1939 when he had fought for England in the air and in the trenches in 1914? Was he wrong to resign from the government and found a new movement when he could get nothing done for the unemployed? Is he wrong now to stand for a complete union of Europe - Europe a Nation - and to say that Britain should lead in uniting instead of dividing Europe?

The war he opposed has weakened Britain, and increased the strength of America and Russia. Is not the union of Europe the only way back to the greatness of the British people? Are not his new ideas since the war worth discussing: ideas like European Socialism, which means the building of a new civilisation in Europe-Africa with its own raw materials and markets and the consequent ability to build up its own high standard of life free from world chaos - the workers' ownership of developed industries instead of bureaucratic nationalisation, combined with much freer private enterprise in new industries - a fair reward for skill and effort instead of reducing all to a dead level - taxation of spending instead of earnings, of the idle instead of the hard-working etc., etc.? These are some of the questions asked about Mosley, as a growing belief that he was right after all leads more and more people to enquire what sort of a man he is.

It is difficult for them to know what he is like because the great vested interests which control the system keep him out of radio and television. The old parties will not give an opportunity to their challenger, despite all their talk of free speech. The great newspapers controlled by the money power seldom give him any mention except savage abuse, though the provincial press, as always remains fair (Chapter 13). There is nothing surprising in all this. Only a complete political innocent would be surprised by the treatment of Mosley. Any real man is bound to be assailed like that, and the people may thus recognise their man when they need him. Any real man who quickly reacts to a situation which require a great change is bound to be treated like that. Such men have been so attacked all through history. Universal abuse (and almost invariably prison at some time as well) is always their experience right up to the hour of their final victory. These revolutionary figures stand for the interests of the people against a corrupt, decadent and dying system. Naturally the defenders of that system, who live and grow fat on its very rottenness, dislike men who challenge their whole position root and branch. The volume and strength of the abuse of Mosley is the measure of his value to England and the people. The fact that he has stood firm through the storm is the proof of his character. In an age of failure and betrayal, we need, above all, proved character.

Foreword

Such men learn to guide great nations through the storms of destiny during the storms which previously beat on their own heads. Their minds and spirits are hardened and tempered, and their judgement cooled and clarified by such experiences, which are unknown to those who have chosen easier ways.

So throughout history has fate discovered and trained the men of new ideas, of faith and character, when the failure of the old system has made great changes necessary.

If crisis come to Britain this is the man who will then be necessary to Britain and to Europe. He will come to that task by reason of ideas which have been proved right, and by virtue of a character which has stood the test. We shall then need ideas which are new, and a character which is strong. Mosley has both.

Preface

Mosley has one great advantage in comparison with most pioneers who believe a great change is necessary in an existing system and long established order. He was an outstanding success within that system, was greatly eulogised by its press and literature and was hailed as the coming man by all the chief figures in all parties of the Establishment. When, therefore, he came to the deliberate conclusion that a real change was needed, it was difficult to give him the customary treatment of dismissal as a lunatic either harmless or criminal. So many words of an almost universal praise could not be lightly swallowed. The silence treatment became more effective than abuse, although any promising occasion for the latter method was eagerly seized. It is particularly instructive to study in the next four chapters of this book what was said about Mosley when he was the hope of the system, and to contrast it with the treatment of him when he became challenger of the Establishment.

A glance through his writings and speeches over the years will clearly indicate to any impartial and competent critic that his mind is far more developed and powerful today than at the time when he was favoured by so many eulogies. So we are led to a conclusion which appears unavoidable. The attitude of the great interests to a man has no relation to what he is in reality. It depends entirely on the question whether they think he can be used for their purposes or not. In time of crisis many thinking people will begin to study these things who had previously been interested in other matters. We hope this book will help them to discover certain facts for themselves and to form the judgement which will then be necessary.

Chapter 1

Mosley In Parliament

Mr. Speaker Lowther *later Lord Ullswater*: "On my left is Sir Oswald Mosley - who became a member of the House of Commons while I was presiding over that body. I think at that time he was the youngest member of the house and he very soon rose to distinction. I remember hearing his maiden speech and remarking to a friend that it was one of the most successful and brilliant I had ever heard in the House, and the promise he then gave is justified." - *Yea and Nay* describing a debate with the Duke of Northumberland.

(19.6.1923)

The Right Hon. J. Ramsay MacDonald, M.P., Prime Minister 1924 and 1929-1935: "I need not tell the electors of your great ability, your brilliance in debate and your comprehensive grasp of every phase of politics; I merely say to them 'We need Mosley in the House, he is one of our most brilliant young men. Free yourselves from the shackles of a worn-out tradition and return a man who has all the qualities of a great leader and the capacity for brilliant service to his party and the country.'"

(23.10.1924)

The Right Hon. Winston Churchill, M.P., Prime Minister 1940-1945 and 1951-1955 on the occasion of Sir Oswald Mosley's resignation speech in the House of Commons on May 28th, 1930: "I come to the speech of the Hon Member for Smethwick, a very remarkable speech and admirable in every way. It would be impossible to have given a more compendious account of the intricate matters with which he attempted to deal."

(28.5.1930)

The Right Hon. David Lloyd George, M.P., Prime Minister 1917-1922, on the same occasion: "We have listened to a very remarkable and powerful speech from the Hon. Member for Smethwick (Sir O. Mosley). He has put his case with remarkable lucidity and force."

(28.5.1930)

Colonel Joseph Wedgwood, M.P., A Labour Minister, and subsequently Father of the House, on the same occasion: "We have listened to one of the most eloquent and one of the most dangerous speeches I have ever heard in the House. No one who listened to it can deny that as he spoke he was converting member after Member in this House to his views. I watched the Liberal party. I watched the Conservative party. Man after man was saying to himself 'That is our leader.'"

(28.5.1930)

The Irish leader, *Joseph Devlin*, M.P. : "In the manner of its delivery, it was the best speech he had ever heard in the House."

(29.5.1930)

The Right Hon. John Wheatley, M.P., Minister of Health, and Leader of the Clydeside Labour group said Mosley was : " A man who was bound to play a brilliant part in British political history ... In his opinion he was one of the greatest and most hopeful figures that the Socialist movement had thrown up during the thirty years if its history."

(14.12.1926)

The Right Hon. J. Chuter Ede, M.P., Home Secretary in the Labour Government 1945-1951: "The alliance of Mr. Oswald Mosley, M.P. for Harrow, with the Labour party is another indication of the rallying of opinion to the side of the Government. Mr. Mosley possesses a brilliant wit, and is one of the few remaining members who can lash his opponents into a fury by the bitter jests that were common when Mr. Healy and Mr. Devlin were in their prime. No one doubts his sincerity, and he has, in addition to his sarcasm, a power of expressing great ideals eloquently that will make him a welcome recruit to the Labour benches."

(5.4.1934)

T. P. O'Connor, famous Irish Nationalist M.P., and leading journalist: "Young Oswald Mosley also made an excellent speech. I was very much afraid that his courage and his violent difference with his own party would have driven him out of the representation of so respectable a Tory constituency as Harrow; but he won a huge majority - a tribute to courageous honesty that one does not see too often in British politics."

(18.2.1923)

Dingle Foot, Liberal M.P., wrote : "He is one of the few post-war politicians with a real command of eloquence. Even in the far-off days when he sat as Independent member for Harrow, M.P.s would flock in from lobbies and smoking-room when the tape announced that 'Mosley was up.'

"I recently listened to a debate from the Visitors' Gallery. Next to me sat an ardent Conservative who persistently cheered the Opposition under his breath. After a time Sir Oswald rose to denounce the feebleness of the Government and the feebleness of all three established parties. When he sat down my neighbour drew a long breath and jerked his thumb towards the Conservative benches. 'Just fancy', he whispered, 'and we have been spending all these years looking for a Man over there.'"

(8.8.1931)

Chapter 2

Distinguished Opinion: Pre-War

Lord Chief Justice (Lord Hewart) said (summing up in the *Star* libel case, on 7th November, 1934, in which Mosley obtained damages of £5,000 for a suggestion that he intended a *coup d'etat*): "Do you, or do you not, believe him, whatever you may think of his opinions? Did it not appear to you that he is a public man of no mean courage, no little candour, and no little ability?"

George Bernard Shaw :- "Sir Oswald Mosley - a very interesting man to read just now; one of the few people who are writing and thinking about real things, and not about figments and phrases. You will hear something more of Sir Oswald before you are through with him. I know you (the Labour leaders) dislike him, because he looks like a man who has some physical courage and is going to do something; and that is a terrible thing. You instinctively hate him, because you do not know where he will land you. Instead of talking round and round political subjects and obscuring them with bunk verbiage without even touching them, and without understanding them, all the time assuming states of things which ceased to exist from twenty to six hundred and fifty years ago, he keeps hard down on the actual situation."

(3.12.1932)

Extract from *Inside Europe* by *John Gunther*, published January 1936. "...... He is probably the best orator in England. His personal magnetism is very great. He was competent enough intellectually to draw into his camp, before he turned fascist, some of the best minds in England..."

".....Of his intelligence, his magnetism, there was no doubt"

H. R. Knickerbocker - the celebrated American journalist - who had an almost unique experience of European politics: "He began to speak ... In two minutes he had succeeded in reducing the tumult to isolated cries ...His voice has an insistent quality, similar to the greatest Russian orator, Trotsky. The style of his opening sentences reminded me to Dr. Joseph Goebels, the best Nazi speaker. Towards the end, as the hostility of the audience more and more yielded, he worked into the passion of Adolf Hitler. He is decidedly a better speaker than Hitler. He is a least as good as Goebels. Englishmen who hate him, admit that he is the best people's orator in the British Isles."

John Scanlon, the well known Labour and Socialist journalist in his book, *The Decline and Fall of the Labour Party*, published October, 1932, gives this account of the Labour Party Conference in October, 1932, soon after Oswald Mosley resigned from the Government : "By the time Sir Oswald rose to make his speech, the conference had returned to normality, and the volume of cheering which greeted his rising showed the amazing hold he had acquired on the minds of the delegates. Next to the Prime Minister, he was the most popular man at the Conference, and for the first time all the dislike of the Right Wing had been transferred from Maxton to Sir Oswald. His speech was a masterly indictment of the Government and a clear lucid explanation of his own scheme...

Sir Oswald's vote was the biggest challenge ever delivered to the governing machine. But for the fact that the issue was regarded as a vote of confidence or no confidence in the Government, Sir Oswald's vote would have been very much bigger. Delegates who were weary of the Government's inactivity and would have liked to show their disapproval, hesitated to show the country that they had no confidence in their leaders...

In the Press and the labour Movement itself, the discussion now centred round the question of how long it would be before Sir Oswald became the Party Leader. Even without a crash in the

Party's fortunes it was easy to see that changes must come soon. The controllers of the party, mostly old men could not stay the inexorable march of time any more than ordinary mortals. No other leader was in sight. Mr Wheatley was gone. Mr Maxton had none of the pushful qualities which carry a man to leadership in Labour politics and nobody from the Trade Unions showed the slightest sign of being able to take charge. Therefore every prophet fixed on Sir Oswald as the next Party Leader. Even Socialists, who had no particular love for Sir Oswald, were saying nothing could stop it. All the prophets, however, had overlooked the one man who could stop it - Sir Oswald himself."[1]

Extract from *Beverley Nichols'* book, *Men Do Not Weep*, 1941: "I have heard many great speakers: Lloyd George at his fiery best, F. E. distilling the attar of his vitriol, Asquith floating most delectably over his Latin waves. I have heard none to touch Mosley. He had also considerable personal courage, and that indefinable quality that can only be called 'leadership'."

And from his *News of England*, 1938 : "The first attempt to murder Sir Oswald Mosley, leader of the British fascists, was made at Hull, in July 1936. On this occasion a man in the crowd, who escaped, fired a bullet which penetrated the windscreen of his car. This attempted murder is interesting for several reasons. Firstly because political assassination is a very rare phenomenon in British politics. Secondly, because it was entirely ignored by the press, of every shade of political opinion...."

"From 1934 onwards the violence has increased so rapidly that a recital of it would only be monotonous. The first attempt at murder, as we have seen came in 1936 at Hull, but there were many other occasions when his life was in danger. Very few of these occasions were ever reported, though now and then a paragraph would creep in, paying a grudging tribute to his

---

1   Oswald Mosley stopped it because he had no more faith in a party the majority of which upheld leaders, when they broke the pledges the party had made to the people on unemployment, until those leaders joined the Tories in the National Government of 1931. He left the Labour Party to found the new movement.

personal courage, while deploring his principles. One does not
need to be a fascist to wish to see fair play done even to one's
opponents. And the treatment of Sir Oswald Mosley, by the
British press, makes one wonder if 'fair play' is an expression
which, in these islands, is obsolete.

For Mosley, whether you regard him as a limb of Satan or a
potential saviour of this nation, is one of the three most dynamic
personalities in the Empire today. And the men he has inspired
are animated by something akin to religious faith.

Anybody who has ever gone to any of the smaller fascist meetings
... not the sensational meetings of the leader but the ordinary
gatherings of the rank and file ... will find himself in the presence
of men and women to whom this creed is a matter of life and
death. And that, whether we like it or not, is something new in
British politics.

What are the reasons for this advance ... of which you will not
read one word in the British press? One of them lies in the
personality of Mosley himself ... You would have realised you
were in the presence of a figure of tremendous importance. Some
will say a figure of great danger, others of great promise.

If you are interested you might read Mosley's own book, *The
Greater Britain*. Do what you like with it. Riddle it with criticism.
Laugh at it. But do not ignore it. For the views it sets forward are
held, with religious conviction, by thousands of Englishmen who
are prepared to die for them.

For he is the only man I know who has in him the qualities of
that hero for whom the country has waited so long, and waited
in vain."

Professor H. Laski, Chairman of the Labour party in 1946, wrote :

"He has obviously great qualities. As a speaker, he has charm and rhetorical gifts of a very high order. He knows how to debate; and he has the manner of the man born to play a part in the House of Commons. He has more than the gift of eloquence. He has courage and energy and enthusiasm. It took courage to cross the floor of the House; it took courage to risk his career by resigning from the Government ... He organises himself for the end he has in view with a relentless vigour it is impossible not to admire. Anyone who sees him with his followers cannot help but see he has great gifts of leadership. He makes his associates want to follow him."

(24 May 1930)

Sir William Morris, afterwards Lord Nuffield, the famous motor manufacturer, and Chairman in 1930 of the National Council of Industry, issued the following bulletin on the night of December 16, 1930:-

"There is one bright spot on the gloomy horizon, the forceful gesture of a young and virile section of the Labour Party. In Sir Oswald Mosley's Manifesto I see a ray of hope."

(17 Dec 1930)

The Right Hon. John Strachey, M.P., Secretary of State for war in Labour Government 1950-1951. In the dedication of a book, *Revolution by Reason* (1926).

"To O.M., who may one day do the things of which we dream."

Chapter 3

Distinguished Opinion Post-War

Heinrich Sanden writing in the German journal *Nation Europa* (May, 1954) :-

"Happy memories from a sad period are particularly unforgettable - and among them, for us Germans, is the fact that since 1945 Sir Oswald Mosley had been the first, and for a long time was the only Englishman, who spoke and wrote, in his own country, passionately and with clear vision for us Germans, without any regard to the burning hatred he thereby evoked.

His great book, *The Alternative*, published in 1947, is one of the most courageous and far-seeing books in the English language; it is one of those books to which one constantly returns, and is never laid aside without the greatest admiration for the mind of a statesman who points the way to a new future for Europe. The watchword 'Nation Europe' which later gave our review its name, was here formulated as a policy for the first time.

This fact alone makes Oswald Mosley a prophetic phenomenon and directing spirit in the otherwise confused thinking of our time.

The picture of this man cannot be too often brought before the German reader, who during this century has not frequently found friendship or understanding in England. In 1918 the youngest M.P., in 1929 a Minister; in 1930 resigning from the Government; since 1931 the founder of and fighter for his own political movement; during the war imprisoned for years, and since the war once again untiring in his struggle for the idea of a greater European unity - this is the outline of a character, whose destiny with others of this kind may be that greatness which only future generations can fully recognise."

Extract from *British Politics since 1900* by *D. C. Somervell*, (published 1950), the famous historian who produced the abridgment of Toynbee's *Study of History*.

"He was now the hero of the rank and file and was looked upon by many as the future leader of the Party. At the Annual Conference in 1930 a Resolution in favour of his policy was nearly carried against the Party Leaders. But Sir Oswald's patience was too easily exhausted. Some day, I suppose, posterity will have an impartial and discerning biography of this extraordinary man. Presumably he lost patience with the Parliamentary system, and he obviously lacked the 'team spirit' without which Parliamentary institutions will not work. Had he possessed that virtue he might quite conceivably be where Attlee is today."

The explanation of Mosley's conduct is contained in Mr. Somervell's next sentence.

"As the number of the unemployed rose, etc."

Mosley resigned because he was not permitted to deal with the unemployment which the Labour Party had pledged itself to tackle at the previous election. The warning he gave when he resigned as a young minister is coming true in the developing crisis, which was only postponed by two armament booms and a war.

Extract from *King George V : His Life And Reign*, by *Harold Nicolson* (published 1952)

"For the execution of his gigantic task Mr. Thomas had been accorded three gifted or prominent assistants, Mr. George Lansbury, Mr. Tom Johnston, and the new Chancellor of the Duchy of Lancaster, Sir Oswald Mosley. From the very outset it became apparent that the exuberant dynamism of the Chancellor of the Duchy was ill-attuned to the cheerful lethargy of the Lord Privy Seal. Having battled for months in the hope of interesting his chief in his schemes for the state-aided public works, Sir Oswald resigned his appointment in despair:-

'Sir Oswald Mosley', the King noted in his diary for May 24th, 1930 'gave up his seal of the Duchy of Lancaster, he having resigned the Chancellorship. Major Attlee was sworn as the Chancellor in his place.'

It was not long before Mr. Thomas also relinquished his task as Minister of Unemployment and restricted himself thereafter to the more sedative functions of the Secretary for the Dominions. The ordinary honest Socialist was distressed to observe that so little was being done to redeem the promises made at the election, whereas so much was being done to encourage the heresies of those deviationists who contended that employment or unemployment had less to do with capitalism than with trade cycles: and that these inhuman cycles were as tides, waning or waxing to the dictates of some occult economic moon. The feeling within the rank and file became manifest at the Annual Conference of the Labour Party held at Llandudno in October 1930. Mr. James Maxton brought forward a motion to the effect that 'This Conference views with alarm the failure of the Government to apply the bold unemployment policy outlined in *Labour and the Nation*. Mr. MacDonald, in a speech vibrant with emotion, was able to swing the Conference to his side. 'My friend,' he pleaded, in that wonderful voice that seemed to blend all the veracity of a Scottish engineer with all the self-pity of a Welsh revivalist, 'My friend, we are not on trial; it is the system under which we live. It has broken down, not only on this little island, it has broken down in Europe, in Asia, in America; it has broken down everywhere as it was bound to break down. And the cure, the new path, the new idea, is Organisation.'

"Sir Oswald Mosley, whose words had a great effect upon the Conference, replied that it was this very organisation that he had sought so desperately to obtain from Mr. J. H. Thomas and the Cabinet; that it was this very incapacity to organise firmly that had convinced him that the present Cabinet were too ignorant, too lazy, or too timid, to take the drastic measures by which alone the rising wave of unemployment could be checked. The Llandudno Conference remained loyal to Mr. MacDonald; yet those who were present were well aware that a gulf had been disclosed between the leaders and the ranks. Significantly enough, it was Sir Oswald Mosley who at the conclusion of the Conference was elected to the National Executive; not Mr. J. H. Thomas.

On his retirement from the Duchy of Lancaster. Sir Oswald Mosley had prepared a formidable indictment of Mr. Thomas, together with a memorandum setting out his own ideas as to the action that ought immediately to be taken. This Memorandum was, on January 27th, 1931, considered at a special meeting of the Parliamentary Labour Party, held in Committee Room 14 of the House of Commons. The speech which Sir Oswald delivered on that occasion was valorous and forceful. Had he not, encouraged by cheers with which he had been greeted, insisted on putting the issue to a vote - thereby arousing all the inhibitions of party loyalties and discipline - he might well have rallied the bulk of the meeting to his side. As it was, Mr. Arthur Henderson was able, by deft compliments and appeals to solidarity and commonsense to undo some at least of the damage that Sir Oswald had occasioned. Yet had the latter been less easily swept away by his own impatience, he might have forced the government to accept his terms. His error, at that critical moment, deprived him of an unrepeated opportunity; and the country of a great Parliamentarian."

His *impatience* was of course his refusal to betray the unemployed.

Mrs. Beatrice Webb's Diary (published 1952).

Mrs Beatrice Webb wrote of Mosley when he first joined the labour party in 1924. :-

"We have made the acquaintance of the most brilliant man in the House of Commons - Oswald Mosley ...

Here is the perfect politician who is also a perfect gentleman ... If there were a word for the direct opposite of a caricature, for something which is almost absurdly a *perfect type*, I should apply it to him ... He is also an accomplished orator in the old grand style: an assiduous worker in the modern manner - keeps two secretaries at work supplying him with information but realises that he himself has to do the thinking!"

She concluded by fearing that "so much perfection" might one day "sweep" her "cause" "out of the way." As her fellow Fabian, Bernard Shaw remarked, he looked "like a man who is going to do something; and that is a terrible thing."

In the next volume of her diary (1956) she wrote again of Mosley after his resignation from the Labour Government :-

"Has MacDonald found his superseder in Oswald Mosley?"

She enquired hopefully after Mosley's resignation speech in 1930, which she states was "acclaimed as that of a distinguished Parliamentary orator."

By that time she was very sick of MacDonald and looking round for someone to take his place. But a few months after she was to write that Mosley had left the Labour Party "slamming the door with a bang to resound through the political world."

He was then in her view guilty of an "amazing act of arrogance" and "so much perfection" was written off with the remark that "he would be beaten and retire." She concluded her study of Mosley by observing: "in the chaos of our political life today there will be many meteors passing through the firmament. There is still Winston Churchill to be accounted for. Have there ever been so many political personages on the loose?"

Nine years later Sir Winston Churchill became Prime Minister and twenty-five years later Mosley has still not retired, despite quite a few defeats. This record indicates the degree to which even a mind so fair and distinguished as that of Mrs. Webb is influenced by purely personal consideration. Mosley was "perfection" when he was on her side, and she felt when he first joined the Labour Party that he could be used for her purposes. Her view of him varied constantly, whenever he tried really to get something done within the Labour Party and thus came up against her innate resistance to change and action. (*Vide* Mr. Cole's epigram: The Webbs, at least, have the courage of their obsolescence). But when she despaired of the party leader and of the party itself as then constructed, she turned hopefully again to Mosley when he resigned from the Government, and she required his dynamism to save something from the wreck. Nothing was too bad for him, however, when he carried her perfectly correct opinion of the whole structure of the party and personnel of the Labour leadership to its logical conclusion, and resigned from the party to form a new movement capable of real achievement. Like so many of the intellectuals, she willed the end but not the means. Finally, she spent her old age applauding Soviet Russia, after using her maturity in obstructing those who sought to build a constructive alternative to communism in England and Europe. She could applaud a bad thing done, but always resisted anything, good or bad, in the making. Despite her many gifts of mind and character she followed the herd of politicians who always decided quite simply that Mosley was an angel or devil according to the equally simple test whether he was on their side or not.

Extract from *As It Happened* by *Earl Attlee* (published 1954).

"Yet another group in the Labour Party was forming round the personality of Sir Oswald Mosley. This was at first not much more than a 'ginger group' which attracted such young men as Aneurin Bevan, John Strachey and John Beckett, but the fact that it depended mainly on the personality if its leader, who had considerable dynamic force, brought it into line with the Fascist ideas prevalent on the Continent."

It is interesting to note concerning the young men who are mentioned as being led astray that Mr. Bevan is approximately the same age as Mosley, Mr. Beckett a few years older, and Mr. Strachey a few years younger.

Extract from *Harold Laski*, by *Kingsley Martin*, (published 1953): "The most remarkable feature of this letter" (15 Jun 1929) "is Harold's report that MacDonald considered Sir Oswald Mosley as a possible Foreign Secretary."

At this time, when he was considered for the post of Foreign Secretary, Mosley was still only 32 years old.

Extract from *Earl Winterton's* book *Order Of The Day* (published 1953): "... He was a first-class debater, able to make an angry House, however bitterly opposed to him, listen to his view..."

"... He could hold his own in the most hostile and disorderly House. He also possessed the personal magnetism which is a necessary accomplishment of the successful orator."

Extract from *Doctor In The Whips Room* by *Sir Henry Maurice Jones*, M.P., Chairman of Welsh Parliamentary Party, Whip of the Liberal Party: "... Mosley had a talent above the ordinary. Had he remained with his team there is no office in the State which he could not have reached. He resigned in 1931 because his government would not adopt the drastic steps which he had formulated to deal with unemployment. Looking back over the years, after listening to many Ministers addressing the House from the corner of the third bench below the gangway on the government side, on their retirement from office on some issue or other, I can recall no speech more outstandingly brilliant in matter and delivery."

Chapter 4

The Press: Pre-War

Hannen Swaffer, the leading journalist of the Left before the war, stated when Mosley was in gaol and in his opinion finished, that British Union would have won power if the war had not come.

Writing in the *World's Press News* (5 Aug 1943) under the heading 'Saved by the War' he stated that it was "left to the war and 18B" to deal effectively with Mosley and his movement, and concluded "Yes, but for the war we might today have been a Fascist country."

Labour's view of Mosley was very different some years before when he was a member of the party and they did not feel that it was necessary to have a war to stop him.

S. V. Bracher, Parliamentary Correspondent of the *Daily Herald* in *The Herald Book of Labour Members, 1923-4* wrote :-

"Mr. Oswald Mosley's decision taken at the end of March, 1924, to join the Labour Party was adjudged by seasoned critics the most notable event of its kind since Mr. Winston Churchill at nearly the same age (Mr. Mosley was scarcely 28) went over to the Liberals.

Time may prove it by far the more important conversion of the two. The Member for Harrow has the Churchillian brilliancy in debate - and much besides ...

The fine diction, the keen sarcasm, the flashing wit of Mr. Mosley's speeches are notorious. Less known, but equally characteristic, are their close reasoning, their original thinking, their economic and historical knowledge, their wise idealism and high sense of moral responsibility. We who have watched him see no limit, within the possible, to his future political eminence."

The *Daily Herald's* report on Mosley's speech of 29th May 1930 justifying his resignation from the Labour Government because the Government would not deal effectively with the unemployment problem, was as follows :-

"... Sir Oswald Mosley impressed the whole House with a dignified and urgent statement of the reasons that led to his resignation ... At an early hour it became obvious that the House was facing up to the problem with a new seriousness. An insistent sense of national emergency breaking down Party barriers seemed to sweep over the Members ... Sir Oswald Mosley entered a brilliant defence of his attitude followed by a vigorous and detailed offensive ... When he sat down there was a long and continued cheering from every section of the House. Rarely, if ever, has a Junior Minister retiring under such circumstances achieved such a remarkable personal triumph. Whether Members agreed or not, there was a general consensus that he had provided a real basis for a constructive debate."

The *Daily Herald* Lobby Correspondent: "Undoubtedly Sir Oswald Mosley's speech was the event of the debate. Tory members discussing it with me afterwards seemed almost awed, such was the impression it made on them."

The *Daily Herald* (21.5.1930) further commented: "The resignation of Sir Oswald Mosley will be regretted throughout the Labour Movement."

And again on 22.5.1930: "Sir Oswald Mosley will be 34 in November ... Make good he assuredly will, for he has a first class mind, great industry and courage of a rare kind."

Sunday Express

"Sir Oswald is a very powerful figure in public life. He makes a bigger platform appeal than any other individual in this country."

(31.7.1930)

"Mr. Mosley has already secured the confidence of the country in a marked degree, and I venture to predict that, when he has shed a few of his illusions about the League of Nations and settled down, he will prove of the stuff out of which Prime Ministers are made."

(18.8.1923)

"No one could 'draw' Mr. Winston Churchill in the last Parliament more effectively than he, and as a matter of fact, young Mr. Mosley is very much of the Churchill type. He has a daring mind, any amount of courage, and is a master of jibe and biting sarcasm."

(15.7.1923)

"The House of Commons is extraordinarily interested in the definite crossing over to the Socialist Party of young Mr. Mosley. It is a tribute to one of the most challenging personalities in Parliament ... He is a valuable a recruit as the Government could well have - young, politically ambitious, remarkably able and with a gift for stinging, vitriolic eloquence with which Mr. Winston Churchill used to be able to deal, but which nobody in Parliament can quite match."

(6.4.1924)

Daily Express

"If I were asked to pick out two men from the back Socialist benches whom I thought to have as much chance as future Prime Ministers as any others I should name Mr. Maxton and Mr. Mosley. They both take politics seriously, and both have great gifts of expression and manner. (Labour lost both).

(12.7.1924)

New Statesman[1]

"I should say that at 28 he is as ripened an intelligence as was Mr. Churchill's at the same age, and that in his case mind and heart go well together, they offer a rich promise of good for the state. Nor is there anything sudden or impulsive in Mr. Mosley's act.

He has spoken the language of what is called 'sane idealism' ever since he began to think about after-war politics."

(5.4.1924)

"Mr Mosley is a bird of rather dazzling hackle. He can think and he can feel, and while he has shown himself a singularly quick and able student of politics, his intelligence lacks neither breadth nor distinction. He will be of the greatest value to his new party, especially, but by no means exclusively, in foreign affairs; and it is of importance that he should be brought, as early as possible, into its inner counsels."

(26.7.1924)

The Nation[2]

"After wandering on the brink of political waters, Mr. Oswald Mosley has taken the plunge at the deep end. His formal entry into the Labour communion is the most interesting personal event of the sort, since Mr. Churchill joined the Liberal Party 20 years ago ... He has great courage, considerable gifts of speech and unquestioned sincerity ... With again the exception of Mr. Churchill no one now in politics has travelled so far at 27 as he has done and among the men of the future he is certain to have a conspicuous place."

(5.4.1924)

"Oswald Mosley's decision to join the Independent Labour Party brings to that organisation one of the ablest and most promising young men in England, whom some are already describing

1   The *New Statesman*, edited by the late *Mr. Clifford Sharpe*.

2   *The Nation*, edited by the late *Mr. H. J. Massingham*.

as a future prime Minister ... Quite aside from personalities, however, the accession to Labour ranks of men of this type gives the greatest hope for that party's future."

(16.4.1924)

"The resignation of Sir Oswald Mosley is an event of capital importance in domestic politics ... We feel that Sir Oswald has acted rightly - as he has certainly acted courageously - in declining to share any longer in the responsibility for inertia."

(24.5.1930)

Week End Review[3]

"The defection of Sir Oswald Mosley was a great blow to the Government; for he is the one man on the Labour side who increased his reputation last session."

(9.8.1930)

"Sir Oswald Mosley's Manifesto, published last week end, came pat upon the issue. In principle it is exactly right ... The great gain is that Sir Oswald and his advisers have sensed the first need of the hour and have fulfilled it. They understand two things: first that the nation is sick to death of party routine and effete political machinery - sick to death in the literal sense that it is dying of them; secondly that unless we can quickly pull ourselves together as a people and unite in a supreme effort of reconstruction and national planning, we shall go down into the pit. In recognising this the Mosley Manifesto sounds a new and ringing tone in current politics. For months politicians have been content with a cry that 'something must be done.' Here is a man with the courage and the sense to face the music."

(13.12.1930)

The organ of Liberalism the *Westminster Gazette* at that time edited by Mr. A.G. Spender, author of *The Public Life* (1925, *Journalism and Politics* (1927), *Life of Lord Oxford and Asquith*

---

3   *Week End Review*, edited by Mr. Gerald Barry.

37

(1932), *Fifty Years of Europe* (1933), *Great Britain, Empire and Commonwealth* (1936) etc.

"Although in his 27th year, Mr. Mosley is spoken of by old and skilled Parliamentary hands as composed of the stuff of which Prime Ministers are made. The most polished literary speaker in the Commons, words flow from him in graceful epigrammatic phrases that have a sting in them for the Government and the Conservatives. To listen to him is an education in the English language, also in the art of delicate but deadly repartee ... he has human sympathies, courage and brains."

(26.6.1923)

"There is no more polished speaker in the House than Mr. Oswald Mosley ... who is steadily gaining the ear of the House."

(16.2.1923)

"It was an indication of the way in which the House of Commons is beginning to anticipate Mr. Oswald Mosley's clever wit that although there were shouts of 'vide' when Lord Robert Cecil sat down, they were instantly silenced when the member for Harrow was seen on his feet."

(30.5.1923)

Daily News

"Behind the over-cleverness of Mr. Mosley's style lies an intense passion for social justice, and it was for that reason, as well as for the sake of entertainment, that the House had again filled to over-flowing before he sat down."

(18.1.1924)

Daily Mail

"The one outstanding case of an advanced prestige is Sir Oswald Mosley, who has provided us with a rare example of a man who has steadily advanced in importance since retiring from

Ministerial office ... Sir Oswald has proved himself more and more of a force to be reckoned with."

(4.8.1930)

Daily Mirror

"One of the few who has displayed gifts of the highest oratorial order is Sir Oswald Mosley."

(2.8.1930)

Morning Post

"Mr. Mosley who is to combat the Duke of Northumberland tonight in debate ... is one of the most promising but most uncertain of our young Parliamentarians. In many respects Mr. Mosley reminds me of Disraeli before he had taken his political bearings and was eager to attract attention by his waywardness, brilliance and audacity. Mr. Mosley never shouts, but like his predecessor, he does not 'sit down' until they have heard him. Mr. Mosley will go far, when he gets his marching orders."

(19.6.1923)

Manchester Guardian

"Who could doubt, when Sir Oswald Mosley sat down after his Free Trade Hall speech in Manchester on Saturday and the audience, stirred as an audience rarely is, rose and swept a storm of applause towards the platform - who could doubt that here was one of those root-and-branch men who have been thrown up from time to time in the religious, political and business story of England.

First that gripping audience is arrested, then stirred and finally, as we have said, swept off its feet by a tornado of a peroration yelled at the defiant high pitch of a tremendous voice..."

(26.10.1931)

John Bull

"There are two men on the Labour benches who will make their mark before long. No party could afford to keep Mr. Oswald Mosley and Mr. James Maxton on its back benches forever."

(26.7.1924)

Church Times

"Few politicians have added to their reputation during this year, but Sir Oswald Mosley is certainly one of them."

(24.12.1930)

Methodist Recorder

"The manifesto fulfils expectations concerning Sir Oswald Mosley which have been more than once expressed in these columns; it constitutes a challenge to traditionalism ... It is not difficult to criticise certain details of the manifesto. But the spirit of the manifesto is stimulating and courageous. It is the embodiment of that vital energy which, at present lacking, youth of whatever party must supply in our national life, if industrial prosperity, the well-being of our land and the unity of the Empire are to be saved from the blight of traditionalism."

(11.12.1930)

Christian Science Monitor

"Despite the fact that no political party upholds it and that it received but a chilly reception at the hands of the party press in England, the demand of Sir Oswald Mosley for an emergency Cabinet of five members to direct the Government of Great Britain during the continuance of the present depression has in it a good deal of intelligent common sense. The 'Cabinet of All the Talents' is what Sir Oswald seeks, and it is not certain that such a plan would not be advantageous were it adopted in some other countries than Great Britain ... Among the masses in England and among the thinking people in England not too closely bound by party ties, Sir Oswald's suggestion is awakening an active and intelligent discussion."

(10.12.1930)

Observer

"Sir Oswald Mosley himself has taken his political life into his hands with brilliant fearlessness. He is the only leader of his generation who has the courage to strike a new path though it may lead him temporarily into the wilderness."

(7.12.1930)

Manchester Daily Dispatch

"Sir Oswald Mosley is the outstanding Socialist figure of this Parliament. He has imagination ... and an immense intellectual equipment. The speech in which he revealed the work plans over which he broke with the Government was easily the most distinguished Socialist performance of last session."

(31.12.1930)

Manchester Evening Chronicle

"There was a consensus of opinion that on the Government side Sir Oswald Mosley is the member who has definitely enhanced his reputation."

(1.8.1930)

Liverpool Post

"Is there a place in life for a man who can think, and can feel, and at the same time can build a bridge between human sorrow and human sympathy? One man in England does think and feel this more intensely than his fellows, for he was born in a class far apart from the poor. And his name is Sir Oswald Mosley ... Anyone who studies Mosley's face will see that he is a strong personality - a man who never suffers fools gladly. He bubbles over with energy of mind and body; hence, one can imagine his scorn of fools in authority ... It is a new form of Socialism of which we shall hear more in the future, and its boldest and most eloquent exponent will be Sir Oswald Mosley ... it will inevitably make him Prime Minister of Great Britain and leader of the British empire."

(18.10.1930)

Yorkshire Post

"They noted his superb command of language, his elevated phraseology, his extraordinary power of invective, and they conferred among themselves regarding his various graces and power, exulting in the brilliance of his attacks, and agreeing as to the indication of future parliamentary greatness which in those days he provided so amply..."

(25.2.1929)

Western Daily News

"Mr. Mosley is a clever young man who is quite obviously destined to make a big name for himself in politics."

(26.2.1923)

Scotsman

"In phrasing and argumentative construction he is as careful as he is industrious in reading up his case."

(14.3.1923)

Notts Journal

"Sir Oswald Mosley's speech is praised all round ... because it contained evidence that the speaker still believed in his party's election pledges and believed that they could and should be attempted. It was a breath of honest politics for which the nation was waiting."

(31.5.1930)

Notts Guardian

"The resignation of Sir Oswald Mosley was the principle topic of conversation in the lobby of the House of Commons last night. It is conceded generally that he has shown considerable spirit in taking this step."

(21.5.1930)

Edinburgh Evening News

"When Sir Oswald Mosley said he felt his position in the Government to be inconsistent with honour, he meant it from the bottom of his heart. He has before made great sacrifices for his faith and will make them again."

(28.5.1930)

East Anglian Daily Times

"Before he had finished he had got the House into that state in which it even forgets to applaud. Every effort was concentrated on listening. One secret of his success was his complete but businesslike naturalness."

(29.5.1930)

Bristol Daily Press

"Whatever may be the ultimate fate of the proposals put forward by Sir Oswald Mosley and his friends, they are likely to command the earnest attention, if not necessarily the approval, of thoughtful people of all parties."

(8.12.1930)

Pembroke Telegraph

"In our opinion Sir Oswald Mosley has got a grip of the situation which others have not. His remedy lacks nothing in thoroughness ... Only by the application of the principles he suggests will the various component parts of the state function again and prosperity be restored to the land."

(18.12.1930)

Hanley Sentinel

Sir Oswald Mosley is an outstanding figure in the political parties of the day; he has the gift of oratory, and the capacity of swaying his hearers; he has a proper discontent with things as they are; and he has courage sufficient to face the wilderness. Whatever may be said of his memorandum - both as to plan and detail - it throws *laissez faire* to the winds, and proposes concrete schemes in place of acceptance of existing conditions ... Sir Oswald's manifesto is a sign of the times and expressive of the trend of thought and belief among the working people."

(8.12.1930)

Chapter 5

Violence

It will be clear to any reader of the foregoing chapters that, in the opinion of those best qualified to judge, Mosley was a speaker without equal. For many years before he left the Labour Party he had addressed many of the largest and most enthusiastic meetings ever held in this country. After leaving that party and founding a new movement, public meetings were the only means available to him for stating his case; he had neither press nor any other propaganda medium which big money commands. It is therefore obvious that he had no interest in preventing himself from making speeches. His ability as a speaker was his only means, and his enemies at once resolved to deprive him of that means. The method was organised disorder. When Mosley eventually took steps to prevent the disorder, it was surely the strangest charge ever made in British politics, that a speaker of his ability should hire a hall and advertise a meeting at considerable expense, for the sole purpose of beating up the large audience which came to listen to him. Yet Left-wing propaganda, with the aid of some sections of the Conservative press, was successful in convincing the gullible of the truth of this fantasy.

In fact, of course, meetings had been broken up all over England for years before Mosley began his movement. Many will remember this, and some of the quotations we shall now publish will prove it. No Conservative leader could make his voice heard, except at ticketed meetings where the faithful were carefully screened before entry. Supporters of the Labour party made a habit of breaking up all meetings of other parties, and in so doing they were often led by the highly-trained militants of communism. This did not matter so much to the Conservative leaders, because they had a large and powerful press to report what they said and to spread their views. But the closing down of public meetings would have been death to a new movement which had to rely solely on the spoken word, and had to win new adherents from the general public to build the party.

Mosley was faced with the plain alternative of resisting violence or closing down. He began his meetings with a few stewards to show people to their seats, as was his custom when in the Labour Party. He continued to do so even after being threatened by a responsible official from Labour headquarters with lynching, if he dared to walk through the large crowd of Labour Party supporters collected from all over Lancashire after the Ashton-under-Lyne by-election. In fact, he got through with his life, but it was a rough passage. However, it was not until his meetings were systematically smashed in the manner described in the Conservative press account of his meeting in the Rag Market, Birmingham that he organised to prevent violence.

For the first time for many years red violence was then brought to an end in Great Britain. No disorder occurred at any indoor meeting addressed by Mosley for the last three years before the war. But very heavy fighting took place first at meetings all over the country, in which Mosley's young men threw out with bare hands hooligans armed with every kind of weapon.

The procedure was always the same in the event of disorder. Ordinary heckling or interruption was never checked or resented. On the contrary, as thousands have heard, Mosley always welcomes an interruption because it gives him a chance to drive home his point in reply. It was not until an organised body of men stood up with steady chanting to drown the speech, or tried to rush the platform, that measures were taken to preserve free speech. Mosley then warned them as chairman of the meeting under the law of the land, and, only if these warnings were ignored, instructed the stewards to eject the interrupters with the minimum force necessary to secure their removal. The organised bands reacted violently, and used weapons. Mosley's men were forbidden to use weapons and, in suspected cases, were even searched to prevent their use. With their bare hands the Blackshirt movement triumphed over the red violence which had brought free speech in Britain to an end. These fights were the origin of the Blackshirt movement in Britain, as in every European country which suffered the same experience of red violence. When a few have to deal in this way with armed roughs, they must be able to recognise each other and to act together. This requires some distinguishing mark or uniform. The black shirt was first used for this purely practical reason. After the comradeship of sacrifice and suffering in these struggles, it became a symbol sacred to many who were proud to wear it.

Eventually the black shirt was suppressed by an act of parliament. The Public Order Act forbade the wearing of uniform for political purpose; but it had done its work, and the red terror at indoor meetings was by then over. Also in such halls stewards still retained the same right to deal with disorder as before, although without the aid of uniform. But the Act removed from political movements the right to organise the defence of their own meetings in the open air. That duty was imposed on the police, who in some areas had no experience of such matters for the good reason that no party before Mosley's movement dared to hold such meetings in red areas. Mosley had held open air meetings all over the country, and despite many attempts on him, had come through unscathed owing to the defence measures of his experienced comrades. The passing of the Public Order Act, however, was the signal for a renewed outbreak of red violence on the streets. Very soon after the passing of the Act Mosley was in hospital for a considerable period with a head injury, which would have been fatal if it had occurred even an inch further along the head. The process on this occasion was simple. Mosley's supporters were ordered by the police to close round the platform, and were then ringed round by the police to prevent them from moving. Highly organised red rogues from behind the ring of police then put down such a barrage of every conceivable missile on the platform that it could only be a matter of minutes before Mosley was hit. It was not, of course, the intention of the police that this should happen. The whole thing was due to their inexperience. It is not so simple to deal with situations like that if you do not know the business.

So the Public Order Act proved in practice to be an act for the promotion of disorder. Violence on the streets became far worse, and the removal of the uniform from Mosley's supporters contributed to the general confusion. They had been a disciplined body, obeying the order to leave their opponent's meetings alone. Until that point no Labour Party meeting had ever been broken up by Mosley's supporters. After the passage of the Public Order Act Labour meetings were broken up all over the place. For some time no Labour meeting at all could be held in East London, and Messrs. Attlee and Morrison vacated their seats in that area in favour of quieter localities. Times had changed since placards were carried in procession from East London to Olympia with the words: "March with us and smash fascism." Soon after the passing of the Public Order Act in 1936 the placards of the evening papers bore the words: "Labour M.P.s in East London ask for police protection." The Labour Party was reaping the whirlwind it had sown. Also the removal of the black shirt had taken away the old discipline from Mosley's movement, and men without discipline are naturally more inclined to hold bitter memories and repay old scores. Mosley did his utmost to prevent such occurrences by discipline while the law still permitted it, and by appeals for order when the law no longer permitted discipline. But a long tradition of disorder begun by the Left - which existed long before Mosley's time - had then gone too far to be checked except at his own indoor meetings where order had become a method and a habit.

Post-War

Since the war Mosley has held many meetings without any disorder. Particularly in his first full scale campaign through London and the industrial areas in the Spring of 1956 - which was a return to large indoor public meetings - he took the greatest trouble and showed the utmost patience in order to prevent any possibility of disorder. He was rewarded by the fact that not a single person had to be ejected from these meetings. After the war there seems to be a good hope that the old tradition of disorder is over among the British people, who are now wise to take their politics with deadly seriousness. It will never revive unless it is organised. In fact there was never disorder, even before the war, unless it was organised. The British people will always listen fairly to a man who puts his case courteously. They did so even in the worst days before the war. It was always only a small minority which organised the disorder. Very often only some fifty men in a meeting of some five thousand. But the minority was strong enough to drown the voice of the speaker, and to prevent an audience which had paid for their seats from listening to the speech they had come to hear. So it was then necessary to deal with the red violence. We can only hope our English people have now outgrown this childish nonsense. But we are now telling an old story, and the following quotations prove the facts of the case we have stated.

We give quotations from Conservative M.P.s who had such experiences long before Mosley even began. We deal with the breakup of Mosley's early meetings and with such events as the much discussed Olympia meeting. Medical evidence is given in detail to show who suffered injuries on such occasions, and how the injuries were caused. Statements from many Conservative M.P.s and other witnesses who were impartial or opposed to Mosley in politics, are given in detail. Finally we give the measured statement on the Olympia Meeting of the ex-Prime Minister Lloyd-George.

At the end of this section the reader will find the relevant passages from the Public Order Act which prevented Mosley maintaining order at his outdoor meetings, and of the subsequent, and consequent attack on him at Liverpool which put him in hospital. He was still left with the right to maintain order at his own indoor meetings which were held in perfect order for three years before the war, and subsequently, up to the time of preparation of this book.

Four quotations are sufficient to reveal the atmosphere of the period in which Mosley began his movement. They show that any man who had to rely solely on public meetings for the advance of his cause, must face the choice of organising he defence of free speech, or closing down and retiring.

T. Howard, M.P. for south Islington, in the House of Commons on June 14th (Vol. 290, Hansard) 1934, said:

"I challenge any leader of the Conservative party, or of the Liberal Party, to organise a meeting in London, except in Westminster ... and to advertise the meeting as an open meeting and then to get a hearing. In the General Elections since 1918 until now the Labour party in my Division had led the opposition to prevent free speech."

Cecil Pike, M.P. for Attercliffe Division of Sheffield, in the House of Commons, June 14th (Vol. 290, Hansard) 1934, said:

"I have seen in my Division meeting after meeting wilfully broken up, and I am perfectly convinced that every other member of this House has had the same experience."

Lord Beaverbrook's experience at Camberwell:

"Lord Beaverbrook was shouted down last night at an eve-of-the poll meeting at Camberwell ... As the meeting proceeded it was obvious that the labour opposition was strongly in evidence, and when Lord Beaverbrook rose to speak his words were inaudible beyond the front of the hall, owing to the stamping on the floor and persistent shouting and singing. It appeared at one time that the platform would be rushed, but there was a strong bodyguard of stewards. After a further attempt to make himself heard, Lord Beaverbrook sat down amid opposition cheers. Later he left the hall after shaking hands with those on the platform ... Later several free fights took place in front of the platform ... several stewards were knocked down in the rush, and afterwards one was carried out battered and bleeding. The police were called in, and the hall gradually cleared."

Manchester Guardian (8.3.1934)

An L.C.C. candidate's experience:

"A barbed wire entanglement erected in front of the platform ... police posted round the walls of the hall ... a hostile crowd of six hundred keeping up a continuous barrage of shouting, stamping and singing ... the Red Flag hoisted. These were the extraordinary scenes at an L.C.C. election meeting held at the Old Kent Road Baths last night. The barbed wire had been put up earlier in the day by Mr. Bateman (the candidate). He told a *Daily Express* representative last night that at a meeting last week the platform was rushed and he has taken the precaution for the safety of his daughter."

Daily Express (6.3.1934)

Evidence On The Use Of
Weapons Against Mosley's Meetings

Four quotations are sufficient to show the methods used against Mosley's meetings and the weapons employed against his unarmed followers.

Mr Philip Toynbee: Mr Philip Toynbee's evidence on the use of weapons in the attempted break up of Mosley's Olympia meeting,

June, 1934. (His statement is taken from his book *Friends Apart*, published by Macgibbon and Kee, March, 1954 - page 21.)

"In the afternoon we bought knuckledusters at a Drury Lane ironmongers, and I well remember the exaltation of trying them on."

His account of the meeting (7th June, 1934): "Tier after tier of the curious and the enthusiastic, and the enthusiastic in great majority."

His description of the organised attempt to break up the meeting and of his own consequent exit: "tearful, bruised and broke, I was at last thrown out onto the street."

Mr Jack Spot in the *Sunday Chronicle* (16.1.1955) describes his preparations to oppose the procession of Mosley's movement through Aldgate in the Autumn of 1936, for which police permission had been given in accordance with the law. "On the day before the procession was due I went to an old cabinet maker in Aldgate and asked him to make me a weapon ... the old cabinet maker did a beautiful job. He made me a short, turned sofa leg and filled the top, wider end with lead. I slipped this into a paper carrier bag." This story was carried by the *Sunday Chronicle* under the heading: "Jack Spot begins today: Britain's No. 1 gangster tells all ... Jack Spot reigns, and there is peace."

The *Daily Herald* on 12.8.1955 gave another account of Jack Spot in the same incident which concludes: "The outcry that followed these disorders enabled police to take action to prevent processions by Fascists." (The Labour Party, of course, had built its movement with such street processions.)

This was Jack Comer - known as Jack Spot, king of Soho - the top member of the underworld, but he had helped the police to break up the Blackshirts.

Mosley's Early Exprience Of
Disorder At Meetings

Mosley's own experience began at a meeting held at the Rag Market, Birmingham, after his break with the Labour Party. He had previously spoken to orderly and enthusiastic meetings for the Labour Party, in this same hall and all over Birmingham. The meeting was organised in exactly the same way, and only 60 stewards in plain clothes were present to show an audience of fifteen thousand to their seats. The following is a description of what occurred in the *Birmingham Post*, which was a strong supporter of the Conservative Party: "There were amazing scenes at a political meeting at the Rag Market, Birmingham, last night ... The platform was rushed, and its framework broken down by those seeking safety from the struggle in the body of the hall, and women and children were got through the crowd in a hysterical condition to safety in the greater portion of the market at the rear of the platform.

There were about fifteen thousand people in the market, and it was fortunate that no serious casualties occurred. The vast bulk of those present were orderly, and the trouble arose through a small body. The wild disorder which arose midway through Sir Oswald's speech lasted half an hour or more, and at the end, when a cordon of police held back the crowd at some distance from the platform, the scene in front was one mass of over-turned and broken chairs over a considerable area.

Arising out of this meeting and the disorder, Sir Oswald was summoned for an assault on two men during the disturbances. The evidence for the prosecution broke down under cross-examination, and after hearing Sir Oswald's evidence, the Stipendiary indicated that he did not wish to hear more witnesses for the defence, and he dismissed both summonses, remarking that he was satisfied the defendant did not do anything more than he was entitled to do."

(19.10.1931)

Olympia.

It was to deal with this situation, and to ensure that those who attended his meetings should be permitted to hear what he had to say, that uniformed stewards were organised. After many meetings in which such stewards were able to deal with the situation with comparatively little trouble, a meeting at Olympia was announced for June 7th, 1934. Left-wing journals immediately appealed to their readers to turn out in force and break it up.

Daily Worker

"In connection with the great anti-Fascist demonstration which is being organised by the London District Committee of the Communist Party on June 7th, when Mosley's Blackshirts are holding a Fascist rally at Olympia, the following are the arrangements. Marches will be organised from five different parts of London in the late afternoon, to arrive in Hammersmith Road, in the vicinity of Olympia at 6.30 p.m. Workers who cannot participate in the marches are asked to rally to Hammersmith Road from 6.30 p.m. onwards after leaving work. Arrangements should be made in the localities for parties of workers to travel on the Underground and to obtain cheap facilities for parties. The District Committee of the Communist Party have sent letters to the London Labour Party, London Trades Council, the I.L.P. and District Committee of the Trade Unions, inviting their co-operation in the counter-demonstration."

(26.5.1934)

Manchester Guardian

"A press statement issued by the London District Committee of the Communist party of Great Britain says the announcement of the decision of Sir Oswald Mosley to follow up his recent Blackshirt rally at the Albert Hall[4] by a demonstration at Olympia on June 7th will be taken as a challenge by the London

---

4   *Packed meetings had been held in the Albert Hall, which were perfectly orderly.*

Violence

working-class political and trade union movement ... the Communist Party is confident that the workers[5] in the capital city will resist with all means the Fascist menace."

(31.5.1934)

Daily Worker

"In this campaign a number of local working-class organisations are co-operating, including the Labour Party and their Parliamentary candidates, the Socialist I.L.P., the Communist Party and the Y.C.L. ... to arouse support for the workers' counter-demonstration to the Blackshirt rally for Olympia. Every militant worker in London should put his whole energy into mobilising the masses of London against Mosley on Thursday, June 7th."

(31.5.1934)

New Leader (Organ of the I.L.P.)

"Workers challenge Blackshirts." "Great counter-demonstration at Olympia." "The workers are going to be all out at Olympia on Thursday week, June 7th, when Oswald Mosley and his Blackshirts hold their monster demonstration. Get to work at once. Raise the question in your Trade Union branches, Co-op. Guilds, local Labour Parties, Leagues of Youth and Socialist League branches. Talk about it to your factory mates. Get as many as possible to come along to Olympia on June 7th ... The workers must have as big a demonstration as the Blackshirts."

(1.6.1934)

Daily Worker

"Labour Party Youth join with Communists against Fascism. The South Harrow branch of the labour Party league of Youth has officially decided to take part in the workers' counter-demonstration to Mosley at Olympia on Thursday ... It is

---

5   At least 90 percent of Mosley's movement were, and are, manual workers.

reported that a number of Labour Party League of Youth in North Tottenham, East Islington and Stoke Newington were taking part in the anti-Fascist activities. This is the result of an appeal of the London Young Communist League to the London membership of the Labour League of Youth, I.L.P., Guild of Youth and other young workers to come into the counter-demonstration."

(2.6.1934)

Daily Worker

"London's counter-demonstration to Mosley's Fascists. Workers march to Olympia tonight. Thousands of London workers will demonstrate their hatred of fascism tonight by counter-demonstrating against the Blackshirts at Olympia. The East End is chalked white with huge slogans against Mosley, and yesterday the counter-demonstration was being enthusiastically discussed by the workers. Inside the large hall and outside the challenge of Mosley will be met by the determined workers ... But the workers' counter-action will cause them to tremble."

(7.6.1934)

On June 6th and 7th the *Daily Worker* printed a map showing the easiest route to Olympia. These inflammatory publications had the effect intended; thousands marched to Olympia on the evening of June 7th, determined at all costs to prevent Sir Oswald Mosley's speech being heard by an audience of 15,000.

Outside Olympia.

Long before ticket holders could enter the hall it was obvious that counter demonstrations had been organised, with a view not only of preventing the speaker from being heard, but also with the intention of preventing them from attending the meeting.

The force of police on duty before the meeting was, beyond any doubt, desirous of protecting the public, but was, nevertheless too small to be capable of achieving its object. Had the police resources used at the close of the meeting been employed outside before it began, the general public would have been able to enter with very little inconvenience. After the difficulties encountered in entering the building, nobody was very surprised that, from the moment when the speaker began his address, organised attempts were made to prevent a single word from being heard.

According to the law of the land, there exists the right to eject those who attempt to prevent the business of a meeting from being transacted. If this fact is understood clearly, it follows that the only remaining question to be answered concerns the degree of force to be used against interrupters.

The nature of the injuries inflicted upon Fascists showed very clearly, apart from any other evidence, that weapons were used, and a man who is engaged in the struggle with an individual who is prepared to use weapons which may cause death must, if he can, decide the appropriate degree of force to be used.

Allegations of Blackshirt Brutality and Evidence to the Contrary.

Wild allegations of unnecessary brutality in the ejection of interrupters were made. The following statements were from men in the first aid dressing stations.

L. Doelberg. (Medical Student of St. Thomas's Hospital): "Sir, I assisted at a dressing station established by the B.U.F. at the request of one of the orderlies, on the night of the Olympia meeting.

I personally dressed twelve Blackshirts, of which four were serious cases. The details of these four cases were as follows: Kicked in the stomach and sent to the West London Hospital. Kicked on the head and in the stomach and laid up for three weeks. Kicked in the thigh and unable to stand. A girl, who was hit in the eye and had her glasses broken into the eye and was sent to hospital.

I treated only one communist, who had a black eye. I can definitely state that no doctor, other than Dr. Duff-Miller, attended any of the injured during the whole evening."

A certified first-aid worker and military hospital trained nurse orderly: "We treated in our dressing station 63 Blackshirts for injuries, mostly abdominal, and injuries caused by blunt and sharp instruments, also a few communists were treated at my station with minor injuries."

Statement by M. Lord, in charge of fist aid arrangements at Olympia: "I went to the station in the gallery and found there a fascist in an unconscious state, and I was told that he had been kicked in the stomach. I also found a girl fascist with a scratch commencing under her eye and running down her cheek and neck, and finishing on her back, between her shoulder blades. I do not think this scratch could have been done with a fingernail, but that some sharp instrument must have been used. While treating this case, another girl fascist was brought in; she had been struck by a man and her glasses smashed in her face. She was bleeding from the region of her left eye.

The last case I attended was a fascist who had the palm of his right hand cut from the thumb to the third finger. He was removed to hospital by L.C.C. ambulance."

Charges of Brutality by Blackshirts Disproved.

A careful search was made for any communists or interrupters of any kind who had suffered serious injuries. They were invited to come forward and politicians who alleged brutal treatment were challenged to produce evidence. If their statements had been true it is clear that the dressing stations and local hospitals would have been full of interrupters of the meeting. A careful inquiry failed to produce any cases. Eventually in response to repeated challenges, the opposition produced one case, Mr. Jacob Miller. This man was produced at Sir Oswald Mosley's meeting at Sheffield Town Hall on June 28th in an attempt to create a sensation. The *Sheffield Daily Telegraph* of June 29th, 1934 contained the following report:-

"The most piquant situation during the meeting was created when a man on the floor of the hall stood up at question time and said he was severely handled at the Olympia meeting a few weeks ago. The man rose in his place at the invitation of Sir Oswald, who had received a written question from him, in which he asked if Sir Oswald would deny that he was beaten on the head at Olympia and remained in hospital for nine days.

Thereupon Sir Oswald replied: 'You have recovered quickly. Thank you, very much. I am glad to see you here as the man who was supposed to be beaten until he was nearly dead with wounds about the head. I see that you are perfectly fit and without trace of injury that can be seen from here.' Turning to his audience, Sir Oswald then said: 'I challenge him to say why, if he was so badly treated in the way he describes, he did not go to the nearest policeman and charge those inside the hall with assault.' Then, facing the man, Sir Oswald said: 'Do that, if you dare!'

Amid cheering and counter-cheering the man replied that he was not in a fit condition after being ejected from the meeting to make a complaint to the police, being, as he was, half dead. Sir Oswald retorted that he or his friends could have called the assistance of the police. Had a complaint been made to the police it would have been the duty of the police to find and charge the assailant. The man replied that a friend asked the police for help, but that the police did not offer any help at all.

Sir Oswald: 'Now you are challenging not only us but the police. You are now alleging that the police refused to do their duty."

Evidence by Conservative M.P.'s and others present at Olympia.

Many eye-witnesses, upholders of the right of free speech, wrote to the newspapers, or spoke in Parliament, to describe what they had seen.

Sir Leonard Lyle, an ex-Conservative M.P.: "Those who are attacking Sir Oswald Mosley do not give any details as to what happened outside Olympia on Thursday, and as an eye-witness of most unpleasant episodes which took place, I think it is only fair to place on record the fact that in no case did I see or hear of any violence on the part of the Blackshirts; on the other hand, police were assaulted, and at least one mounted officer was un-horsed by organised gangs of 'Reds', and people, like myself, who had come in many cases with our wives to listen, were impeded and insulted in every case by violent Red agitators. I do not happen to be a supporter of Sir Oswald Mosley, but I went to hear him. I was not allowed to do so, owing to the violence and wrecking methods adopted by the people who are now defended by Conservative Members of Parliament."

(13.6.1934)

Hamilton Fyfe, ex-editor of *Daily Herald*:

"Sir, I am not likely to be suspected of any sympathy with Fascism ... Therefore, I feel free to say how unwise - and even unfair - it was to organise interruption at the Olympia meeting. It was organised: that is certain. I saw in Oxford Street, in the early evening, bands of young men, mostly Jews, on their way to the meeting. Every few minutes they shouted in unison some slogan I could not catch. They were clearly in a fighting mood - and they got what they wanted...."

Yours faithfully,

Hamilton Fyfe

(13.6.1934)

Mr Christopher W. Lowther,
Ex-Conservative M.P. (to Sir Oswald Mosley):

"Out of interest I went to your Olympia meeting. With much that you said I agree, with much I disagree. But, however that may be, I think the agitation which has arisen against the Blackshirt methods of dealing with organised interruption is wholly unjustified. I was impressed by the fact that all your stewards whom I saw seemed to be very decent folk, a very good type of British youth. I saw no ejections that were not perfectly justified. I have suffered at several elections from organised interruptions, and I think you have hit upon the proper method of dealing with it."

(15.6.1934)

Eye-Witnesses.

Sir, I am not a Fascist, nor have I anything to do with Sir Oswald Mosley, but I would like to write my experiences of the meeting at Olympia on Thursday last ... The meeting was 35 minutes late beginning, owing to ticket-holders being prevented from entering by unauthorised persons who wished to get in. Directly Sir Oswald Mosley began to speak the row was terrific. He asked very courteously once or twice for a hearing, and finding that the din continued, his adherents very properly rushed the obstructers out ... Whatever the roughness of the young Fascists may have been, they certainly had the most frightful provocation.

Yours faithfully,

Annabel Jackson

(12.6.1934)

Vice-Admiral Powell:

"Sir, There was obviously at Olympia a rowdy element who had gone there to render the holding of the meeting an impossibility. They had been well organised, being in groups disposed in different parts of the hall, each group interrupting every few minutes.

They were asked by Sir Oswald Mosley to cease and to leave the hall. He, in fact cautioned them several times; but it was not until these people had been ejected that one could really pay proper attention to his speech - which, I may add, was quite unprovocative.

I was one of a party of four, well placed for seeing everything, and we certainly did not observe on the part of the stewards of the meeting any brutality in carrying out their duty.

The great proportion of the audience resented the interruptions, and showed that their sympathies were with the Blackshirt stewards by continually cheering when the rowdies were being removed. There was dangerous hustling outside Olympia by Communists attempting to prevent the public who had tickets from entering the building. One of the women of my party suffered from it. In fact, if it had not been for the police, I do not think we should have been able to get in.

Yours etc.,

G. B. Powell

(Vice-Admiral, Rtd.)

(12.6.1934)

Lt. Colonel T. C. R. Moore, M.P. :
"Their plans were skilful in their simplicity - interruption, ejection, resistance, violence; the result - local pandemonium, disturbance of the meeting, and anxious alarm of the women and the old.

I do not know the legal right and privileges of the interrupters but I imagine it will be generally agreed that when a listener - before questions are invited - persistently disturbs the continuity of the speaker's address he merits little consideration, and the stewards, in the interests of the audience, must do their duty.

Violence

In those cases of ejection which I personally noted, the meddlers suffered more from resentful civilians than from the official Blackshirt stewards."

(14.6.1934)

Mr. M. W. Beaumont, M.P. to the Editor of *The Times:*

"Sir,

As one of those present at the Fascist meeting at Olympia on Thursday, I wish to dissent entirely from the view expressed by three of my colleagues in your columns this morning.

They say that the tactics adopted by the Fascists to ensure a hearing of their case are something unusual in this country. The organised noise and interruption with which these tactics are meant to deal are unfortunately not so. While the forces of law and order make no effort to safeguard the rights of free speech in this country, the use of some such methods is the only way in which those putting forward an unknown and controversial case can obtain a hearing. No one present can doubt that the interruptions which were dealt with were skilfully organised with the object of preventing Sir Oswald Mosley from speaking, which, but for the action of the Fascists, they would have succeeded in doing.

While deploring violence in politics (or elsewhere) as much as the signatories of the letter in your today's issue, I was pleased to see the organised hooligans dealt with in the only manner that can be effective and the only one that they can understand.

Yours faithfully,

M. W. Beaumont, M.P.

(8.6.1934)

Mosley: The Facts

Sir N. Grattan-Doyle, M.P. to the Editor of *The Times*:

"Sir,

I have no use for Fascism or dictatorships, but less sympathy for the views expressed in your columns of those who think that the Red hooligans who were present in their organised hundreds were not treated with sufficient leniency. But why were they there? Was it not for the deliberate purpose of preventing a legitimate meeting from being held? Those who undertook the meeting and paid for it knew or suspected that organised attempts would be made to frustrate it, and took measures to meet force with force. Was more force than was necessary used in ejecting the disturbers? Probably there was, and probably also the organisers of the meeting were determined to give an object-lesson to the organised gang who were present for an illegal purpose. If so, and with the view of preventing the same tactics being employed at other meetings in the future, is not the Fascist' psychology understandable?

N. Grattan-Doyle, M.P.

(19.6.1934)

Lord Strathspey:

"... We were very glad to see that such a firm hand was taken to preserve law and order, and if in the future the 'Blackshirts' are allowed to continue to do so, then I am sure that they will give loyal support to the authorities in enforcing peace at future meetings.

It is not a statement of fact to attribute any extra rough treatment to the 'Blackshirts' but if they were rough, then it was only in self-defence, and for the protection of the thousands in the hall. Furthermore, they only gave the wild hooligans what they asked for, and what they right well deserved to get."

(19.6.1934)

Violence

N. Mellor:

"As spectators at the meeting at Olympia, my son and I saw no brutality used in any way in the turning out of interrupters, and we were in the midst of the disturbances. On leaving the hall after the meeting, in Hammersmith Road, we came across Communists and hooligans. One set were attacking a Blackshirt, who was trying to board a bus, and others were attacking a man and woman in a motor-car. My son, who went to their help, had pepper thrown in his face, which was meant for the woman in the car. They were calling the couple in the car 'parasites', etc."

J. Clark Hall:

"Sir,

I, like Mr. Barry, am neither a Blackshirt nor a Communist. At the Albert Hall I listened in peace to Sir Oswald Mosley. At Olympia I was unfortunate to be near a centre of organised opposition and heard little. I agree that the measures taken against interrupters grew very severe. On the other hand, I saw the violence started in every early case by the interrupter.

There were no signs of excitement or brutality during the ten minutes I remained near the main exit - and one policeman. I have been present at disturbances "from China to Peru" but I have never before seen such promise of serious trouble averted by the use of bare fists. If stern measures had not been taken in the part of the hall which was within my vision, and for which I speak, the protesters against violence would have witnessed a serious attack.

Yours etc.,

J. Clark Hall.

(11.6.1934)

C.L. Ricketts:

"Sir,

I, too, was present at the Fascist meeting at Olympia. The interrupters gave such an exhibition of organised hooliganism that I fear they had little sympathy from the vast majority of the audience.

A point which seems to be overlooked is, that each interrupter (at any rate in that part of the building near me) fought and kicked savagely when seized. I myself saw one approaching Blackshirt double up with a vicious kick in the stomach. I feel that with such demonstrators, summary methods are essential.

Personally, I am of the opinion that credit is due to the Fascists for their restraint in abnormally provocative circumstances.

Yours etc.,

C.L. Ricketts

(12.6.1934)

The *Socialist Standard* in an article entitled *Reason or Violence*:

"The meeting held by the Fascists on June 7th at Olympia was the occasion of disorder that has prompted a shower of newspaper correspondence, questions in Parliament, and the suggestion that the police should have the right of entry into public meetings.

As far as the information goes, there does not appear to be any doubt that organised groups went to the meeting with the deliberate intention of creating disorder. Why, then, was so much fuss being made over the fact that they were roughly ejected? The outcry comes from such different quarters as Conservative, Liberal, Labour and Communists. The Conservatives have their own axe to grind, and are not anxious to assist the growth of Mosley's following. The other groups appear to have the wind up.

What is exceedingly curious in the business, however, is the righteous indignation of the Communists - who have gloried in meeting smashing for years, and promised to suppress all discordant voices if they got power.

In our view, those who went to the Fascist meeting with the intention of creating disorder and making the meeting impossible only got what they asked for, and have no reason to complain if they were roughly handled."

(1.7.1934)

Patrick Donner, M.P. to the Editor of *The National Review*:

"Sir,

In view of the many one-sided and consequently distorted accounts of what took place at the Fascist meeting at Olympia, may I, as a Conservative Member of Parliament present on that occasion, make a few comments? I attended as a naturally interested observer, and in no partisan spirit. What follows has no reference to the merits or demerits of Fascism or any other political movement. To describe, as a certain section of the Press have done, organised gangs of hooligans as "hecklers" or "genuine interrupters" who, attempting to elicit further information were brutally assaulted and forcibly ejected, is to give a wholly erroneous impression of what actually occurred.

The Very Reverend "Dick" Sheppard tells us that he rushed in hot haste straight from Olympia to the offices of the *Daily Telegraph*. This precipitate rush, coupled with that gentleman's well-known anti-Fascist bias, perhaps explains that in his statement there is no reference to the one substantial fact that cannot be overlooked if an unprejudiced and just judgement is to be reached. That fact is that many of the Communists were armed with razors, stockings filled with broken glass, knuckle-dusters, and iron bars: that they marched from the East End, the police kindly escorting, with the avowed purpose of wrecking the meeting. A friend of mine saw a woman Fascist with a razor cut across her face, and with my own eyes I witnessed gangs of Communists (some of them dressed in black shirts to make identification of those responsible for the uproar more difficult) resisting ejection with the utmost violence. If then, as cannot be disputed, some of these hooligans were armed, can it in equity be argued that the stewards used their fists, when provoked in this manner, with more vigour than perhaps the situation required. I listened carefully to comments of those nearby, and noted that one woman present referred to the "restraint" shown by the stewards. No one disputes that violent incidents took place in various parts of the hall, but surely it is scarcely surprising if the stewards, faced with organised and armed gangs, reached and passed the limit of human patience.

On leaving the building together with an acquaintance, he was advised by stewards to remove a small Fascist badge from the lapel of his coat because "it is dangerous outside." This man is a cripple, and is so crippled on account of wounds received in the service of his country in time of war. Surely it is intolerable that Englishmen, whatever their views, should not be able to walk with safety in the capital of their own country.

Yours etc.,

Patrick Donner, M.P.

(18.6.1934)

Lloyd George Sums Up

Lloyd George, writing in the *Sunday Pictorial* on June 24th, 1934, gave his view on the Blackshirts: "People began to ask themselves what was the meaning of the Albert Hall phenomenon; what might be the subterranean strength of the Blackshirt Movement, and what its promise or menace for the future government of the country.

But still more startling was the summoning, on June 7, of a meeting of this body at Olympia; for this is the biggest hall in London, only capable of being filled, if ever, in connection with some stirring national crisis. Yet the Blackshirts secured an audience of 15,000 people to pack that huge exhibition hall, and listen to an oration by their leader which went on for more than two hours.

Not all listened sympathetically; a considerable contingent of Communists manoeuvred an entry into the building by dubious means with a view to organising such disturbance as would frustrate speech. Their failure to do so was due to expulsory methods which several spectators have described as brutal in the extreme. This statement is challenged by the promoters of the meeting.

It is difficult to explain why the fury of the champions of free speech should be concentrated so exclusively, not on those who deliberately and resolutely attempted to prevent the public expression of opinion, of which they disapproved, but against those who fought, however roughly, for freedom of speech.

Personally, I have suffered as much as anyone in public life today from hostile interruptions by opponents determined to make it impossible to put my case before audiences. Naturally, therefore, I have an antipathy to that class of interruption, and I feel that men who enter meetings with the deliberate intention of suppressing free speech have no right to complain if an exasperated audience handles them rudely."

Public Order Act, 1936

In 1936 the Conservative leaders - who had permitted such disorder to occur all over the country until Mosley organised successfully to bring Red violence to an end - passed the Public Order Act which deprived him of the right so to organise at outdoor meetings but still permitted stewards at indoor meetings.

Section of Public Order Act, 1936, taking out of hands of private persons right to maintain order at outdoor meeting:

"If the members or adherents of any association of persons, whether incorporated or not, are -

(a) organized or trained or equipped for the purpose of enabling them to be employed in usurping the functions of the police or of the armed forces of the Crown; or

(b) organized and trained and equipped either for the purposes of enabling them to be employed for the display of physical force in promoting any political object, or in such manner as to arouse reasonable apprehension that they are organised and are either trained or equipped for that purpose:

then any person who takes part in the control or management of the association, or in so organising or training as aforesaid any members or adherents thereof, shall be guilty of an offence under this section:

Provided that in any proceedings against a person charged with the offence of taking part in the control or management of such an association as aforesaid it shall be a defence to that charge to prove that he neither consented to nor connived at the organisation, training or equipment of members or adherents of the association in contravening the provisions of this section."

Violence

The passing of the Public Order Act, 1936 deprived Mosley of the right to maintain order at his own outdoor meetings, which until then had been done successfully all over the country. The result of this new law soon became apparent. Below is printed an account in the paper which supported Mosley, *Action*; and an account in the *Daily Mail*. It will be clear that these two descriptions of the same event at Liverpool are similar in all essentials.

Action (No. 87) 16.10.1937:

"By one o'clock in the afternoon everyone must have been aware that a deliberate attempt at disorder by members of the Labour Party and their Communist apron-strings had been organised.

With the arrival of the van the din increased. No sooner had Arthur Greenhalgh climbed to the top than he was met with a shower of bricks of varying sizes one of which so injured his arm it had to be put into a sling.

A few short words heralded the approach of the Leader of British Union. He mounted the van and surveyed the crowd, estimated at more than 20,000, of whom all but a handful had come to listen. Approaching the microphone he waited for the tumult to die down when all at once the air became thick with flying bricks hurled with terrific ferocity by the 'staunch defenders of free speech'.

Quite successfully Mosley dodged the first shower, but was hit on the forehead by a large stone. He stood swaying for a moment, then collapsed on the van top.

In a moment several Blackshirts were at his side and he was being treated by St. Johns Ambulance men amid further showers of bricks from labourites and Communists."

Mosley: The Facts

Daily Mail, Monday, 11.10.1937:

Reds Injure Sir Oswald Mosley
Felled by Brick. Operation in Hospital.
Police Charge. 13 Arrests. Liverpool, Sunday.

"Sir Oswald Mosley is in hospital here with head wounds, being struck down by a firebrick by Red demonstrators during a Blackshirt meeting today.

Tonight a bulletin stated that he suffers from concussion and a punctured wound of the scalp. 'A minor operation was performed successfully and his condition is giving no rise for anxiety at the moment.'

A force of mounted police, hidden in reserve in a high-walled yard, charged the crowds gathered on a piece of waste land in Queen's Drive, Walton, here, as Sir Oswald fell on his face after being hit. He had been standing on the roof of a loudspeaker van trying to make himself heard above the shouts and screams of the Communists.

Howls greeted the men who began to assemble the loudspeakers and microphones on the roof of the van and they were hit many times with stones.

"... Sir Oswald staggered forward, fell on his hands and knees with his hands to his forehead. While supporters and an ambulance man were bending over him they were showered with bricks and Sir Oswald was hit several times on the body.

Stones continued to bounce off the side of the van while he was receiving first-aid inside after being lowered from the roof."

A Conservative Government's contribution to order by its Public Order Act was thus to deprive Mosley of the means to defend himself, without devising any effective means of their own to maintain order. It is clear, therefore, that the description of the act as a measure to promote disorder was not merely an empty gibe of the period. The conduct of the Conservative Party throughout has at least lent some colour to the suspicion that they were well content to give red violence a free hand against their only effective challenger, while they themselves retired from the struggle behind the protection of press and radio monopoly. It is to the great credit of many Conservatives M.P.s and party members that they refused to participate in this disgraceful action, as the quotations prove which are published above. As already stated, Mosley's indoor meetings - where he was not deprived by the act of the normal and legitimate means of maintaining free speech - were held in perfect order for a period of three years before the war. Until the time of publication, also, his meetings since the war have been held in good order and, happily, in good humour.

Chapter 6

The Frame-Up That Failed

On the 23rd May, 1940, Mosley was arrested and thrown into gaol under a special regulation passed the night before of whose existence he was, of course, unaware. Some 800 prominent members of his Movement were held in gaol without charge or trial under this Regulation. Mosley himself was three and a half years in gaol, and another year and a half under house arrest. The facts of this matter are now proved up to the hilt. Mosley and his friends were held in gaol for one reason alone - to prevent them persuading the British people to make peace. It is only necessary to supply two quotations in this section from the overwhelming evidence available.

1. A statement in the House of commons by Mr. Stokes (Minister of Works in Labour Government, 1945/51).

2. A statement by Lord Jowitt in the House of Lords at the time he was Lord chancellor in the Labour Government, 1945/51.

It is not only proved and admitted that Mosley and his colleagues did nothing disloyal to the country; in fact, they did nothing at all except advocate peace at public meetings. It is also proved that for years before the war Mosley led the demand for the re-armament of Britain, and quotations on this subject are also supplied in this section. It is grotesque to suggest that a man who demanded re-armament, even before Churchill did so, could desire the defeat of his country. The suggestion is rendered still more absurd by his instructions to his members at the outbreak of war, to be loyal to the country and to do their duty in the fighting forces where many of them were serving. He re-iterated his own determination to fight again as he had before (in the air and in the trenches in the 1914 war) if Britain were invaded, or the life of the country was in any way threatened. Meanwhile in the "Phoney war" period of 1939/1940 he claimed for himself the right to advocate a negotiated peace; a right which had always been accorded to British statesmen. Chatham did it, Charles James Fox did it, Lloyd George, Ramsay MacDonald and many others took such a stand in time of war.[6] Why was Mosley alone gaoled for doing precisely the same thing? The representatives of Government stated they were afraid his speeches would persuade the people to make peace. But in that case they had many remedies, short of putting men in prison who had committed no offence. They had special powers to prevent anyone saying, writing or publishing anything. Why were they not used? Or they could have called Mosley up. He was a regular soldier by original profession. He has often stated that in time of war he himself would have passed a simple law to place all citizens at the disposal of the nation for the duration. He would not have complained of such treatment. That would have been a clean and honourable action on the part of the Government.

But what did they do instead? They passed a special regulation under their power to suspend the Habeas Corpus Act, and arrested Mosley under it next day before he could even know it had been passed, and certainly long before he could learn the terms of it. That regulation was retrospective legislation at its worst. It was specially designed to enable members of his movement to be imprisoned without charge or trial. We publish in this section the terms of the regulation which enabled any member of any movement to be imprisoned whose leaders had had "association" (before the war, of course) with the leaders of countries with whom we were at war. In fact, it was not even suggested that

---

6   Mr Douglas Jay, Economic Secretary to the Treasury in the Labour Government of 1945/50, wrote when Labour was opposing war over Suez, the following words: "Don't let's forget that Chatham, Charles James Fox, Gladstone and Lloyd George all carried out full-blooded political campaigns against what they judged to be unjust wars waged by Tory governments. It is an honourable British tradition to oppose such wars." (Forward, 14th September, 1956).

Mosley has any "association" at all since 1936, three years before the war, when he saw both Hitler and Mussolini for the last time. Mr. Chamberlain "associated" with them long afterwards at Munich and many other prominent Englishmen saw them much more recently before the war.

Any man could be imprisoned for anything under such principles of retrospective legislation. You could do something perfectly legal - without possibility of reproach from anyone - and then be imprisoned for having done it years later under retrospective law.

Why did the Government stoop to this elaborate humbug in order to get Mosley into gaol? They had many other means to silence him without any necessity for a means so shameful - a means which clearly made nonsense of every principle for which they professed to stand. The answer is surely provided by what happened while he was in prison and what has happened since. While he was held silent and defenceless in gaol an intensive whispering campaign was organised against him. His political opponents took the opportunity to pay off old scores, and, as they hoped, to silence him forever. However even from gaol he answered them, when he had the chance. A Conservative M.P., Sir Thomas Cook, was foolish enough to say in public Mosley was a traitor, instead of whispering it in private like his less courageous colleagues. Mosley sued Cook for slander, and obliged him to make a public apology and pay damages, rather than face a court action in which he was advised he would not have a leg to stand on.

But Mosley could neither speak nor write, and the lies got a long start. It was only after the war that he slowly caught up with the lie and overcame it, despite the boycott of the national press which was meant to perpetuate the lie. The object was, of course, to take advantage of the war and Mosley's stand for peace to finish him politically, as his enemies hoped once and for all. The lie was launched, and at the same time every means taken to smother the answers. The means were to imprison him for as long as possible, and later to deny him all chance of reply through the national press, radio or television. If further proof were needed, Mosley's treatment after the war supplies it. The great smother continued. He must not be allowed to answer the lies. So a complete boycott was organised in the national press, and he alone among well known national figures was denied the use of radio or television. In fact, every Tom, Dick, Harry, clown or charlatan was given these facilities, while Mosley was denied them. Yet, for instance, in the Spring of 1956 he was again addressing packed and enthusiastic meetings all over the country, after leading figures in all parties had failed at meetings to draw handfuls. The simple fact is that the rulers of the system took their chance during the war to "fix" their only effective challenger. They gaoled him by a trick which made nonsense of all their professed principles during the war, circulated every possible diverse and devious means at their disposal, then used the power of money in press and television to deny him even after the war the means to reply. All of which adds up to one thing: this is the man they fear. And consequently this is the one man the public will want when they see through the great racket, as they are now beginning to do in the gathering crisis of the system. The old world failed to get Mosley down because again and again he fought back until the truth won through. They failed, too, because the people of Britain love fair play, and know a man if they get a chance to see him, and came again in their masses to his meetings after the war. The local press, conducted on the honest principle of fairly reporting what is news, gave him the publicity the money lords denied him in press and television. Mosley fought back; the facts broke through; and slowly the lie was killed. The blow which failed to destroy him simply made him stronger. Such are the tests of character that prove a man. Britain will soon need a man of proved strength and character. Mosley's enemies have provided for him that proof.

Statement by *Mr. R. R. Stokes*, Minister of Works in the Labour Government 1945/51, in the House of Commons Debate on December 10th, 1940:

"After 16 hours cross-examination in the private committees to consider 18B cases, Mr Norman Birkett indulged in this conversation with Sir Oswald Mosley, which I think ought to be put on record, whatever one's feelings. Sir Oswald said to Mr. Birkett:

"There appear to be two grounds for detaining us -

1. A suggestion that we are traitors who would take up arms and fight with the Germans if they landed and,

2. that our propaganda undermines the civilian morale"

Sir Oswald Mosley: "Then I can only assume that we have been detained because of our campaign in favour of a negotiated peace."

Mr. Norman Birkett: "Yes, Sir Oswald, that is the case."

The government made no attempt to deny or in any way to challenge Mr. Stoke's statement. Mr. Norman Birkett had been appointed by the British Government to preside over the inquiry, held in camera, into the cases of those detained under Regulation 18B. Afterwards, as Mr. Justice Birkett, he was a judge at Nuremberg.

Statement by *Lord Jowitt*, Lord Chancellor in the Labour Government, 1945/51 in a House of Lords Debate on December 11th, 1946:-

"I am not going to embark on a controversy as to whether Sir Oswald Mosley is an ordinary or extraordinary man, but we all agree that he was a very prominent man, and everybody in this country, and I suppose a very large number of people abroad, know him by name and know the sort of action which he took.

After all, lets us be fair to those people who were imprisoned under Order 18B, and let us remember that they have never been accused of any crime; not only have they not been convicted of a crime but they have not been accused of a crime. That should be remembered in all fairness to them."

Mosley Policy On War

On the 1st September, 1939, Mosley published the following instructions to all members of British Union:

"To our members my message is plain and clear. Our country is involved in war. Therefore I ask you to do nothing to injure our country, or to help any other power.

Our members should do what the law requires of them, and if they are members of any of the forces or services of the Crown, they should obey their orders, and, in particular, obey the rules of their service...

We have said a hundred times that if the life of Britain were threatened we would fight again..."

In May, 1940, he wrote as follows:

"According to the press stories concerning the invasion of Britain are being circulated ... In such an event every member of British Union would be at the disposal of the nation. Every one of us would resist the foreign invader with all that is in us. However rotten the existing government, and however much we detested its polices, we would throw ourselves into the effort of a united nation until the foreigner was driven from our soil. In such a situation no doubt existed concerning the attitude of the British Union."

Action (9.5.1940)

The author of these words was arrested a fortnight later, on May 23rd, 1940.

The Frame-Up That Failed

British Union's attitude before and since the war has been:-

1. We want peace and do our utmost to persuade the British people to declare their will for peace.

2. We are determined by every means in our power to ensure that the life and safety of Britain shall be preserved by proper defences until that peace can be made.

(14.3.1940)

Mosley repeatedly demanded re-armament for years before the war. A few extracts from his speeches on this subject to which he returned continually :-

"The arrival of the air factor has altered fundamentally the position of these islands, and the consequences of that factor have never yet been realised by the older generation of politicians. We will immediately raise the air strength of Britain to the level of the strongest power in Europe."

The Greater Britain (1.10.1932)

This quotation seems to make it clear that Mosley was even before Churchill in his demand for the re-armament of Britain. It is also made clear by the following quotation in 1933 :-

"We are not prepared to leave Great Britain in the helpless position which we occupy today, in face of the overwhelming air strength of other countries. Either their air strength must come down, or our air strength must go up."

Mosley's demand for re-armament continued consistently and persistently right up to the outbreak of war.

"We will immediately mobilise every resource of the nation to give us an Air Force equal in strength to the strongest in Europe. We will modernise and mechanise our Army, and at the end of that process our Army will cost less, but will be the most modern and effective striking force in the world."

(15.6.1934)

He also demanded a National Defence Loan for three purposes:

- To give Britain immediate air strength.

- To modernise and mechanise our Army.

- To put the Fleet in proper condition to defend our trade routes.

(12.7.1934)

On the 15th October, 1938, he denounced the failure of the Tory Party to provide proper armament in the following words :-

"The state of our national defence has alarmed the Tory Party. The state of these defences is a national scandal and disgrace. The Tory Party is, therefore, right to be alarmed; and, having been in power for the last seven years, they should be ashamed."

In an article on the 15th October, 1938, Mosley put his finger on the method which was to prove decisive in the coming war :-

"Modern wars are won by airmen and mechanics not by masses of barrack square infantry."

The old world ignored the importance of the air arm in which Mosley served in the first war, and of the new tank arm. The result was the loss of France. The newspaper *Action* which supported him made it clear that Mosley agreed with Mr. Churchill's attitude at least on the subject of re-arming Britain :-

"*Action* disagrees with Mr. Churchill on nearly every subject under the sun, and particularly in recent years with his foreign policy. But we agree with his indictment of the gross neglect of British defences.

British Union pressed re-armament upon the Government long before they began it, and long before even Mr. Churchill advocated it. British Union believes that Britain should be in a position to defend herself against the attack of any nation in the world."

Summary of Mosley's War Position.

In short, Mosley was against the war but he was for Britain. However mistaken he believed this war to be, he was determined that Britain should be defended from any attack. He put the position in a nut-shell in his book *My Answer*. It was in this book published in 1946 that he dealt with many of the sillier charges made against him before the war, e.g. that he received foreign funds in the thirties, as some Labour leaders did in the twenties. After repeated challenges his opponents failed to produce a shred of evidence for such allegations. But in the passage below he deals with the deadly serious suggestion - whispered but never spoken - that he might have been untrue to his country in time of war. By a very simple argument he shows that such a thing is out of the question for a man of principles, or for any such being:-

"There was never a moment's doubt as to our course; on the one hand to do nothing to weaken or injure our country for whose armament and strength, in a menacing world, we had ever striven: on the other hand, to do everything possible by the open political action, which the law then permitted, to persuade our fellow citizens first to keep the peace, and later to restore the peace. That course was dictated by the profoundest realities of nature which, in this case, are easily comprehended by any who begin to understand her deep laws. A man may not destroy his mother, however mistaken he may believe her to be. He may seek by every art of persuasion to retrain her from a dangerous folly. But, if she persists in that course, he may not join with her enemies to destroy her; on the contrary, he must, if necessary, defend her, however wrong, or even wicked, he may think her conduct. Anyone who does not understand this, is incapable of grasping the profound and divine laws which govern that small part of the universe which is discernible by man...

...Supposing a man's old mother expresses her firm intention to go down in fighting mood to the "local", where a number of tough characters are wont to assemble. He will be alarmed; particularly if his old mother expresses her equally firm intention of slapping "that person's" face, if he does anything of which she disapproves. He may, in fact, foresee a packet of trouble; and his disquietude will be in no way lessened by the fact, that his old mother has seen fit to arm herself for the occasion with nothing more formidable than an umbrella and a shrill tongue. But his course of conduct is perfectly clear. He will do his utmost to dissuade her from an undertaking which he feels can bring no good to her or to the family as a whole; if he fails he will not absent himself, but will accompany her. When the inevitable row begins he will do his utmost (1) to protect her, and (2) to extricate her as soon as possible with the minimum possible hurt. Any other course would be contrary to nature and every normal feeling of man. What an appalling conception that the son should be the first, when trouble begins, to stab his old mother in the back. No matter what his opinion of her behaviour, such action from him is inconceivable."

Yet this is precisely the conduct of which our opponents suggested we might be guilty, if left at large during a war which we believed to be a profound mistake. It matters not, for the sake of this argument, whether we were right or wrong in our opinion; that question will be discussed later. It matters not, in this simple analogy, whether a son's view of his mother's behaviour was in any way valid. All that matters is the acceptance of the principle that, rightly or wrongly, he may profoundly disapprove of her conduct, and yet be inhibited by every law of nature, and every normal feeling, from raising a hand against her, or doing anything except succour and protect her in her difficulty, whatever its origin. He will seek to dissuade her - yes - but he will never seek to injure her. Such was our attitude to our country in the last war. The reader may, or may not, think it utterly mistaken, for the moment that does not matter - but it is, at any rate, a position which he will understand and accept as honourable.

A Post-Script Explanation

The following explanation for the arrest and imprisonment of Mosley and his friends was provided by the Rev. Hugh Ross Williamson, the well-known author and later editor of *The Bookman* :-

"... May I emphasise the truth of the Duke's suggestion that 18B was used 'to pay off old scores against former political opponents ... and, in some cases, to punish anti-Semitism. Few of us who were involved in the pre-war politics of the Left can have any doubt not only that it has been used but that it was designed for this purpose.

At the Bournemouth Conference of the Labour Party in 1940 one of the main subjects of conversation which I heard at 'unofficial' talks was whether or not the Labour leaders had made the arrest and imprisonment of Mosley a condition of their entering the Government. The general feeling was that they had (or, at least, that they ought to) and though the matter is, obviously, incapable of proof, it is still accepted by many of us as the real reason for 18B..."

Hugh Ross Williamson, (17.7.1942)

"... May I be permitted to make an addendum to last week's letter on a matter of fact. At the time of writing I had not, unfortunately, access to Hansard, and was loth to trust my memory in the matter of dates.

The Amendment of Regulation 18B which made possible the arrest of Mosley was made on the evening of May 22nd, 1940 (Hansard, May 23rd, Sir John Anderson's speech, col. 291). This was the second sitting day after Labour joined the Government, and four days after Labour joined the Government, and four days after the close of the Bournemouth Conference of the Labour Party."

Hugh Ross Williamson, (24.7.1942)

Chapter 7

Writings And Speeches : Pre-War

In this chapter we give a few extracts from Mosley's pre-war speeches and writings, followed by others from his post-war speeches and writings (Chapters 9 and 10). The reader will naturally understand that the object here is not to give a comprehensive idea of his policy. For that purpose it is necessary to study such books as *The Greater Britain, One Hundred Questions Answered, Tomorrow We Live,* and his other pre-war writings, together with his books *My Answer, The Alternative, Mosley Policy and Debate,* and pamphlets such as *Government of Tomorrow, The Problem of Power, European Socialism, Automation,* etc., written since the war. The purpose here is to give some picture of Mosley in action, rather in the manner of stills from films.

The continuity of his thinking and feeling in certain vital respects emerges throughout his political life. But his strong sense of realism often leads him to grasp fresh means when circumstances entirely change. For instance, it is clear from these quotes that very early in the present generation he stood for European Union; so early as 1936. But he had in mind at that time some form of federation of the great European powers rather than Europe as an integral nation. He combined this conception for the maintenance of world peace, order and progress with the demand for a rapid development of British Empire in insulation from the chaotic condition of world markets. He believed this the best means then available for preventing the recurrent economic crises of the system and for progressively raising the standard of life of the British people. The fighting of an unnecessary war - which he opposed to the point of prison and obloquy (See Chapter 7: *The Frame-up That Failed*) - left Britain stripped of much of the old Empire and nearly all the resources with which it could have been developed. America and Russia emerged, as Mosley alone foresaw, with a dominating strength. As he had warned so often the Soviets then threatened to crush the enfeebled European powers, who were as hopelessly divided as the city states of ancient Greece, and menaced with the same fate. Mosley's realism at once drew the logical conclusion. It was useless any longer to speak of Britain forestalling economic disaster by development of her own Empire, when she has lost the manpower and the resources to do it. Britain no longer had manpower even adequate for her own agriculture and mining industry and was continually in danger of running a deficit on her balance of trade instead of the large surplus which was the only means to develop the Empire after the loss of nearly all her foreign investments in war.

Therefore Mosley declared in October 1948 the principle of Europe a Nation, after originally advocating the close Union of Europe as early as 1936. Nothing short of Europe organised as an integral nation could overcome internal differences and frictions, give the power of rapid action which the situation demanded, the strength to face the menace of Bolshevik Russia which the war had created, and the inspiring ideal necessary to enthuse the European people with new faith.

Two years later, in 1950, he developed the creed of European Socialism, which aims at the full use of modern science for the creation of a new civilisation. In a policy which far surpasses his economic thinking he finds the solution of such problems as automation within a self-contained system of supply and market in Europe/Africa, and develops the practical means by which the European standard of life can be progressively raised as science increases the power to produce.

The same strong sense of realism led him fundamentally to revise his pre-war concept of the problem of power and the structure of government. It was untrue that he ever stood before the war, or at any time, for dictatorship or a totalitarian system of government.

But he realised after the war that too much could be sacrificed, even to obtain the action which the modern situation so urgently requires. He is ever ready to learn, and always learning. He has purged all errors of the past from his new constitutional thinking. The means of action which the rapid movements of events makes so necessary is secured, but it is reconciled with the most carefully devised and protected system of individual liberty.

As already stated, it is not possible here to describe his creative thinking, or even in these quotations to give more than a light indication of his mind and spirit. Those who are interested should study the brief extracts in this chapter from his pre-war writings and speeches and the longer extracts in Chapter 9 and 10 from his post-war writings and speeches. The thoughtful reader is likely to find his post-war thinking more interesting than his pre-war thinking. This is one of the many paradoxes connected with Mosley; that his mind has greatly developed since the days when he was so much praised by the upholders of the present system. But perhaps it is no paradox; it may be quite natural that any man's thought should be less appreciated in current politics and journalism as it becomes more serious.

Union of Europe

"What then is the alternative to the present League of Nations? The only alternative is the Union of Europe, as opposed to the division of Europe under the old balance of power which now wears the tattered label League of Nations. The Union of Europe was the determination of the war generation at the end of the war, and the hope that the League of Nations would achieve that idea alone led to its support.

Meantime, with cant of League and Peace, the financial democrats divide Europe in their vendetta, which jeopardises the peace of the world, while they neglect the first duty of any government in the present situation, which is to arm Britain with the utmost speed against any contingency and threat. In the confusion and collapse of British foreign policy but one alternative emerges, and that is the Union of Europe, which alone can rest on a bloc of the great powers, united in common interest and inspired by a new world ideal.

The balance of power has returned, with Britain in the wrong scale of balance. We declare instead for the Union of Europe."

(26.6.1936)

"Our generation was sacrificed to bring an end to the balance of power which divided European civilisation into two armed and hostile camps. The avowed purpose of the League of Nations was to consecrate that sacrifice in a new world system. But, from the League mockery of prelates and politicians, emerges the old system in a yet more hideous and fatal form. Again our generation is challenged to save the ideal of which the old men cheat us once again. Shall Europe be divided, or unite?"

(21.2.1936)

"We must return to the fundamental conception of European Union", wrote Mosley in the *World Alternative*, a long study of the world situation which was published in 1937, in which he strongly advocated the Union of Europe. This essay was also published in the German magazine, *Geo Politik*.

Mosley wrote again in his last pre-war book *Tomorrow We Live*, published 1938 :-

"We will give leadership and make contributions to secure the material and spiritual Union of Europe, on which alone world peace and British interest in world peace can rest."

It seems quite clear from the above quotations Mosley was the first modern statesman to advocate the Union of Europe.

"I will begin with a simple proposition which none can deny. Either the confessions of the accused were true or untrue.

Having established that simple but basic fact we can examine the confessions. The accused stated that for years they had organised sabotage of their nation's industries and that, in the course of such acts, many of their fellow-countrymen had lost their lives. They stated that they had negotiated with foreign nations for the partition of their country in war. They further proclaimed that, in order to secure that defeat, they had arranged to release disease germs to wipe out the civil population of their own land. In fact, almost exultingly, they accused themselves of the vilest crimes conceivable to humanity.

Who were these self-accused criminals? They were the flower of the Bolshevik revolution, who made the revolution, and made the new Russia. With the exception of Stalin himself, practically every old Bolshevik was involved in this, or the previous trial. So, if the confessions are true, the men who made the Bolshevik revolution and the new Russian state, are amongst the vilest criminals yet known to history ... Let us then examine the only other alternative, that the confessions are untrue ... In this alternative Stalin is guilty of the deliberate frame-up of his colleagues and companions, and the enforcement of false confessions, for his own purposes, by the torture of his friends. Therefore, if we accept, as we must, the basic fact that the confessions are either true or untrue, but two conclusions can emerge. Either all men who made the Bolshevik revolution, except Stalin, are the lowest criminals yet known to history, or on the other hand Stalin, and those who now support him in the government of Russia, are monsters with few parallels in the annals of human depravity."

(6.3.1937)

"All wars are good to the Socialist Party on three conditions; the first, that the war shall be in the interest of the Soviets and not in the interest of Britain; the second, that our troops have no arms with which to fight; and the third, that socialist leaders are not included among the troops."

(26.6.1936)

"There you have the complete policy of Labour and socialism; scrap all your defences and then go out and fight the biggest man you can find. A very sensible policy! And a very brave policy when you have other men to do the fighting."

(13.9.1935)

"Labour is the party of war without preparation. Labour is the party which makes trouble and leaves others to do the fighting."

(6.4.1936)

"To seek war is a crime: to seek war without the means of war is more than a crime, it is madness."

(6.9.1935)

"Supposing two lots of Englishmen wanted to join up and get together. What would you think of Germany if she said: 'No you can't, if you two lots of Englishmen get together, we will declare war on you.' We would tell Germany or any other country that said two lots of Englishmen cannot get together, we would tell them to go to hell, and you know it. Supposing that Kent were occupied by the Portuguese and that in Kent, the Portuguese were insulting the British flag and bullying British womanhood. We in Britain would not stand for it. We would say those British people are coming home to Britain. What would we say to Germany if she tried to stop us? Yet that is what the Labour Party want to do to the Germans.

Each great nation has got to awake in its own great way. We, the British people, will never copy any other nation on earth, because we believe that with our own people we can make this the greatest nation in the world, that the whole world will look to Britain for an example. I want one day to be able to say to Hitler: "I don't care what you do with the East of Europe - good luck to you. We are going to beat you in the race for higher wages; we are going to beat you in the race to build the fairest, noblest land the world has ever seen."

(8.10.1938)

"First they disarm in an armed world. Secondly, they create a panic by threatening war without the arms to wage war; thirdly, they use the panic to get themselves re-elected on the cry that more arms are needed."

(18.10.1935)

"We ask those who join us to march with us in a great and hazardous adventure. We ask them to be prepared to sacrifice all, but to do so for no small and unworthy ends. We ask them to dedicate their lives to building in this country a movement of the modern age ... We ask them to re-write the greatest pages of British history by finding for the spirit of their age its highest mission in these islands. Neither to our friends, nor to the country, do we make any promises; not without struggle and ordeal will the future be won. Those who march with us will certainly face abuse, misunderstanding, bitter animosity, and possibly the ferocity of struggle and of danger. In return we can only offer to them the deep belief that they are fighting that a great land may live."

(1.10.1932)

"We count it a privilege to live in an age when England demands that great things shall be done, a privilege to be of the generation which learns to say what we can give, instead of what we can take. For thus our generation learns that there are greater things than slothful ease; greater things than safety; more terrible things than death. This shall be the epic generation which scales again the heights of time and history to see once more the immortal lights - the lights of sacrifice and high endeavour summoning through ordeal the soul of humanity to the sublime and eternal. The alternatives of our age are heroism or oblivion. There are no lesser paths in the history of great nations."

(29.3.1935)

"There was an element of farce in the tragedy. Spokesmen of the later Labour Government saw in the crisis that collapse of capitalism which they had prophesied with religious fervour.

'If that were true,' said Sir Oswald, 'the crisis came in a lucky moment for them. Labour was in office, and had every resource of the state at its command. What happened? The great day dawned, and Labour resigned; cleared out just when they had the realisation of their greatest wish. What would we think of a Salvation Army that took to its heels on the day of judgement?' he asked amid laughter."

(14.9.1931)

"The whole socialist conception of party and Government has been so designed that by no possible chance can any man on any occasion ever take a decision and act.

Conservatism has adopted some of the executive instruments such as loyalty and a measure of discipline. But it has used these great instruments, not to secure reforms, but to resist reform. It has sought to secure the stability of the state by resisting changes, in an age which demands great changes, if the state is not to collapse in ruin or degeneration.

So, socialism has failed to lead the nation, because in seeking progress, it has adopted methods which lead to chaos; conservatism on the other hand, by resisting change when change was necessary, has led the country to the same result."

(22.4.1934)

"The system is defended on the grounds that truth emerges from unfettered public controversy. Yet, in the paralysis of parliament and the decadence of the party system, real controversy has practically ceased to exist. All parties are agreed on all fundamentals, and differences arise only in purely artificial dispute.

It is this deep agreement of parties on the outstanding question of the day which is more responsible than any other factor for the absence of real issues between the parties and for the divorce of parliament from reality."

(2.7.1936)

"Some of the Marxian laws do actually operate if mankind is not organised to defeat them and they are operating today in the chaotic society which they envisage. If we rely on the instruments of the Stone Age, we shall be subject to the laws of the Stone Age, and overwhelmed by its forces. In other words if we rely on conservatism to defeat Marxism we shall be defeated by Marxism."

(1.10.1932)

"Marxism is essentially a material creed, denying all spiritual urge. Every motive of man, according to Marx, and every motive of humanity, has an economic and material origin. This may be true of some socialists, but we deny it is true of the normal Englishman. If a donkey jumps across a ditch, it is legitimate to conclude that animal has observed a particularly luxurious thistle on the other side. If a man jumps across a ditch we are disposed to believe that he has another motive. The movement of men throughout the ages has far more often been derived from a spiritual than from an economic inspiration."

(22.4.1934)

"If a business company issued a fraudulent prospectus which they knew they could not fulfil, they would go to gaol. But, if professional politicians issue a fraudulent prospectus to the nation at an election, they go to Downing Street. That is why so many distinguished gentlemen prefer public to private life."

(17.4.1937)

"We ask whether any honest man or movement in politics would not make his first proposal, and his first duty, to create an instrument of Government by which he could carry out the promises he had made, and the policy for which the people have voted."

(26.2.1938)

"If they want executive men to represent them in the modern world, they must vote for a system in which executive men can function. In fact, if the people want a public leader they must cease to expect a statesman to behave like a private clown.

The men of the future must 'live like athletes' because the stress of the modern world demands nothing less. Physically, mentally, spiritually, they must follow the fixed purpose of the dedicated life. Such men and such lives in the end must triumph because steel endures, and cuts clean and clean through."

(26.6.1937)

"The present system, not only by its whole structure, and methods, makes action impossible; more than that, it produces a type of man to whom action and decision are impossible even if he had the power.

We seek to establish a new ideal of public service, and a new system of authority which rests on merit."

(22.4.1934)

"As world markets and resources fail, modern science in their place reveals the limitless resources and possibilities of British Empire. What a moment in which to strike with a cold knife of cynicism, or blunt edged ranting demagogy, at the gossamer threads of tradition, loyalty and emotion which bind it together."

(15.5.1937)

"Britain was awake and soon blazed to her greatest glory under Chatham who, in the brief space of a few years, created the British Empire by a system of personal leadership, supported by an enthusiastic solidarity of the nation which would doubtless be described by present-day financial democrats as a most tyrannous dictatorship. The character of Chatham was as totally opposite to the character of Walpole as the conflicting moods of the nation in the two periods. Yet both were supreme embodiments of the British spirit. One represented Britain asleep and the other Britain awake.

In previous epochs time has been permitted for the nation to wake up under the stress of new and menacing circumstances. In the modern age fate may not permit that time. All things today accelerate and the pace speeds up; the periods and the rhythms of history move faster. The long periods of inaction followed by slow recovery to the plenitude of action, give place to but short periods of slumber, followed swiftly by the hammer-blows of destiny summoning to fresh effort."

(21.1.1937)

"*Can't* will be the epitaph of the British Empire unless we wake up in time."

(9.12.1937)

"They say their system is all right and there is nothing wrong with it. But how are we to judge any system? Surely by the condition of the people. Today we have in England low wages, long hours, rotten houses, unemployment and poverty corrupting our people - all absolutely unnecessary! With the vast imperial resources which are the heritage of this country, in this age when scientific progress and technical advance have increased production, the problems of poverty and want can easily be solved by a government empowered by the people to carry out their will. While democratic governments are giving away the Empire which our fathers won, our people are abandoned to poverty and unemployment. Yet the Empire belongs to you, the people of Britain! The hands of Englishmen won this great Empire which has been the glory of the world; their sacrifice and heroism gained it for us ... Arise and enter your own, and be great, happy and wealthy once again! Arise in your thousands, work with us ... In days to come your children will call down the blessings of heaven upon your heads, because you had the courage in these days of our struggle to stand with us against all the forces of political corruption, and all the hatred of the old world."

(23.10.1936)

"Such are the lessons of division, arising from the war of parties and the war of class, which have set Britons at each others' throats so that disunion may rivet on their necks the yoke of their financial masters. Thus Merrie England in an age which

97

could be golden, fades away in the smoke of the sweat shop and the slum, and the green beloved country becomes the playground of the stock-jobber, while the sturdy yeoman lines up in the unemployment queue ... From the ashes of the past, shall rise a Merrie England of gay and serene manhood, resplendent and adorned by the miracle of the modern age and the modern mind."

(8.5.1937)

"Let me think for a moment of the gay and manly scene of Tudor England on May Day, when a people of genius were first reaching out with a hard and confident challenge to the leadership of mankind; fire in their eyes, while their laughter rang in the face of death. Such men had not trod the mortal scene since the sunlight of the Attic spirit, and the virility of ancient Rome. Contrast such May Days of Elizabethan England with that shuffling procession to Hyde Park, where Labour leaders will declare that China and Spain must be saved by the dreary drip of their drivelling words. Meantime, they will ask the British people, from the depths of their poverty, to make a free present, to any who care to take it, of that boundless wealth of Empire, which the heroism and sacrifice of our fathers won...

Let us think, too, of the early leaders of Labour, marching on May Day in passionate protest against the conditions of the people of Britain. Let us reflect on the spirit of the early martyrs of the people's cause, and contrast it with these little men who lisp of China and Timbuctoo, on the rare occasions when their mouths are not stuffed with high living at the luxurious tables of the oppressors of the British people. Let us on May Day take one look at such creatures, and then raise our eyes from the mud to see again the light of those who died gladly, in every age of Britain's greatness, that the glory of Britain might live forever."

(30.4.1938)

"The decline of an obsolete system is reflected not only in parliamentary leadership, but in the whole conduct of government and parliamentary debate. The Cabinet has become a 'speak-easy' from which collective responsibility, discipline and team work have departed. Every little tadpole struggling for personal position airs his own opinions at the expense of his country, his colleagues, his leader and his party. While, as for parliamentary debate, it was recently described by an old member as a P.S.A. with the Prime Minister in the role of the dear vicar. A cross word is hardly ever heard in its delicate proceedings and the cut and thrust of debate, in the early and more virile days of parliament, is almost unknown. When Mr. Lloyd George occasionally breaks loose, the young Conservatives are reported to sit in silence, with the pained expression of those who witness a public-house brawl in a church. The tedium of the proceedings is relieved, alone, by zoological noises from the socialist benches to howl down anyone who ventures at all vigorously to criticise their policy. Whatever reality parliament ever possessed has departed, and controversy is left to the daily newspapers, while government, as ever, is entrusted to the City of London."

(15.5.1937)

"The majestic symbol of the British Crown embodies the pride of the British people in the past, the present and the future of our Imperial race. It is the Crown not only of Britain but of Empire, and as such it symbolises our immortal history, in which the genius of our forbears reached out from this small island to possess, and to elevate in high civilisation, one quarter of the terrestrial globe. The Crown, therefore, represents an achievement unique in the annals of the human race, and every Briton feels that this achievement of his race is thus represented and perpetuated in the Crown. It is the outward and visible sign of our Imperial splendour, achieved by rare genius. He, who insults the British Crown, thus insults the history and achievements of the British race."

(15.5.1937)

"Small minds and great empires go ill together," observed one of the greatest British orators and thinkers. Small is the mind and mean the spirit which decries the Crown with the shrill giggle of the parlour Bolshevik or snarling hate of the class-war rhetorician."

(15.5.1937)

"The future has no place for idlers, and indeed, it is a contravention of the very laws of nature that a C3 brain should draw an A1 income."

(5.1.1939)

"He (Mosley) was asked the other day to summarise his policy. He did so very shortly in two words - "Socialistic Imperialism.""

(29.11.1918)

"The roots of Britain are being dragged from the soil. Any tempest can blow over the top-heavy structure of the industrial state.

But little acquaintance with history is necessary to the knowledge that the decline of all great civilisations has been accompanied by two main symptoms of decadence. The first is the growth of the international usury system and the second is the decline of the countryside and the drift of population from country to town. Any civilisation that is to endure requires constant replenishment from the steady, virile stock which is bred in the health, sanity, and natural but arduous labour of the countryside."

(24.4.1937)

"Once again the yeomen of Britain will return, and within them will live again the spirit of that breed of man who built the Empire, and lifted to the heights of history the British name. The spirit of the country will remain and the roots of Britain will again grip and dig deep into British soil. Let tempests come: the oak will stand."

(24.4.1937)

"In the reign of Queen Elizabeth it was the law of the land that no man might starve. Nearly four centuries later thousands are half-starved, and their physique permanently impaired, by the protracted want of the essentials of life. That is the scandal of the modern age to which financial democracy has reduced us. The wrong cries for redress at the moment when fish are flung back into the sea and milk is poured down the drain, or used to make handles for walking sticks. This monstrous thing is permitted in an age when science has solved the problems of poverty, if government had the wit and the will to organise the proper distribution of the bounty of nature and industry.

A fraction of the present luxury spending would provide sufficient for the needs of life to those who are below the border-line of human existence. This I declare not because I have ever suffered from the illusion that mere redistribution can solve the problem of existence. On the contrary, my whole policy and my every speech and writing has advanced a policy by which greater wealth production provides the solution of the poverty problem. But during the organisation of that system we cannot and will not permit luxury to be flaunted in the eyes of the stricken.

Nothing can stop the disgusting spectacle of bemused sots swilling and guzzling to the strains of a highly-paid American-Negro band, while British folk starve in hovels, except a new movement of national renaissance backed by the will and conscience of an awakened nation. They shall neither swill nor shall stuff while others starve. Not a night club shall open its doors or ball be given, until the needs of the suffering have been tended. The first charge on the nation shall be those whom this system has cast on the scrap heap of plutocracy..."[1]

(29.11.1936)

"The march with bands and banners, followed by a mass meeting was a socialist technique unknown or rendered impossible to conservative opponents. I learnt the technique of street propaganda when elected annually to speak at miners' galas

---

[1]   At the end of 1936 there were 1,749,000 unemployed in Great Britain.

and other great open-air meetings of the Labour Party, long before I had ever witnessed a fascist or Nazi demonstration. We perfected that technique and carried far beyond the Labour Party methodology to defeat them on their own ground. Our bands, banners and marches, with the aid of uniforms and other novel methods of propaganda, have been far more colourful and attractive to the mass of the people than the dreary spectacle of a few pot-bellied trade union officials, and long-haired intellectuals, waddling along in a procession to an open-air meeting of the Labour Party. So we have beaten them on their own ground and where they drew a thousand, we drew a hundred thousand."

(31.10.1936)

"We may leave cynicism to the poor creatures of the pseudo-intellectual world, the feeble operations of whose minds have quickly vitiated their still feebler bodies. For mechanism so fragile cannot withstand the strain of thinking and feeling at the same time, so they discard emotion in favour of what they erroneously believe to be thought. The full man can both feel and think, because his vitality of mind, and strength of spirit, can carry learning as a gift and an adornment and not as a burden."

(15.5.1937)

"In the public affairs of national life we have disorder and anarchy; in the private affairs of individual life we have interference and repression. At every point the private life of the individual is invaded by busybody politicians who have grossly mismanaged their real business - which is the public life of an organised nation. It is, of course, a simpler task for limited intelligence to keep the public-houses closed than to keep factories open.

We live on public anarchy and private repression; we should have public organisation and private liberty. The moral and social law and convention of Britain provide the most startling of all contrasts with the Briton's strange illusion that he is free. The plain fact is that the country is hag-ridden.

(1.10.1932)

"The slow soft days are behind us, perhaps forever. Hard days and dark nights ahead, no relaxing of the muscle of mind and will. It is at once our privilege and our ordeal to live in a dynamic period in the history of man. The tents of ease are struck, and the soul of man is once more upon the march."

(1.10.1934)

"Do we envy those who have lived in the lotus moments of the past? Do those of my generation regret their own short youth; that brief bright moment between storm and storm? No! we regret nothing. Those, who have lived in the quiet valleys of blissful, peaceful periods in the history of the world have never known our depths, but they have, also, never known our heights. They have never stood on the topmost pinnacle of sacrifice where thunder threatens and lightning strikes. They have never felt on their brow the beckoning wind of the future, nor seen with their eyes the land that is to come. They have shared happiness with the animals of the field, but they have never felt the fierce fires of danger, and of suffering, urging forward and upward the spirit of humanity. Therefore, we would not change with them, even if we could. Hard is our road, but on our march we feel the rhythm of the universe."

(1.10.1934)

"The future is with the strong and the brave, the resolute, who have found themselves by the oblivion of self in a greater cause and destiny."

(2.1.1937)

"Supposing people had stood on the shore when the ships of Drake and Raleigh, or of Clive, set to sea and said, "Don't go. The sea is very rough and there will be trouble at the other end." There was no old wife on the shore then, whispering Mr. Baldwin's favourite slogan "Safety First.""

(29.3.1935)

"When we began we could not tell whether it would take us three years or thirty years to make our Movement. For our own part we did not care how long it took; we only meant to do the job that had to be done."

(25.10.1935)

"I have never made prophecies on the time and chronology of things. It is sufficient to hold a faith so deep that it carries with it the certainty of victory. Leave prophecies of when and where, and talk of today or tomorrow, to the little jobbers of the market. For us it is enough to know that without our faith Britain cannot live, and that to live Britain must turn to us."

(2.10.1937)

"Great struggles await us, and from time to time in the future as in the past no doubt we shall experience our reverses. These things do not matter. What does matter is that a spirit has been created in Britain which in the end cannot fail."

(1.10.1932)

"We take the view that the patriot is not only the man who loves his country, but is determined to build a country worthy of that love, and who dedicates himself to the service of the nation which he loves."

(17.5.1935)

"We vowed to our comrades who fell, that from their sacrifice, and from their ashes a nobler land should arise - a land in which their children might live in peace and happiness. To the dead we keep our vow. In memory of those men who died, we who are left must relent not nor relax till peace be won and Britain be reborn. In the name of the dead, in the name of the living, in the name of our children and of Britons yet unborn, we give ourselves to England."

(17.3.1938)

"We must call in the new world of science to redress the balance of the old world of industry."

(1.10.1932)

Menace of Russian Communism

Speeches and writings before and during the war which warned that the outcome of that war would only increase the menace of Russian Communism.

"And what is Russia doing? - playing the old oriental communist game of the last twenty years and more with all the old oriental cunning and skill; luring the poor old Tory government deeper and deeper into the bog of commitment until at last they have them where they will; dangling the carrot in front of the old donkey's nose, who is plunging and blundering further and further and then, when she has guaranteed not only Turkey, Greece and Rumania, but all the Baltic states, when they have got Britain into any quarrel that is going on anywhere in the world, then they will provoke world war, let it loose upon us and at last achieve the objective of the communist leaders to overthrow Britain and western civilisation in suicidal war."

(16.7.1939)

"Russia believes that by playing about between the Axis powers and the financial democracies she can most effectively promote the world war to bring the destruction of western civilisation for which the leaders of Russian communism have worked consistently for over twenty years. Committed to neither side but playing with both is a familiar role in their type. If in the process they can drag both sides to ever deeper and more fatal commitment their objective is achieved.

In Russia they clearly must seek a new means of destroying their first and greatest antagonist, which is British Empire in the East."

(26.8.1939)

"Some observers state that Stalin feels now like the greatest of the Csars; others that he is still a simple and original Russian communist. Whichever be true, either the old Russian imperialism or the old Russian communism has always held, as its first and main objective, the smashing of the British Empire in the East."

(2.10.1937)

"While the two great white giants, Britain and Germany, lie in the dust panting, gasping, streaming with their wounds, the yellow bandits and the Slav jackals will seize our eastern Empire."

(16.10.1939)

"Not only Russian engineers, but Russian propagandists have long been appearing in these parts of the world. The new oriental horde moves with its scouting force well in front in the shape of a storm of propaganda. What prize of her (Russia's) western borders compares with the objective which has been held throughout the ages by both Russian tsardom and Russian communism - the overthrow of British Empire in the East? To a half-oriental power could any reward for greater risk in the West compare with the long desired access to the southern seas of Asia and the complete domination of the Middle East?

Will they, on the other hand, prefer a strategy which suits well the nomad character which they still retain from their ancestors, in a gradual filtering down towards the ocean through the great broken spaces of the East, preceded by wave after wave of propagandists, against an enemy who has to fight over sea-borne communications at enormous distances from his base?"

(16.1.1939)

Prediction of Economic Crisis.

The following extracts from speeches and writings long before the war, show that Mosley accurately predicted the economic crisis which is now beginning to occur. It was postponed by a war and two armament booms (pre-war and post-war). The H-bomb has closed the traditional escape from economic breakdown into war.

"We were the first nation to pass through an industrial revolution, and for long we enjoyed something approaching a monopoly of world trade in manufactured goods. Long before the war[2] that monopoly had passed away, and under the stress of war and post-war development the process has been progressive and accelerated. Nevertheless, our export of manufactured goods still amounts to nearly 30 per cent of our total production...

In actual fact, each nation is striving hard to make itself as nearly as possible a self-contained economic unit. Behind every kind of artificial barrier they seek to create a variety of trades to supply them with as large a proportion as possible of the goods which they consume ... we have to face the fact that nearly every civilised nation is striving to produce at home that ever-greater quantity of the goods which it consumes. Further, the backward and undeveloped areas of the world, which we previously supplied with manufactures for their consumption and with the capital goods for their development, have mostly reached a point of development in which they need such services in ever-lessening degree.

In addition to all this industrialisation of former markets, we have to face in whatever markets remain an intensity of competition without precedent in previous experience. Many of these competitors, too, are nearer than we to the markets for the goods concerned, and better fitted to appreciate the problems of manufacture and sale arising from geographical and racial differences. In addition, a country like America, which hitherto

---

2   *World War I*

has disposed of only some 8 percent of her surplus production, in export trade, has a clear advantage in a price-cutting scramble for markets over a country such as Britain, which has diverted a 30 percent margin of her total production to export trade.

A country, like a business, may dispose for a time of a small proportion of its total output at a loss, in order to invade further markets and to crush competitors. There is another point. Protected industries, such as those of the United States, provided that they have a substantial market at home, can charge prices which allow them to pay overhead charges and the interest on all their capital by selling the bulk - but not the whole - of their output. It then pays them to sell the rest, for export, at prices which merely pay for the labour and materials used. A business, or a nation, can do this with 8 or 10 percent of its output; but Britain, in order to compete, would have to adopt the same policy with 30 percent - in many industries more - of her industrial production. To attempt such a course is the direct road to bankruptcy.

We are faced, in fact, with a new and intensive competition for foreign markets. The intensity of the struggle for foreign markets is further increased by the shrinkage of home markets, which drives the industrialists of every nation ever more desperately to seek a foreign outlet for their surplus production. The shrinkage of home markets, of course, is in turn aggravated by the race in wage reduction, in order to lower costs and capture foreign markets, which sets up a vicious circle of shrinking home markets and greater pressure to sell abroad.

It is now the declared aim of every great nation to have a favourable balance of trade. Every nation in fact seeks to sell more to others than it buys from them - an achievement which, it is clear, all nations cannot simultaneously attain. So a dogfight for foreign markets ensues in which the weaker nations go under, and their collapse in turn reacts upon the victors in the struggle by a further shrinkage of world markets. A continuation of the present world struggle for export markets is clearly the road to world suicide, as well as a deadly threat to the traditional basis of British trade.

Underlying all these phenomena is a deeper sociological fact which destroys for all time the illusion that our old supremacy can be regained in the old way. In the past British goods gained their ascendancy, partly because they were first in the field, but also because they were the best.

Mass production has altered the criteria; the skill of the handcraftman is no longer the leading factor in industry and buyers are increasingly influenced by price. Here we are at many disadvantages. In the past, export has been our main problem, and we cannot afford to sell goods abroad except at a full economic price. In each market we are apt to encounter some nearby competitor who is simply getting rid of his surplus at any price which will pay him to keep his mass-production machinery going.

Again, most of our workmen are of a good type, capable of rising to the heights if skill which earned them their reputation in the past. For modern, cheap mass production, such labour is unnecessary. No limits are now set to the exploitation of the backward labour of the Orient in competition with the skilled labour of the West. An oriental can work for ten hours a day, in exchange for a few bowls of rice, provided that such labour does not exact too much from his fragile physique or from his undeveloped intelligence. To press a button at regular intervals in the simplified process of mass-production while he dreams of other things, is to him most appropriate and congenial labour. He is actually, in some way, better suited for the monotony of mass-production tasks than is white labour, which cannot endure that monotony, at any rate for more than very short hours. That tendency is bound to increase and to become a deadly menace to the whole white standard of life and indeed to the whole structure of Western civilisation.

The Greater Britain (1.10.1932)

Prediction of Automation Problem.

Even if we make the immense assumption that all the problems which are now so much canvassed as barriers to trade were surmounted by the statesmen who are now discussing them, we should still have to overcome certain bedrock facts for which the existing political system and existing statesmanship offer no solution whatsoever. We should still be faced by the fact that the industries of the world can today produce, without running at nearly their full pressure, far more than any conceivable effective demand of the present system can absorb. That is the central fact which neither talk nor conference has escaped.

The process of rationalisation[3], advanced as it is, has still far to go. Broadly speaking, it is furthest advanced in the United States. Twenty American families, working on the land, Mr. Hubert Blake has estimated, can produce the food needed for themselves and eighty other families; in France it takes fifty families to produce the food needed for themselves and fifty others ... the Czechoslovakian workman, in the highly mechanized factories of the late Herr Bata, produces twice as many boots per day as does the workman in British boot factories. The movement of the future will be towards a higher world average per workman, and thus to increasing rationalisation in Britain.

In face of this evidence, it is quite clear that the power to produce has far outstripped the mechanism of distribution. The relatively slow increase of productive capacity during the last century gave time for the automatic adjustment of demand to supply; this has now given place to a sensational advance in science, technique and productive potentiality, which makes irrelevant all hope of the automatic adjustments of the past.

Nothing but the rationalised state can hope to overcome the problem created by rationalised industry. It is idle to denounce

---

3   Rationalisation is now called automation. The process remains essentially the same; man's labour is replaced by the machine. The only difference is that is those days the machine did part of the task; now it does nearly the whole task in some cases.

rationalisation, because it simply means the modernisation of industry, and industries which are not modernised cannot live at all in present conditions. Further, to prevent rationalisation is to prevent any reaping of the fruits of science which, in any rationalised society, would vastly benefit mankind. The way to meet industrialisation is not to put back the hands of the clock, but so to organise society that its effects are constructive rather than destructive.

It cannot be denied that every day new processes of rationalisation displace fresh labour. The displacement of labour creates more unemployment, reduces the number of those earning wages, and thus yet further reduces the market for which industry produces. The power to produce goods increases, but the power to consume does not increase - at least in anything like the same proportion. If the power to consume increased in anything like equal ratio to the power to produce, the labour displaced by rationalisation would of course be absorbed in industry again by the greater demand for goods.

(1.10.1932)

The Economic System: What is Wrong? [4]

"Every boom of the present system grows shorter and lesser; every depression grows deeper and longer. The crazy machine of the present economy rocks ever more violently towards a final disaster. The plain and simple reason is that the international system is a century out of date. That system is responsible both for the evils and for the danger of the present time.

The facts are precisely the opposite to a century ago; yet the system in all fundamentals is precisely the same and the attitude of the parties is the same. To the international parties everything

---

4   From Oswald Mosley's 'Tomorrow We Live', published in 1937, the policy of the pre-war movement, British Union.

that has happened in the interval might never have occurred. The arrival of the technician, the introduction of the age of steam and later the age of power, has altered forever the economic environment of mankind. Yet all parties, including the Labour Party, support the international system of trade which preceded this vast revolution in fact and circumstance.

So our unfortunate industry is compelled to serve the international system and at all costs to national economy to fight for the export trade on which that system rests. In the battle for exports modern science and modern conditions have again confronted our trade with an entirely new set of facts which have built such insuperable obstacles that the fight for exports ever since the war has been a steadily losing battle. The spread of modern science and technique has enabled our former customers to industrialise themselves. These new foreign industries are protected not by the obsolete weapon of tariffs but by barriers of complete exclusion which have not yet been lowered in response to the pious request of British statesmanship, at innumerable international conferences, that these foreign nations should ruin their own industries in order to provide us with the markets which we lack. In remaining markets still open to us we are faced with a competition, unprecedented and irresistible, which has been created by the vile exploitation of modern science by finance power in the industrialisation of the Orient. Western finance has provided the loans which have equipped the East with equal machinery to the West, and have hired the western technician to teach the oriental to perform the simplified tasks of mass-production with modern mechanical technique at a third of the wages and for longer hours of monotonous toil than white labour can endure. The result has been a stream of sweated goods under-cutting British products on the markets of the world.

How can we raise or even maintain British wages in the face of competition from sweated labour supplied with the same machinery but paid a third of the wages and working for far longer hours? Whether industry be capitalist and owned by the unrestricted individual, or socialist and owned by the state, how can it function in modern conditions if the system be international? This question is the epitaph of international socialism, for it drives every thinking socialist, together with men of all parties who seriously study modern conditions, into the ranks of British Union, which organizes industrial freedom within the insulated bounds of an Empire economic system.

The wages and salaries of the British people are held down far below the level which modern science and the potential of production could justify because their labour is subject to the undercutting competition of sweated labour on both foreign and home markets.

In economic results every blessing with which science endows mankind becomes in fact a curse. The rationalisation of industry with higher wealth potential should be the greatest benefit of the period. In fact, it is dreaded by the people because it brings ever increasing unemployment with every increase in the power to produce. The reason again is plain to see, because each increase in the power to produce goods is not accompanied by a corresponding increase in the power to consume goods.

On the contrary, because internationalism restricts purchasing power, rationalisation results in a lesser rather than a greater power to consume the wealth it produces. Rationalisation enable industry either to produce more goods with the same amount of labour, or to produce the same amount of goods with less labour. Because the purchasing power of the people is held down by the unfair competition of the international system, purchasing power cannot increase at the same time that rationalisation increases the power to produce. As a result only the same amount of goods as before can be produced after rationalisation, and they are produced with less labour. More are thrown, with loss of wages, on to the scrap heap of unemployment, and purchasing power is further diminished, just at the moment when it is essential that it should be increased if the victory of science is to be a blessing and not a curse.

Labour is prevented by an obsolete international creed from pursuing the only solution of building high British wages within a British economic system to enable the British people to consume what the British people produce. Any fool can inflate, and appropriately enough this is the only remedy now left to the Labour Party.

International socialism has always rested on the theory summarized in the slogan *Workers of the World, Unite*. After 80 years of this appeal the workers of the world are farther than ever from unity. On the contrary, in the interval, capitalism has got on with the task of introducing new and sweated workers who are incapable of reading even a socialist manifesto.

The whole conspiracy of politicians, press and economists teaches the British people to believe that to send steel to a remote country to build a bridge over a faraway river, and send bicycles for savages to ride over the bridge, without any hope of repayment for this exported wealth, is a transaction of sound economy and finance. While to keep that steel at home to build British dwellings, and the bicycles at home for Britons to ride along well made roads, is a principle of wild-cat finance. The greatest of all bluffs put over the British people is the loan-export bluff, for it has induced them to alienate from themselves forever an enormous proportion of the wealth they have produced by the genius of their technicians and the sweat of their workers. Late in the day they begin to see that the export machines which they created, and taught the world to use, is today resulting in the equipment of sweated labour to undercut them on every market of the world. Finance, secure in the equipment of the East by the effort of the West, cynically deserts the origin of its strength and wealth for fresh oriental pastures, where the yield of usury from the sweated is greater than the return of interest from the civilized. So in the final frenzy of the system finance drives the West to produce the means of its own destruction, and, not content even with this classic business of the money power, our financial masters now make the primary commodities and raw materials which serve our stricken industries the subject of world gambles whose fluctuations create chaos in which industry is paralysed. But internationalism and the parasite which drives it to destruction have gone too far; and today greed and folly bring their nemesis in the threatened destruction of the body on which they prey. That body is the industry and life of western man."

System of Government - What is Wrong?
(Further extracts from '*Tomorrow We Live*')

"Decisions and movements of international finance on Wall Street, and its sub-branch in the City of London, may send prices soaring to create a speculators' paradise at the expense of the real wages to the people, or may send prices crashing to throw millions into unemployment as the aftermath of some gigantic gamble. In the terms of the things that really matter to the people, such as real wages, employment, the hours of labour, food prices, and the simple ability to pay the rent, finance, under the present system, can affect the lives of the mass of the people more closely and more terribly in the decision of one afternoon than can Parliament in the course of a decade.

Good wages, good houses, short hours of labour, opportunity for culture, recreation and self-development, a chance for the children of the family equal to the chance of any children in the land: these are the realities of liberty in the homes of the people. Who will deny on the one hand that the people do not under this system possess this liberty, and who will deny on the other hand that such liberty in the age of modern science is within the achievement of the human mind and the human will?

The technician with the genius of the modern mind and the inspiration of the modern spirit within him carries in his hands for the people this priceless gift of liberty for the first time in history.

It is the task of government to keep the ring for the technician and protect him from the forces of chaos while he solves the problem of human liberty - which can primarily be solved only in economic terms. Yet this is precisely the duty which at present government is incapable of performing. The forces of chaos and of predatory anarchy are loose in the world and they are stronger than government. The problem of human liberty cannot be solved until government is stronger than they.

So the small man continues to be crushed by the combines and the worker continues as industrial fodder, for fear that they may lose their freedom. The householder will not employ a policeman because he is persuaded that to give policemen power is dangerous. So he is ruled and finally crushed by the tyranny of finance which he has not elected and which he cannot control, because he fears that to give a government, which he has elected and which he can control, the power to act, is to deprive himself of liberty.

There stands the Briton in the street, gulled into the acceptance of slavery by words about liberty, and boasting of freedom, while in truth denied the freedom to call his own even the soul of which alone his masters have not robbed him, for the simple reason that it has no cash value.

Parliamentary Speeches.

Brief extracts only are printed from Mosley's Parliamentary speeches to give some idea of his Parliamentary style which differed considerably from his platform method. The two speeches selected are his resignation speech (28th May 1930) and his speech on the economic crisis of 1931 (8th September 1931). These extracts, of course, give no idea of his argument as a whole on these momentous occasions. Any reader who is interested in the subject must read the whole speeches, copies of which are available.

From Mosley's Resignation Speech, House of Commons (28 May 1930):

"General surveys of unemployment I have always distrusted, because they are liable to degenerate into generalities which lead us nowhere. If we are to discuss this matter with any relation to realities, we must master the actual hard details of the administrative problem, and to that problem I desire immediately to proceed.

I submit to the Committee that, if anyone starts in any business or enterprise, his first consideration must be the creation of a machine by which that business can be conducted; and, when a Government comes into power to deal with unemployment, its first business is the creation of an efficient and effective machine.

The machine which I suggested - it is impossible to describe it in great detail on this occasion - was a central organisation armed with an adequate research and economic advisory department on the one hand, linked to an executive machine composed of some 12 higher officials on the other, operating under the direct control of the Prime Minister and the head of the Civil Service himself, and driving out from that central organisation the energy and initiative of the Government through every department which had to deal with the problem. It is impossible really to expound such a scheme to the House in detail unless it is seen in the graph form in which I submitted it.

It is admittedly a complex organisation. I was told that to carry such an organisation into effect would mean a revolution in the machinery of government. My only comment is this. The machinery which I suggested may be right or may be wrong, but this I do suggest, that to grapple with this problem it is necessary to have a revolution in the machinery of government. After all, it was done in the war; there were revolutions in the machinery of government one after the other, until the machine was devised and created by which the job could be done. Unless we treat the

117

unemployment problem as a lesser problem, which I believe to be a fallacious view, we have to have a change in the machinery of government by which we can get that central drive and organisation by which alone this problem can be surmounted.

The Government throughout have pinned their hopes to rationalisation.[5] For my part I have always made it perfectly clear that, in my view, rationalisation was necessary and inevitable. It has to come in the modern world. Industries which do not rationalise simply go under. It is agreed among most people that rationalisation is necessary, but do not let us proceed, from our view that rationalisation is necessary, to the easy belief that rationalisation in itself will cure the unemployment problem.

I have been at some pains to examine the facts in trades which have at any rate partially rationalised, and I think we can take, as a criterion of a rationalised trade, those trades which, in a relatively short space of time, have greatly increased their production for a profitable market. I applied this criterion to trades of that character - four big groups of trades - and I found, between 1924 and 1929, an average increase in production of over 20 percent, but an average decline in the insured workers in those trades of over 4 percent. Over five years you have that immense increase in production - a very great achievement - and over the same long period a steady decline in the efficiency in expanding their markets. It would appear, therefore, on the evidence which exists, that rationalisation in itself is at any rate no short and easy cut to the solution of the unemployment problem.

There is a further point. The whole emphasis in this matter of rationalisation is thrown by the Government on the export trade.

I submit that this hope of recovering our position through an expansion of our export trade is an illusion, and a dangerous illusion; and the sooner the fallacy is realised, the quicker can we devote ourselves to a search for the real remedy. There are

---

5   Now called automation.

innumerable factors beyond these which I have mentioned, militating against any increase of our export trade to that extent. There is the industrialisation of other countries for their own home markets; there is the industrialisation of countries which had no industries at all a few years ago.

The intensified competition all over the world is making more and more illusory the belief that we can again build up in the world that unique position which we occupied many years ago.

If our export trade on its pre-war basis is really no longer possible, we have to turn to the home market. We must always, of course, export sufficient to buy our essential foodstuffs and raw materials.

We have to get away from the belief that the only criterion of British prosperity is how many goods we can send abroad for foreigners to consume.

I want to suggest that that policy of controlled imports can and should be extended to other trades, for this reason that if we are able to build up a home market, it must be agreed that this nation must to some extent be insulated from the electric civilisation and a standard of life which can absorb the great shocks of present world conditions. You cannot build a higher force of modern production. If you are subject to price fluctuations from the rest of the world which dislocate your industry at every turn, and to the sport of competition from virtually slave conditions in other countries. What prospects have we, except the home market, of absorbing modern production?

Apart from the effects of rationalisation, which I have already endeavoured to describe, we have to consider this great fact, that since the war there has been a tremendous spring of scientific invention. All through the last century it is true these things happened, but they happened gradually. You had an adjustment of production to consumption over a long period of time, albeit with considerable dislocation of industry. Now you have this tremendous leap forward in a few years in your productive capacity which has absolutely upset the industrial equilibrium of the world and demands entirely different measures to deal with it. A great scientist said to me only a few months ago, "In the last 30 years the scientific and industrial capacity of the world has increased more than it did in the previous 300 years" and rather unkindly he went on to add, "The only minds that have not registered that change are those of the politicians."

Governments, officially at any rate, have never done any thinking. It is very difficult to analyse and get at the facts of the modern situation unless you have at your disposal the information and the research which government departments alone can supply. That is why it is so essential to have at the centre of things machinery that can undertake that work. What machine today is undertaking the work of reorganising industry? Not the Government at all, but the banks. It is the Governor of the Bank of England who is doing this work. I admit at once that, in any effort of the Government in present conditions, the co-operation of the banks is very necessary and that efforts should be made to secure it as the Lord Privy Seal has tried to do, but co-operation between the Government and the banks is a very different thing from abdication by the Government in favour of the banks, and we are perilously near that point.

The first duty of the Government is, after all, to govern. The worst thing that can happen to a government is to assume responsibility without control. After all, the impression has been created in the country that in some way or other the Government is promoting the system and is responsible for the activity of these banking efforts, but effective control is absolutely lacking.

When you are setting out on an enterprise which means nothing less than the reorganisation of the whole basis of the industrial life of the country, you must have a system. You must, in a word, have a machine, and that machine has not yet even been created.

I begged the Cabinet to make up its mind how much it was prepared to spend on unemployment, how much money it could find, and then allocate the money available according to the best objects we could discover. As it is no such system has ever been adopted. Departments have come crowding along, jostling each other with their schemes, and, like bookmakers on the race course, the man who can push the hardest, make the most noise and get through the turnstile first, gets away with the money. It is absolutely necessary to make up our minds in advance in any national reconstruction, what our resources are and how they are to be allocated.

I am one of those who believe that the great main roads of this country should be national concerns, and that it is as much an anachronism to leave these roads in local hands as it would be to leave the railways in local hands. I admit that that raises a large controversy, but I try always to face reality and a practical situation, and I believe you can get round that difficulty and get agreement quickly in this way - leave the question of the nationalised roads until you settle the major question later, when you have to face the whole transport equilibrium of this country, as we have not begun to do. What matters in the building of roads quickly in relation to this problem is not the construction of the roads but the maintenance of the roads. Let the state construct and hand over to the local authority for subsequent maintenance.

But before you launch out on any such programme you have to make up your minds in broad outline, what the permanent transport equilibrium of this country is to be. On every turn when we want to build roads we are told that it will damage the railways. What is to be the relationship between railway, road and canal in the future? No research, no thinking beyond the Commission - which has been sitting for long, and is to report later - is going on in this country; no examination by government; not faced up to by government, and so at every turn your road programme and your immediate unemployment programme is thwarted because it is said that any great development of the roads will injure the railways. That matter has to be decided.

This is not the permanent problem of unemployment. We are merely bridging the gulf before the fruition of our long-term measures. Directly our permanent reconstruction is achieved this emergency programme will come to an end, at the end of three years or more, you will not forever be getting assistance from the state to do your job. In these circumstances you would get every local authority coming forward with schemes, if you face them with a now-or-never position and urge them forwards with machinery of government, which must be rather similar to the machine of the Right Hon. Member for Carnarvon Boroughs (Mr. Lloyd George) under the National Health Insurance Act, when I believe he had machinery going into every constituency and to every local authority, explaining it and gingering up the locality.

There is a tremendous struggle, an incessant struggle, going on in every government department to put every penny they can off the taxpayer and on to the rate payer. What holds up these plans for months is the struggle for these pennies, these minor details. What does it matter? What is the use of shifting the burden from the taxpayer to the ratepayer? What is the use of lifting the burden from the right shoulder to the left? It is the same man who has to carry it, and the economic fact is this, as the Colwyn and every other authoritative inquiry upon the economic side has said, that the burden on the ratepayer is more onerous upon industry than the burden on the taxpayer. If this burden has to be carried, need we struggle and waste time in deciding whether it is to be carried by the taxpayer or by the ratepayer?

Hanging over all that policy is the great conception of conversion. There are two ways of achieving conversion. One through the inherent financial strength of your position, leading to a strengthening of government credit. The other is by the simple process of deflation to make all industrial investments unprofitable, and drive your investor into government securities because he has no other profitable outlet. But there may be another effect of that policy; that the money goes abroad, and then you get the logical effect of that policy suggested by the President of the Board of Trade as the only means of solving our industrial problems, when he said on the 14th May:

"During the past fortnight alone £16,000,000 of new capital has been authorised or raised for overseas investment and so I trust the process will continue."

Why? Why is it right and proper and desirable that capital should go overseas to equip factories to compete against us, to build roads and railways in the Argentine or in Timbuctoo, to provide employment for people in those countries while it is supposed to shake the whole basis of our financial strength if anyone dares to suggest the raising of money by the government of this country to provide employment for the people of this country? If those views are passed without examination or challenge the position of this country is serious indeed.

This nation has to be mobilised and rallied for a tremendous effort, and who can do that except the Government of the day? If that effort is not made we may soon come to crisis, to a real crisis. I do not fear that so much, for this reason, that in a crisis this nation is always at its best. This people knows how to handle a crisis, it cools their heads and steels their nerves. What I fear much more than a sudden crisis is a long, slow, crumbling through the years until we sink to the level of a Spain, a gradual paralysis beneath which all the vigour and energy of this country will succumb. That is a far more dangerous thing, and far more likely to happen unless some effort is made. If the effort is made, how relatively easily can disaster be averted. You have in this country resources, skilled craftsmen among the workers, design and technique among the technicians, unknown and unequalled in any other country in the world. What a fantastic assumption it is that a nation which within the lifetime of everyone has put forth efforts of energy and vigour unequalled in the history of the world, should succumb before an economic situation such as the present. If the situation is to be overcome, if the great powers of this country are to be rallied and mobilised for a great national effort, then the Government and Parliament must give a lead. I beg the Government tonight to give the vital forces of this country the chance that they await. I beg Parliament to give that lead."

Short extracts from speech in Parliament on economic crisis, 8 Sep 1931.

"For my part, I have to say quite clearly that I believe those measures are inadequate to the situation and will not meet it, and in fact are likely to make it worse. But, in having that opinion, for my part again I would not oppose this Government with factious opposition. However wide our differences of opinion and our views as to remedies, we can at least be united in the belief that action, and speedy action, alone can meet the situation. Therefore, whatever Government for the time being is trusted with the confidence of this House, should, in my view, not be opposed with parliamentary obstruction, but should be given opportunities to carry its measures, and we who do not believe in those measures should content ourselves with putting forward a contrary opinion and registering our dissent. This is not a moment for parliamentary obstruction; this is a moment for rapid action. I hope that the measure of the Government will be successful in extricating the nation, but I do not believe that they will be.

I am not going to burden the House with very many figures; in fact, I shall mention very few. But I would like to quote one or two figures which give the whole reason for the crisis. If we take the first seven months of this year and compare them with the first seven months of 1929, we find a 45 percent drop in the exports of this country. That is really your crisis. That is why you have panic on the markets of the world. Even if you make all allowances for slight monetary changes in the interval, that figure is startling and almost appalling. In the same period imports have fallen by only 30 percent. It is the comparison between imports and exports, what the Right Hon. Gentleman referred to as the balance of trade, which is the really alarming aspect of the situation. Imports for this year have more than doubled exports. In 1929, only two years ago, they were little more than 50 percent above exports. In manufactured goods we now import as much as we export. In 1929 we exported twice as much as we imported.

That extraordinary change in the balance of trade, illustrated in those very few and obvious and simple figures, accounts and accounts entirely for the present financial panic. In view of the progressive deterioration of the industrial position what is the use of trying to balance your Budget on the present basis of revenue when, unless you have an active industrial policy, your revenue is bound again to collapse within a measurable distance of time? That is why the one thing I want to urge upon the House is the immediate adoption of some constructive industrial policy.

If the Labour Party had said that it was the banking policy of the last 10 years, a policy which they supported, that was responsible for this situation, a policy which their Chancellor of the Exchequer supported and which they supported him in supporting, then they would be getting at the root facts of the present situation. Over and over again the solid ranks of Labour closed up behind him, supported the policy of deflation, supported the policy of the Cunliffe Committee to which he adhered, supported the policy which led to wage reductions in 1921 and 1926, which led to the doubling of the burden of the National Debt, which led to the doubling of the interest of every debenture holder, rentier and bond-holder, and which placed upon British industry and trade a burden which no other industries in the world had to carry. The Labour Party again, and again, in the Division Lobby, at party meetings and conferences, supported the Chancellor of the Exchequer. They did not walk out of the bankers' palace until it fell about their ears.

It seems to me that Britain in her crisis is being asked to turn her face to the wall and to give up like an old woman who knows that she has to die. I want to see this country at least make an effort. I do not believe and never have believed that the way out is not the way of the monk but the way of the athlete. It is only by endeavour, by a great attempt to reorganise our industries, that this country can win through, and I venture to suggest that the simple question before the House in this Debate is whether Great Britain is to meet its crisis lying down or standing up."

Chapter 8

Writings: Post-War

Various quotations printed in this book make it quite clear that Mosley was the first statesman of modern Europe to stand for the Union of Europe. The idea, of course, is as old as the age of Charlemagne or the Roman Empire. Henri IV, Napoleon and many other Europeans of vision and will have striven for this ideal. The merit of Mosley in this matter is that he stood for the Union of Europe when our continent was being riven by the nationalism which culminated in the disaster of the second world war. He was strongly for the Union of Europe before the war, at a moment when statesmen were busy dividing Europe who, since the war, have been acclaimed as the protagonists, if not the inventors, of European Union. Those divided with such disastrous results can never unite; their actions have left behind a legacy of too much bitterness. The only force that can unite is a consistent faith in the essential oneness of Europe, and this Mosley has always shown. It was to him the ideal of the first war generation, the soldiers and airmen to whom he belonged, and who resolved that the sacrifice of their comrades should not be made in vain by a recurrence of fratricidal war in Europe. Particularly the airmen in the first world war - at first a small band on either side - had that sense of the deep community of European youth. It was in those days that Mosley began to become a European. He stood for the idea in speeches before the war and in such essays as *The World Alternative* (1937) which was a powerful effort to divert fascism from nationalism to a sense of European communion which would have made impossible the second world war.

After the war he turned to European Union as his first theme directly he was free of gaol and restrictions. He developed the idea far more fully and consciously than before the war and finally summarised his belief in the phrase 'Europe a Nation' which concentrated the aim of the European movement and gave its name to an outstanding German journal. Today his argument is that only the United States of Europe can face the United States of America and the Union of Soviet and Socialist Republics. "England must grow bigger and not smaller" (Trafalgar Square, 1.7.1956) becomes the stark reality that for thousands is the only solution of Britain's present troubles. In this long fight for Europe Mosley has marched always between the ideal and the practical. Tomorrow he will unite both in a great fact.

Directly he was free to speak or write after the war Mosley continued his advocacy of the Union of Europe. This is best made clear by brief extracts from three speeches and a press conference, before we come to his post-war writings. Extracts from his main post-war speeches are given in Chapter 10. Mosley spoke on November 15th 1946 as follows:

"The Union of Europe becomes not merely a dream or a desire but a necessity. The Union of Europe is no new conception, the only novelty is its present necessity."

On November 15th 1947, he said:

"We must realise that science has rendered any pre-war policy entirely irrelevant in a new age."

The idea he now advanced was far beyond both the fascism and democracy of 1939 as the jet propelled aeroplane was beyond the nineteenth century steam engine. The movement of science since 1939 compelled a commensurate development in political thinking. Politics must bring in a new world of science to redress the balance of the old world of Europe in the development of Africa. The boundaries of thought must enlarge and they must conceive the future in terms of two continents. The Union of Europe was now necessary to the survival of every nation in this continent. The new science presented at once the best opportunity and the worst danger of all history. It had destroyed forever the island community of Britain and compelled the organisation of life in wider areas. It had accelerated evolution, and imposed union with their kindred of Europe if they were to survive. But science had also given them a great new power of rapid economic progress in such projects as opening Africa. If they linked the Union of Europe with the development of Africa in a new system of two continents they would build a civilisation which surpassed, and a force which equalled, any power in the world. It was in the interests of America to have a partner rather than a pensioner. It was in the interests of the world for a power to arise which could render hopeless the Russian design for the subjection of Europe to communism. They would thus combine in an enduring union the undying tradition of Europe and the profound revolution of modern science. From that union would be born a civilisation of continuing creation and ever unfolding beauty that would withstand the tests of time.

The advocacy of the Union of Europe was carried a stage further at a Press conference with Mr. Oswald Pirow, South African Minister of Defence, 1933-39, Minister of Justice, 1929-33. He told a crowded press conference on April 12th 1948: "He has come to this country for the express purpose of consulting Mosley with regard to his Union Movement and his proposed development of Africa." When asked why he had chosen to consult with Mosley on the subject of the Union of Europe and the development of Africa, rather than with Mr. Churchill or the Labour Government, Mr. Pirow replied that "He did so because Mosley had been the first to suggest western union." He also pointed out that "Mosley's scheme alone included Germany and the other European states, such as Spain and Portugal, which had a great part to play in the union of Western Europe."

Mosley first used the phrase *Europe a Nation* in a speech on 16th October, 1948:

"European Union is sinking in the restrictions, jealousies and petty manoeuvres of the old nationalism. An early and decisive act is needed to save the great idea...

This is the only road to peace; history provides the proof. When Englishmen and Scotsmen thought, felt and acted as Englishmen and Scotsmen, ceaseless wars occurred between them. When they learnt to think, feel and act as Britons, in a wider union, they ceased to fight, except with words in their united deliberations. A similar process is now required in Europe to lift us beyond nationalism, and teach us to think, feel and act as Europeans...

Communism can never be met and defeated by a negative; communism can only be defeated by a great positive.

It is this positive idea which must emerge from the Assembly of Europe, whose high task will be to fulfil the will of the people to union. The great affair must be lifted beyond the intrigues of the lobbies and the manoeuvres of diplomats. Trust the people and let their voice be heard in their assembly.

Let us turn from the old internationalism, which always failed and the old nationalism which is now obsolete, to the new idea of Europe a Nation."

These few quotations make clear the background to his post-war writings. The following brief extracts can give an impression of Mosley's mind but can give no idea of the logical structure, order and sequence of his thinking in the system and doctrine of his post-war writings. To understand him properly it is necessary to study the books which are listed at the end of this book.

Mosley reviewed the past and reiterated his faith in union in January 1947, in an essay entitled *The Extension of Patriotism, the idea of kinship*:

"We were divided and we are conquered. That is the tragic epitaph of two war generations: words which should adorn the graves of the youth of Europe. That was the fate of my generation in 1914, and the doom of a new generation of young soldiers in 1939. The youth of Europe shed the blood of their own family, and the jackals of the world grew fat. Those who fought are in the position of the conquered, whatever their country. Those who did not fight, but merely profited, alone are victorious.

What, then was the truth concerning the national socialist or fascist movements before the war? Our fault was exactly the opposite of that suggested against us. How often in politics is that the fact? How rarely are the people permitted to know anything except the reverse of truth. It was suggested that we might set the interest of other countries before our own: that was an absurd lie. In reality, we were all too national - too narrowly concentrated upon securing the interests of our own nations. That was the true fault of all national socialist or fascist movements; whether in Britain, Germany, France, Spain, Italy. So far from being willing to serve each other as "fifth columns" in the event of a clash between states, our political ideology and propaganda were far too nationalistic even to mould the minds of men in this new sense of European kinship and solidarity which might have avoided disaster by universal consent. So far from fighting for other countries in a war, we none of us argued with sufficient force in favour of that new sense of European Union which modern fact must now make an integral part of a new creed. Our creed was brought to the dust because the fascist outlook in each land was too national.

How did it happen? How did that creed, which might have brought the renaissance of western man, confine itself within the limits of a too narrow nationalism?

There were two reasons; the first practical, the second ideological. The attempt to solve every problem by bigger and better committees of wider and more diverse nationalities ended in the grotesque failure which our realism foresaw. Their procedure in the face of difficulty was ever to introduce more and more people who were less and less like each other in tradition, thought, feeling and instinct. Consequently and inevitably the difficulties became ever more insuperable until the whole attempt broke down in tragic absurdity. That did not appear to us a practical method. So we tried the opposite approach of each nation building in its own area a system suitable to its own tradition, culture and feeling.

But the revulsion from current errors led most protagonists of the new European creed back into what should have been regarded as the obsolete paths of ultra-nationalism. The idea which will become the creed of the future is to reject the old internationalism on the one hand, and, on the other hand, to transcend an exclusive nationalism which divides natural friends and relatives.

The idea of kinship is the true idea; the reaching out to those who are kindred or of the same kind. The idea of kinship can bring the Union of Europe where the old internationalism failed. As a family of the same stock and kind, Europe should always have been united. Today the real as well as the ideal faces Europe with the alternative of union or disaster. So must come a new union of mind and spirit, not only to avoid destruction, but for further purposes of construction. Yet the idea of kinship carries us far beyond Europe; there are kindreds of ours in both Americas. Their spiritual life is also ultimately based on nearly three millennia of European history and culture. In the deep realities and further ideal of this age all nature impels them in their final test to feel and think as we do.

We love our countries, but we must extend that love; the ideal and practical now compel it. The extension of patriotism; that is the necessity and that is the hope. The new patriotism will extend to embrace all of like kind, but will not destroy the values of its kind by seeking the unnatural mingling of the old internationalism.

(1.1.1947)

The Third Force[1]

"In 1948 I stated the policy - Europe a Nation - because it seemed to me at this point in history to be both the deep desire of the European and the practical necessity of the present situation. It is right and natural for related peoples to unite when they have grown and developed enough as individual nations. This is an organic process of nature which has occurred again and again. To such events in the past all present nations have owed not only their greatness but their ability to live a full life, or to live at all. It was inevitable that England should join with Scotland and Wales after centuries of strife to form a British nation. It was equally inevitable that the German states should come together into a German nation. It is not only inevitable but materially and spiritually desirable that great peoples should find ever higher opportunities for their thought, work and mission in ever higher forms of life.

Europe has nearly been destroyed by brothers' wars, just as the internecine wars of the Greek states destroyed the greatness and beauty of Greek civilisation. Before they reached that stage both the classic Greeks and the early Europeans had a deep sense of the honour and duty imposed by membership of the same community in a great culture and tradition; indeed, in a great brotherhood. The wars of the Greek states destroyed that sentiment and with it Greek civilisation. The question in Europe today is whether we succumb to the same fatality, or rise above it and move beyond it to a new and higher union. This is the way of nature and of destiny; to deny these divine forces of life is to perish.

There can never be conflicting states within the state, if the state is to endure. Europe must be a great unity imbued with a sense of high mission, not a market place of jealous, battling interests. This is the only way to achievement and the only way to peace. There was no peace within Britain while the national divisions remained; there was no peace within Germany while the state

---

1   Extracts from Mosley's essay 'The Third Force', published March, 1950.

divisions remained; there was no peace within France until France reached nationhood. There will be no peace in Europe until Europe becomes a nation.

Then and not before can the Europeans give all their mind and will and genius to the real task of this age. That duty is to lift the mass of the people to the level which modern science makes possible and the European desires. How can we begin this greatest work and deepest duty until national strife within Europe is ended? The work of saving and serving the people in their desire for a better life is prevented by national divisions within Europe.

The living room of Europe is in two great spaces. The first is the Eastern homeland of Europe. There is space which is European space. There is wealth which is European wealth. It belongs to Europe and not to the Orient. Europeans alone have the energy and ability to develop it. We claim it back.

The second space is in Africa, which will be the Empire of Europe. In these two areas are the raw material and mineral wealth with which the European will build the greatest civilisation the world has yet seen.

Europe wants freedom and certainly deserves it. The question is how to get it?

The chief barrier to European Union is still the memory of past wars. This is the barrier between France and Germany. It is the supreme tragedy of modern Europe. In the new conditions it is not only tragic, it is entirely without reason. France remembers the numerical superiority of Germany; a decisive factor in the wars of the past. What have numbers to do with wars of the future? They will be settled by mind not mass; by scientific and political talent, not by weight of divisions. We are entering the age of pure intelligence.

Obsolete minds are now a menace not only to themselves but to the world. We need new thought both in strategy and politics, which are now more than ever inter-connected.

By comparison with the external threat all questions between France and Germany are now insignificant, and can easily be solved within the brotherhood of Europe. When the new and decisive facts of this period are realised, France and Europe will yet live to be thankful for the genius of will and energy which is Germany. That hour will come with the calm certainty of destiny. It is the duty of all who love Europe to assist the friendship of France and Germany; from that great event all else will follow.

In the turmoil and surprises of this epoch the bedrock principle on which we rest is the Union of Europe. Division is death; union is life. Let us strive for union physically, intellectually, spiritually; we have no time to lose.

Europe lies helpless between the powers of America and Russia; and is chiefly occupied or controlled by the former. Until Europe is free some are indifferent which is the occupying power. That attitude reveals an inability to grasp realities and an error in tactics. Lets us regard facts and nothing but facts. Under Russia, European freedom is killed, and under America, European freedom can still exist and even grow. That is the basic difference which must determine the question of attitude. On the one side is a police apparatus which crushes all opposition and prevents the expression of all contrary opinion; one the other side is a limited freedom which varies in degree between the occupied or controlled countries - e.g., Germany and Britain - but, on the whole, permits some expression of opinion and liberty of action. It is possible for a decisive idea to grow within a money-democracy; that growth is not possible within a bolshevist prison. There is only one choice in Russia - the grave or the underground movement. This is the fact which settles this first question between West and East."

(1.3.1950)

135

"How often in life the principal debit can be turned by time and energy into the principal asset. It is those who stood true to Europe by representing in dark days its deepest necessity who will hold the key to the future."

(1.10.1947)

"All of European stock throughout the world will find in the new union a source of material strength and spiritual inspiration. All overseas communities of Europeans which are now associated with European countries, such as the British dominions, will be invited to participate and will bring worldwide connections. Close association is inevitable and desirable with the European nations of South America. But the new nation of Europe will be no all-consuming machine of the state. Within Europe every diversity of life and culture which has been the expression of individual nations will be retained and encouraged. The new life must seek infinite variety, and never permit the imposition of a grey uniformity and monotony."

(1.3.1950)

"Within an area so great as Europe/Africa we have room in which a people so great as the European can live and grow freely. A smaller room is not enough in this age of modern science which reduces size and space. A larger area is too big for healthy development; it would be unworkable and unmoral, without plan or principle. When we consider the difficulties inherent even in the union of the Europeans it does not take long to find the answer to those internationalist who talk of an immediate world union. In this phase of world affairs family life is not only a healthy thing, but the only practical means of existence. Europe is a family of similar peoples. Why should not the world develop along family lines of similar peoples living together in adequate space for their own development? If all have enough we can live in friendship with other peoples, without ruling others or interfering with other systems; modern science, joined to the sufficiency of food and raw materials which certainly exists in the various living spaces of the earth's surface, should provide more than enough for all; let us live and let live. But let the first decision to live, and live greatly, be the European. We can again show they way to mankind."

(1.11.1954)

"Most of the troubles of the Western world are due to the root difficulty that England under the old parties is unwilling to enter fully and completely into European life. The excuse was that such participation in the Continent to which England belongs would jeopardise the Commonwealth. In the result a scattered and divided Commonwealth is protected from Soviet pressure by special arrangements with America from which Britain is excluded. A strong lead from England would not only have united Europe but would have brought a united Commonwealth into the European community. Europe would then have been more than capable both of protecting herself and of solving the economic problem within the great area of supply and market provided by Europe/Africa, the British dominions and the overseas relationships of all Europe. But the Foreign Secretary and his Tory-Labour friends found that this opportunity was a little too big for them. Mr. Eden said that he and his friends could not enter Europe because "they felt it was wrong in their bones.""

(1.8.1954)

"The Eden technique of little by little leads to interminable debate and, consequently, postpones all discussion of everything that really matters; it plays straight into the Soviet hands by providing them with unlimited material for delaying action in the realm of reality and for noisy demonstration in the sphere of propaganda. We need on the contrary to bring them right up against decisive principles in the realm of reality, whose negation will be a disaster for them in the spheres of propaganda. All this is very shocking to the old diplomacy which learnt over centuries that a conference which failed, behind the usual closed doors, put things back a long way; of the old gentlemen who once got cross with each other, it took quite a time to get them together round the dinner table again. But this ancient situation has no relation to the modern scene in which great mass forces depend for their momentum on the opinion of the peoples. The shadow of the homburg hat and monocle will pass from diplomacy in favour of rougher shapes, who have been nurtured in mass struggle and can speak in language which the people can understand."

(1.11.1953)

"Britain's permanent absence from Europe - interrupted only by the sporadic clowning of the Foreign Office on the German stage - is of course primarily responsible for the disillusionment and indifference of many Germans. If Britain went right into Europe as the essential unifier of the French-German mind and interest a dynamic union would be born from which all else could follow. But we must be right in; we must become European and embrace the European cause. European Union is the only hope in reality; but it is the chief fear of the fantasy world of the old English ruling class. They dread being mixed up in European causes and quarrels; although they have inevitably been involved in all recent troubles, after standing apart so long that it was impossible to influence events. In particular they fear being drawn into the struggle for the return of the lost German territories and other European territories which were betrayed to Russia by allied policy at the end of the war."

(1.9.1954)

"For reasons which are now being realised even by the slowest that struggle can never now assume the form of international war; nothing is gained by the death of everyone. But it will inevitably continue, not in a military but in a political form; until the lost lands are regained. English influence can play a decisive part in this struggle, and, if fully exerted in the cause of Europe, can both win the abiding friendship of the real Germans and finally unify our continent. Naturally the Germans care more about the union of their people than anything else. But that is a European cause; that cause is our cause. Let us all grant that war in Europe is excluded in the new conditions, while taking all precautions against accidents. Let us then affirm that we will never consent to the mutilation of Europe, that we will never rest in our intensive political struggle until Europe is a whole and a union. In such faith and determination we shall gain something more than twelve divisions from the lobbies of Bonn; we shall win for Europe the will and spirit of all the German people."

(1.9.1954)

"The family of Europe, has been divided and destroyed by internecine conflict, exactly as the related communities of early Greece were rent by the clash of the city states until even the radiance of Hellas was extinguished.

In the past the division of the soil has been the strongest thing in all our lives. In the future the division of the soul will transcend the division of the soil: in the end the soul will be stronger than the soil. This new advance in the mind and spirit of men can only come after the Union of Europe, which is a vital necessity if this continent, and every nation within it, is to survive."

(1.10.1947)

"No country has a greater interest in the creation of a United Europe than Great Britain: no government has done so much to impede it as the British government. The present Prime Minister "felt in his bones" that we did not belong to Europe; the prejudice of conservatism and the comically belated nationalism of Labour has combined to frustrate the Union of Europe."

(1.12.1955)

"The policy of Europe a Nation has now long been debated in strenuous controversy. We are, at any rate, emerging from the period when everyone paid lip service to the ideal of the United Europe while most sabotaged it in practice. The nominal adherents who came from the old world parties have fallen away in a variety of directions, or so reduced the concept of union that it becomes meaningless. In fact, this is an occasion on which an all or nothing policy poses a true dilemma. This Union of

Europe will not work in any form less complete than an integral nation. Scores of conflicting local interests will generate friction and ill-will enough to destroy union a score of times if the conflicting local interests still exist; if separate nations still exist within Europe. Post-war experience has proved this again and again. What was regarded as our extreme emerges as the plain sense of the matter. It is Europe a Nation or nothing. Then let it be nothing, answer the men of the old world, and will so answer until their old world falls about their ears. Ideas so great and so decisive as the Union of Europe are only fully implemented with the aid of some compulsion from events. Few men are ready to step into greatness without that persuasion."

(1.5.1956)

"What, then do we all want? The Russians say they want the Americans out of Europe and peace. So do we, but not on the condition that instead we have the Russians in Europe. American occupation is a humiliation: Russian occupation is death. Suicide is not the only escape from shame.

Let all Europe be the buffer area between West and East, the Third Force that holds the balance of the world. That is the final solution for which we have always stood."

(1.9.1955)

"The greatest argument for Europe is the great market; except for those who are capable of feeling that it is worth even the last effort of mind, heart and will to carry three thousand years of the most exalted culture the world has seen to yet further heights of the human spirit."

(1.11.1955)

"But if Britain take the lead in a decisive policy, we can maintain order in this area because we can carry with us America and the rest of Europe. European interests in the Mediterranean are no longer antithetical; they have become identical. We are not interested to fight other Europeans for lifelines which no longer lead anywhere. But we are interested to maintain a strong position of a United Europe on the flank of Russia, in case that country ever advances against the West. And we are interested in together preserving supplies which are vital to us all, until we have together built the independent civilisation of Europe-Africa. Once again, unity is strength."

(1.4.1956)

"As the mind of man grew and his circumstances enlarged, his sense of patriotism extended always in the same natural manner of first embracing his nearest kin, unless the process was traversed by conquest.

Europe requires a new synthesis; in all things eternal synthesis.

The shrinkage of the world compels the Union of Europe: and that will bring, in time, the union of the best, whose division has made possible the triumph of the worst.

The great shock, which derives from the soil of Europe and is animated by the ideal of service and not of profit, stands like a rock of stability across the course of flux and chaos. Personally incorruptible, because he has values beyond money and is a representative of steadfast continuity in nearly three millennia of culture, the higher European is the final enemy of both finance and communism, because he can neither be bought nor frightened.

Europe was divided and thus alone the men of Europe could be conquered. Their love of country was used to destroy their continent. The best elements in Europe were divided by love; the worst elements were united by greed."

(1.10.1947)

"The Englishman, who regards us with fury because we ask him to unite with Frenchmen or German, must be gently told that his glare of patriotic passion merely reflects the equally inspired light in the eye of the Mercian when he was told to stop killing his hereditary enemies in Wessex and to unite for resistance to the Dane.

The division of the soul will replace the division of the soil: in the conditions of the present time it has become more natural. This is bound to happen directly the peoples decide to merge in a large reunion and so to extend patriotism; and, when that is done, it is right that it should occur. From this great shake of the dice of destiny will be thrown a new dynamism in the service of high achievement."

(1.10.1947)

"If the verdict of opponents were accepted as final, nearly everyone would be guilty of the most revolting crimes in greater or lesser degree. Further, if all these charges were subject to impartial examination by a neutral court, it is possible, and probable, that no nation would be entirely free from any charge which would in varying degree, be the subject of shame under any high code of morality."

(1.10.1947)

"Revenge is the hallmark of small minds; recent experience adds an observation which such minds can understand - revenge does not pay."

(1.12.1953)

"The fault really lies in nothing except ourselves that we are not only "underlings" but very possibly doomed. Give to our lost continent will, union and spirit, and our Europe can yet win this new world. If Europe is really too old, tired, prejudiced and bitter to consider such action, let us at least question what is now happening until we get the truth. If we refuse to live let us at least face the facts of death."

(1.6.1953)

"The first and basic principle must be the freedom of Europe. The second principle must be that freedom means the right of any people to vote freely and by secret ballot for the government it desires, after hearing every opinion which anyone dare to state. The complete freedom of elections in all the occupied countries - west or east - must be guaranteed by commissions whose neutrality is beyond question; many precedents exist for such procedure.

Directly European freedom is granted we can legitimately assume that the Soviets really mean peace. We would then reduce armaments to any extent if the Soviets would accompany us with proved measures on their side; the desired goal would then be that both sides should as far as possible be incapable of attack and should give every guarantee of this which was technically possible."

(1.7.1953)

"The disaster in the Middle East is due to the failure to think and act as Europeans. If we cannot now learn to think and act as Europeans we shall be divided, conquered and destroyed by the barbarians as certainly and finally as the city states of classic Greece. Any European truly regarding the Middle Eastern problem from the European standpoint would have pursued an entirely different policy, which would certainly have avoided present errors and could have brought us to unity and security. This is not wisdom after the event for it is the policy we have advocated throughout. Europeans in the present period have but two interests in this region. The first is to check a Russian advance aimed at the invasion and conquest of Europe. The second is to preserve in peace, and war, the oil supplies of this area, which have importance for all Europe until we can develop in Africa, or elsewhere, alternative sources of supply.

All of this depends on the unity of European policy, and the recognition of two clear truths. The first is that, for us all, the maintenance of the life of Europe is the most important thing in the world. The second is that the strength of Russia is a vital threat to this life, and that it is the final and unchanging policy of the

143

Soviets to destroy our European life. If the massacre of the heroic Hungarians at last brings home these truths to the mind and spirit of Europe the vast tragedy of that superb death will not have been in vain. In place of the great policy of European Union, we have had small, obsolete national policies which have pursued the personal vendettas of the pygmy leaders. The present government of Britain and their predecessors have proved themselves quite incapable of thinking and acting as Europeans. They have not only pursued a selfish national policy, but a policy which in terms of simple British interest is many years out of date. They still talk of the Suez Canal as the "life-line of British Empire", but they gave away the Empire at the other end of the "life-line" in the course of fighting a fratricidal war with Germany. The Cape route even to the oil lands of Persia always has to be used in time of war or trouble. The Mediterranean was closed to such shipping during much of the last war, and one A-bomb, not to mention H-bomb would have put it out of action for good in another war. When Sir Anthony Eden speaks of the Suez Canal as a "life and death" interest of Britain, he is as obsolete in his military as in his political thinking. It was Bonaparte who first recognised that in the conditions of his day the Middle East was the key to the world, and in this matter very few people in Western Europe have done much thinking since he died; in terms of politics and strategy the arrival of the submarine, A-bomb and H-bomb have passed almost unnoticed.

Hypnotised by the past, the British Government has thus abandoned the present. They have failed to devise a united European policy, and they have quarrelled with the Arabs over something that did not matter. Those of the Musselman faith are our natural friends and allies in the face of communism which challenges equally their beliefs and their civilisation. It was a monumental folly to discard that friendship for the illusion of an obsolete policy. There is but one true policy in the Middle East; the union of all the European powers in strength and solidarity on the left flank of Russia, and the closest friendship with the sister Arab peoples whose interest is identical."

(1.12.1956)

"The chief intellectual barrier to European Union is the memory of the quarrel between fascism and democracy. That quarrel belongs to an age which is dead; it is gone with the facts which gave it birth. We have passed beyond fascism and democracy. I stated that simple truth when I became a European. Fascism belongs to that nationalism which proved the ruin of all its great work and high aspirations. In becoming Europeans we pass beyond nationalism and beyond fascism. We seek a union of nations and a synthesis of creeds at a higher level, which can truly unite all that is best in the mind and spirit of Europe. Those who believed with sincerity in the old democracy will, also, pass beyond democracy as they realise that their system serves no longer the will or interest of the people, and has once more degenerated into a "money-democracy". Fascism and the old democracy will both pass because neither is adequate to the facts of a new age. The mind and spirit of the European goes beyond them to a new thesis of life. Already the thought and the act of the future take shape. We reconcile the old conflicts and begin to achieve, today in thought and tomorrow in deed, the union of authority with liberty, action with thought, decision with discussion, power with responsibility, vigour with duty, strength with kindness, and service of the people with the attainment of ever higher forms of life."

(1.3.1950)

"When struggle deepens the men and parties of the money-democracies will make way for men and movements with a decisive idea; or these countries will succumb to communism. They will make way because vital peoples will dismiss them by their votes; and what "democrat" can deny their right to do it? When the present system fails, great peoples will determine to save themselves. They will seek the answer to communism."

(1.3.1950)

European Socialism

"European Socialism combines the revolutionary policy of workers' ownership, in place of nationalism, with complete freedom for private enterprise to work whenever it can, without the restrictions and burdens imposed by the present state. In a synthesis of two extreme opposites we shall achieve a system of constructive action, of creative realism. We shall combine the strong urge of the workers towards syndicalism with the strong urge of the striving individual to make new things, just as the pioneers of the old system made new things in return for this just reward; both these urges are traditional and have been the mainspring of the effective action that has taken place on either side. Syndicalism was really the inspiration of the guild system of the Middle Ages, which in both England and Germany created great enterprises that were free from the vices of both capitalism and of bureaucratic socialism. Syndicalism lived again in the early trade union movement when the workers first learnt to manage their own affairs in their own organisations; they soon did it well enough to win from capitalism an altogether different standard of life. Free enterprise in the hands of creative individuals was responsible for the whole wonder of the industrial revolution. Does anyone imagine for a moment that science would have achieved what it has for mankind if every invention had perforce been submitted to a committee of modern bureaucrats? It was the freedom of capable industrial pioneers to seize opportunities which others did not see and to turn new ideas into great industries, which created the modern world. We are not dealing with crude and untried novelties, but with two of the deepest urges in human nature; the two inspirations which have so far worked. Both are now entirely thwarted, and turned back upon themselves in a disease of frustration."

(1.12.1954)

"The principle of European Socialism is a synthesis at a higher level of the old conflict between individualism and socialism. The method of European Socialism is to use the

146

motive of power of both ideas at the appropriate stage of industrial development. Individual initiative is necessary to found a new industry; the willing co-operation of many is necessary to the successful conduct of a developed industry. At present the individual is fettered by bureaucracy and taxation in launching a new enterprise, while the workers in an established business are employees of capitalism, or of the state, without personal interest in the concern. The result is the worst of both worlds; the creative individual is thwarted, and the mass of the workers are discouraged. The remedy is to free and to encourage the industrial pioneer who creates a new enterprise, and, also, to give the workers a real incentive to do their best for the developed industry in which they work - by making them owners of it.

These proposals may seem both extreme and puzzling to the old political world, which is now visibly failing. Politicians think always in terms of "Right or Left"; an unfettered private enterprise which is free from repressive taxation, will seem to them a proposal of the extreme Right, a workers' ownership of industry will seem to them a policy of the extreme Left. They will see nothing but paradox in a plan to combine the two policies.

Is it not rather the solution of plain sense; a plan in accord with present reality, which develops rapidly, and with human nature, which develops slowly?

No man is fit to be a manager in a great concern if he cannot get along with the workpeople in it. He has to persuade the workers and carry them with him at every turn of modern industry; he will not find this more difficult, but much easier, if the workers' interest becomes identical with the interest of the firm. The workers will be on the lookout for brains which can help them to make money. High salaries will be paid more readily to managers who are saving money to go into the weekly pay packet, or end-of-the-year workers' dividend, than to mangers whose ingenuity is saving, or making money for the "bosses".

The position of the competent manager would be greatly strengthened. The only manager with anything to fear would be the man who seeks to command, but cannot persuade; and he is not an incompetent. When it comes to great affairs, command is persuasion. To do great things, in politics, in war, in business or in anything else, leadership must give confidence and arouse enthusiasm; that is why command is persuasion in the complex mass movement of modern life.

Could any sanction be more powerful than the strike (notice given) of a successful manager whose departure would certainly mean a considerable fall in the profits of a worker-owned industry? Is not this a reversal of all values which the managerial revolution might find quite desirable, and the workers would find at least comprehensible.

We found our industrial structure upon the free individualism of the creative pioneer, and we crown it with the collective individualism of the workers who co-operate with each other to mutual benefit."

(1.5.1954)

"The managerial revolution will be an integral part of European Socialism; managers and workers together - workers both - will conduct developed industries. Managers will find it easier to persuade the workers not to strike when the first thing hit is the workers' profits, and their own. But in all new enterprises, at all early stages of industry, the creative individual will operate with complete freedom and for a full reward; he will not only be free, he will be cherished. Such brains and such spirits must be attracted to the system, preserved, encouraged by every possible means; they are the fuel of the future, the very essence of achievement."

(1.12.1954)

"I gave recently a broad definition of European Socialism as follows:- "European Socialism is the development by a fully united Europe of all the resources in our own continent, in white

Africa, and in South America, for the benefits of all the peoples of Europe and of these other European lands, with every energy and incentive that the active leadership of European government can give to private enterprise workers' ownership or any other method of progress which science and a dynamic system of government finds most effective for the enrichment of all our people and the lifting of European civilisation to ever higher forms of life."

The principles of European Socialism are a constant advance, not a frigid *is*, nor, worse still, like the policies of the old parties in the present world, a frozen *was*. We have direction which is very definite, but not rigidity; our principles are flowing, not frigid. So we seek accord with nature which is ever evolving and developing to higher forms, and reject the artificial systems by which small men seek to imprison both science and the forward urge of humanity within their narrow and transient pre-conceptions.

May I now recapitulate very briefly the main principles of this thinking as they stand after a decade of development since the war.

1. *Europe a Nation.* I first used this phrase after the war to describe the complete integration of the European peoples which I believe to be essential to the survival and advance of European civilisation. No lesser degree of union than that of an integral nation can give the will and power to act on the great scale, and with the decision, which are now necessary. No lesser space than all Europe, and the overseas possessions of Europe in a common pool, can give the room within which to act effectively. The necessity for the close union of the European peoples as a third power has been emphasised by the appearance of the rival giants, America and Russia.

2. *Government with the power to act.* The revolution which science has brought can only be faced by government armed with the

power to act by the free vote of the people. This does not mean dictatorship or any form of totalitarian state, as I have made clear in my essay *Government of Tomorrow* and on previous occasions. But it does mean a clearly defined division of function between judiciary and legislature, and that within the limit so prescribed, the executive shall have a free hand to carry out the mandate conferred by the people's vote. Opposition parties will have every right to criticise, and to enter elections at regular intervals, in an attempt to change the government, but they will not be able by obstruction to impede the work of an elected government and thus to thwart the people's will.

3. *The deliberate equation of production and consumption within the viable area of Europe-Africa.* We have long believed that the individual nations of Europe would founder in the chaos of world competition when normal conditions returned. Each strives to export more than it imports in order to pay by competition on world markets for the raw materials and supplies which none possess in sufficient quantity within their own borders. We propose therefore that the economy of Europe-Africa shall be insulated from world chaos; it will form an area large enough to supply both its own raw materials and its own markets. The aim of government and of a new trade unionism will be deliberately to equate production and consumption by raising the standard of life equally through comparable industries, as science increases the power to produce. This is impossible while they have to face on world markets the competition of labour with a far lower standard of life which is equipped by international finance with modern, simplified machinery. The isolate nations of Europe will also, in the end, not have the strength to meet the dumped surpluses of great industrial countries like America with large home markets, or the below-cost sales of large slave industrial systems like Russia, directly the full force of the coming competition is felt. Developments such as automation will also oblige the active leadership of government in a constructive wage-price policy to prevent production outstripping demand and causing an economic crash. The part of government will be

to lead to the utmost, but to control the minimum, the necessary industrial organisation.

4. *The method of industrial organisation will be a dynamic pragmatism.* We shall experiment, find out what works, change a method if it does not work, and follow success with every energy. We will be bound by no preconceptions or economic shibboleths of the old world. Science has made them all obsolete. We believe the development of new enterprise is best done by an unfettered private enterprise which should not only be free but by every means encouraged. When private enterprise is exhausted and the concern becomes too big for any individual management, we prefer workers' ownership to state ownership or nationalisation. What is begun by a creative individual should finally be continued by a collective individualism of workers who own the enterprise to which they have given their lives, and not by a state bureaucracy without interest or contact with the workers or industry.

5. *All reward should be according to effort and the acceptance of responsibility.* The present tendency to reduce all reward to the dead level is fatal. Reward for skill, effort and responsibility in industry should not be reduced but increased. We clash here fundamentally with all egalitarian doctrine. But it must be reward for work, skill and service and for that alone. In all European countries the extra reward for skill, effort and the acceptance of responsibility is tending to disappear. It must be restored and emphasised. The future must rest on those who can, and not those who do.

6. *The burden of taxation should be shifted from income to spending.* A man should be taxed not on what he earns but on what he spends, not on what he brings in but on what he pays out. Thus saving, thrift, the power of the individual to accumulate the fruits of his labour, and, himself, thereby to develop new enterprises would not only be preserved but be increased, and by every means encouraged. But the luxury spender and the spendthrift,

the fool with money to burn, should carry the burden which today cripples the hardworking. We propose that this should be done by a graduated expenditure tax on all high spending groups, coupled with indirect taxation of everything except necessities. All direct taxation of earnings would be eliminated. All basic necessities of life to the mass of the people would also be freed from tax. The definition of necessities would vary naturally with national prosperity. For instance the standard of life would be much higher within the developed union of Europe-Africa than in an economically beleaguered island. There are various effective administrative plans for implementing the principle: tax spending, free earning. We propose a combination of expenditure tax and indirect taxation which would be graduated sharply on luxury articles."

(1.5.1956)

"The above six points are simple to the verge of crudity, but they give a brief summary of principles evolved in our thinking since the war. If we are to discuss effectively particular aspects of European Socialism, we have to regard them in relation to the whole.

Many cogent arguments have been advanced against the whole conception (workers ownership), which really can be reduced to the simple proposition that you cannot run a factory by an anarchic, obstructive, chattering mob. After some recent experience of the degeneracy of great states this may very often be true in present conditions. It is, indeed, difficult to imagine anything working with the spirit abroad in some quarters. But these critics overlook one decisive factor; the revolution we intend to make, and to whose struggle our lives are dedicated. It is not a law of nature that when workers own a concern it becomes a rabble-driven nonsense, it is only a rule of society in decay. For instance the workers of our own Movement. They made it, and they own it. More than 90 percent of our members have always been workers in the narrowest definition of that term. They have always been volunteers who can leave at any

152

moment, but, in fact, remain in conditions of great sacrifice and hardship, work for nothing and pay to be members. No one by any stretch of the imagination could call our Movement, or any similar band of workers, a rabble. In fact our Movement of workers has been violently denounced for being a highly disciplined army, and a special Act of Parliament was passed to deprive it of that character. The law was obeyed and we are not so organised, but we certainly have the spirit of an army and not of a mob. The point of all this is that it has been proved again and again in movements with which many of my readers will be familiar that the workers are perfectly capable of acting in union and discipline for greater ends which they clearly understand; in fact, they have often proved themselves much more capable of so acting than some of the middle class people who regard them as anarchic mobs.

Our Movement and all similar movements if they are to be effective, depends on the organised workers acting in a voluntary union and co-operation. Without them such movements could not exist. But that knowledge does not turn them into a chattering mob, a discordant rabble. On the contrary, in such movements the workers move in calm and self-disciplined solidarity under leadership they have selected and trust, to objectives they have studied and know. It is true that the details of policy are not always known to them all, and that only the deep principles are universally known and accepted. Decision in many matters needing rapid action is, also, left to the leadership, because it becomes trusted over a period of time as judgement appears correct, and character is proved under hard test. But trust comes, too, from the capacity for constant consultation with colleagues and supporters before decisions are taken. This enables leadership to know what the workers are feeling and thinking and, therefore, continually to interpret their best ideals and, on occasion, to lift their eyes to yet higher aims. I write this to illustrate that leadership which is constantly and completely dependent on the support of the workers can be very remote from a waste of time in constant debate, or from continual danger of upset owing to the anarchic debate, or from continual danger of upset owing to the anarchic impulses of mobs. But such leadership must not be, and cannot be, remote from the workers. The day of the remote boss has gone; certainly in real politics and almost certainly in industry. Even in war it is gone, and some successful generals were recently much concerned to explain and to popularise their measures.

It may be argued that the workers to whom I refer are a self-proved elite, moved by an idea and not by present materialism. But the answer is surely that before we can succeed this elite and their ideas is the premise of all achievement. They will, of course, be aided in this struggle by the manifest breakdown of the present system which will open the way to their ideas. When the mass of the workers have learnt in bitter experience than an anarchy of chatter means industrial death, they will be more disposed to accept both the leadership and the ideals of those who have devised the means of action and recovery. In short, a revolution in thinking is a necessary prelude to a revolution in action. That is the present task of our Movement, everywhere.

Point 6 contains the suggestion for shifting taxation from income to expenditure. This is not original to our thinking; in principle, it has been debated by English economists for generations and was reduced to a practical administrative system by the contribution of American economists during the war. It was at this point that America entered with a constructive thought which could be of great benefit to Europe. In America apparently it provoked a storm of opposition from various interests who find the present system of taxation more convenient. Our only contribution in the matter has been to relate this traditional thinking and its recent development in transatlantic practice to our basic position of sustaining the creative individual. It is inherent to our thinking that he must be free of the burden of mob impulse and mob jealousy, that he may perform his destined service for the wellbeing of the present and the elevation of the future. The creative spirit, whether scientist, technician, individual pioneer or deviser of new forms of service to people which enrich or illumine daily life, is the key of our system because he is the key to higher forms of life. All devices that free and encourage him in his task must be welcome additions to our thought and method. Their discovery and development become imperative at a moment when this main hope of the future seeks release from the burden of taxation."

(1.5.1956)

"We should only syndicalise industries which are now described as ripe for nationalisation; this should mean only industries which have become so big that they have passed beyond any kind of private management and are now controlled by the officials of monopoly capitalism or by the officials of the state.

At the other end of industry is the great multitude of small men with their own concerns, which are rapidly being reduced in favour of the big businesses of monopoly capitalism. These small men range from individuals who manage their own industrial firms, to farmers, small shopkeepers, etc., and it must be admitted that only a few are likely to emerge from their present occupation to found a great new enterprise. Nevertheless, they should be maintained and encouraged, and in such affairs the hereditary principle is desirable. It is right for instance, that a farm, or any enterprise which depends on personal management, should be handed down from father to son; death duties and all forms of repressive and destructive taxation should be lifted from them. The hereditary principle is only vicious when it reposes wealth and considerable power in idle and incompetent hands. Such accumulations of wealth in a hereditary system are a waste and a danger. We should discriminate between the sterile and the creative; this means preventing such accumulations of hereditary wealth but encouraging hereditary management of family concerns.

The guild tradition in the mediaeval cities of England, Germany and other European countries is inherent in our new syndicalism, and will serve the organic life and growth of Europe better than the mandarin system of bureaucratic socialism. We give freedom until it is abused; then we act, and believe me, we not only ask for the power but will have the will to act."

(1.5.1954)

"Here is the crux of the immediate problem. The present system could not work under any condition. We have reached a point where skill is not rewarded, and the acceptance of responsibility is even penalised. Not only have the whole managerial and professional classes a far less proportionate reward than they had before the war. In addition, workers who take responsible positions very often now draw less than the man who refuses it. Add this new factor to the steadily developing tendency to reduce the skilled to the level of the unskilled, and you have all the elements of disaster. In short, you have a system which denies nature itself; a premium is placed on inability and a penalty on ability. It is not only the able men in the old middle classes who are so suffering; able men in what are narrowly described as the working classes are hit in the same manner, if not in the same degree. It is the rule for the hindmost, and the devil take the foremost. Such a system is bound to crash. It would come to an end even if capitalism had not failed to solve its basic problem, even if the British economy were not entirely out of equilibrium. It is as easy for a jumping donkey to defy the laws of gravity as for any man to make such principles work. Under any conditions or any system they would not work in the long run. We must restore the main incentives, reward for skill, effort and responsibility to British industry.

The second essential is to shift taxation from income to spending. It is a revolution in thought and action, but it is necessary. Present taxation kills incentive as surely as the present system of rewards. To reward all fairly is a useless reform if taxation then removes the results from those who earn most. Men and women must be allowed to earn what they are worth, and to keep what they earn."

(1.3.1956)

"We begin with a big reduction in direct taxation; the abolition of P.A.Y.E and a much lower standard rate of income tax. That is the basic principle. To achieve it we are ready to cut clean through the current prejudice and to use novel methods.

In essential principle our taxation will fall on spending, not on income; on what a man gives out and not on what he brings in. Several ingenious systems have been suggested at various times and in diverse places to secure this end. Our method would be a dynamic pragmatism; as I have often explained, we do not treat economic principles like the old tablets of stone. Practical questions of how to sweep the kitchen floor in the best and quickest way cannot become for us articles of eternal faith; these are matters for the engineers and mechanics of statesmanship, whose role is vital but not priestly.

Our approach to the social services and what is called the welfare state starts from the statistical fact that the average working family at present pays more than double in taxes what it receives in benefit from the welfare state. We would therefore organise voluntary services in a contributory system which would be accompanied by our guarantee that reductions in taxation would exceed the contributions people would pay in order to draw out present benefits. We should thereby restore the sound and honest principles of self help and self reliance of national life. The same measure would restore freedom for individuals to decide for themselves what benefits they want, instead of being mulcted by taxation they cannot avoid and handed back in return a lesser value in benefits they do not want."

(1.11.1954)

European Socialism and Communism

It is clear at last to the general public that Russia has made a remarkable technical advance. This is due on part to the free present of so many German scientists at the end of the war, but not wholly. The Russian success is due to two principles which have nothing to do with communism; in fact, we have recommended them for years. The first is that their civilisation rests largely on the scientists; these men and women have been consciously rewarded, promoted, cherished as an elite of the nation. The second is that Russia has space and resources which are large enough to provide an independent civilisation, and has used them to develop another way of life in economic insulation from outside interference and world chaos. These are the real lessons of the Russian situation, which are now revealed; our readers will not find much mention of them in the rest of the press, except by implication.

Europe can easily attain a far greater success by use of these same two principles, without adopting communism in any degree or the denial of liberty in any way. We have far more potential scientists and technical possibilities; we have in Europe-Africa a greater space, and twice the population of far more advanced European peoples. The Soviet results can be left standing, once the European peoples take into their hands with set purpose the living room of Europe and white Africa, and decide science is so important that statesmen (in the words of my book written nine years ago) should live "in the company and inspiration of scientists, as the Medicis lived in the company and inspiration of artists."

Our resources in space, natural wealth and skilled population are far greater than the Russians'; our means, too, will in the end be more effective, because they will derive from the leadership of free peoples by a government charged by these peoples with a high task, and not from the bureaucratic machine of an eastern tyranny imposed on peoples accustomed to slavery and rendered submissive by physical division and illiteracy. Tyranny had a flying start but its troubles now begin, partly by reason of its own achievements.

These are the lessons. The European peoples must emerge from these small separate rooms, which have now become as obsolete as the division of men in the Middle Ages, into a living room which can give them strength of union, and the means to develop a twentieth-century civilisation in freedom from the death throes of nineteenth century capitalism. Let the scientists be given not only the pay but the status of an elite of the nation; scientist, like soldiers, work rather or honour or, like artists, for the pure joy of creation."

(1.6.1956)

"Communism seeks to turn itself into an army and its opponents into a mob."

(1.10.1947)

"Communism appeals to people with their noses in the mud, when no other means exists of getting out of the mud, and until they can lift themselves far enough out of the mud to see something else.

What is the creed of the Soviet apart from materialism? The answer is that it does not exist. The creed of the Soviet is "let us get out of the mud"; once the lowest stratum of society is out of the mud the "creed" comes to an end - its purpose is fulfilled. You might as well call it a creed to travel from London to Surbiton. The "creed" appears altogether absurd when you reflect that you would have reached your destination years ago if the railway service had been efficient.

It became a creed because to organise the elimination of poverty was a bit too difficult for Russians, and regarded as inconvenient by the western financial racket; that is all. So, when everyone has a full belly the creed must come to an end; what a creed!

Would the heaven of the Soviet creed be reached when every Russian lived in a villa with almost the same standard of life as the lower-middle class in a London suburb, but without any of those intellectual interest, or spiritual hopes, which are, at least, offered to vary that monotony? Is the final Soviet paradise "Acacia Row"? If not, what then? Where does their creed of material things take them next?

The struggle to raise the lowest from beneath unnecessary poverty and oppression has set up every complex of enmity, jealousy and hatred which can only be satisfied by an effort to pull down everything above the lowest. To drag life down not merely to the level of the ordinary, but below it is the basic interest of communism. It is the exact contradiction of our creed which seeks to lift life above the ordinary as a necessity of survival, and a fulfilment of the divine will which is revealed in the process of nature.

They reject the God of the Christian churches and the great world creeds, the élan *vital* of some moderns and the more purposeful phusis of the Greeks. Their purpose begins with "fill the belly", and ends with the malice and hatred engendered by long frustration in this simple and intrinsically desirable task.

To that fixed end, discipline and a compulsory co-operation were necessary to an extent that should replace the religious urge. The busy diurnalism of the ant heap became, at last, the substitute of the Greek phusis reaching out from Hellas through three millennia of European growth and culture to the achievement of ever higher forms in union with the higher purpose which directs all earthly existence.

So far from any striving for higher forms within the high design of the higher purpose, their first action is to destroy any high form which now exists. Instead of attempting to build the future on the highest types that now live, they seek to build their state on the lowest types, which today subsist.

We begin with the premise that the values of the spirit oppose those of pure materialism: the values of communism. They learnt from Marx the materialist conception of history, and from their early atheist teachers a denial of any element of truth in any religion: that negation, itself, soon assumed the force of a religion. All was material, whether the past, present or the future of man; he became a mere conditioned reflex of material things. The soul of man as an eternal force became a quaint illusion for analysis in Soviet laboratories, or humour in the comic papers. Any higher striving, in harmony with a higher purpose flowing through earthly things, was reduced to an animal urge to fill the belly.

Here we come to the root of the matter; our values are those of the spirit and their values are those of materialism. If our values are not spiritual values, our struggle and our sacrifice have no purpose. We strive, not merely for the material satisfaction of a transient generation; we strive for the emergence of ever higher forms upon this earth.

When we conceive the earthly mission of man as a conscious striving for higher form, we challenge every fundamental of a creed which is not only material but denounces as the final crime any effort to create, or even to preserve, forms above the ordinary.

The main purpose of communism is to reduce all to the ordinary, or below it, to that lowest common denominator where even envy becomes exhausted; our main purpose is to surpass the ordinary, because we believe than an accelerated evolution of a higher type is essential to man's survival in face of present circumstances. We believe, too, that only through the emergence of ever higher forms can the divine will be served, and that it is our task to serve this purpose.

No matter what the system of government may be the peoples of the West must unite in a European patriotism to throw back the red death that will come from the East. All argument and all dispute about the future system of government would have to wait until that is over."

(1.10.1947)

The Doctrine of Higher Forms

"In some humility, I suggest that our duty is not to ascribe our thought to God, but rather to try to perceive some part of the thought and will of God.

The foundation of our belief must be our perception of the available evidence; we have no other instrument.

In an unemotional estimate of probability it is far harder to believe that no design exists in the universe which modern science reveals, than to believe in a mind and purpose which has conceived it.

The more intricate the pattern of the universe, as demonstrated by modern physics, the harder it becomes to believe that the whole cast mechanism assembled itself by chance. The more remarkable the rise of men from the most primitive of life forms, as revealed by modern biology, the harder it is to believe that no purpose directed the attainment of the present human form throughout so many vicissitudes. Finally, even the blind forces which appeared to drive man forward in contradiction of any divine guidance or solicitude, appear as precisely the challenge which was required to evoke the response that led to a higher life form."

(1.10.1947)

"It is only at a much later, and presently rare, stage in human development than man can advance without the stimulus of pain or menace of destruction by motive only of the fire within.

Nature drives man until he is sufficiently developed to advance under his own power, when the flame of the spirit is ignited. By such compulsion of nature has been secured the evolution of present man from the earliest and lowest forms life forms.

Progress cannot be observed in a measurement of our generation against the classic Greeks in the brief term of history, but it can be discerned in a comparison between this period and the stone age.

The purpose of nature comes in like a great tide of destiny: one wave may not reach so far up the shore as some precursors, but, in the longer vision of science, the deep sea advances.

It is enough to discern sufficient of the purpose of God on earth to be able to place ourselves at the service of that aim. It is certainly clear that the purpose, and the proved achievement, of this will on earth is a progressive movement from lower to higher forms. When we assist that process we serve the purpose of our God, when we oppose it or seek to reverse it, we deny the purpose of God."

(1.10.1947)

"All reproduction and all growth is organic: nothing great occurs without long effort and striving. Life itself is a process of eternal becoming, and never of some sudden and effortless attainment of completion.

The deity appear to work, in the long and mysterious process of this purpose, as nature works in every way of reproduction and evolution to higher forms."

(1.10.1947)

"Is it a crime to hasten the coming in time of the force which, in the long, slow term of unassisted nature may come too late? We go with nature: but we aid her: is not that nearer the purpose of God than the instinct to frustrate instead of to fulfil? A new dynamism in the will to higher forms is the hard and practical requirement of a man to rise higher or to sink forever. He can no longer stand still; he must transcend himself."

(1.10.1947)

The Three Wills

"The "will to comfort" man belongs to a power elite which has attained power, or has been born to it in stable and agreeable conditions. His commanding motive is to stay there, his love is the *status quo*; he hates the disturber of things as they are. His technique is toleration and a general aura of pleasant good-fellowship.

The "will to comfort" was never an admirable type; but in a certain sense, it was all right for a fine day. When the barometer changed from fair to stormy, it became an anachronism, an absurdity and a tragedy. They stand in the gale of our age bereft of every garment which previously impressed and deceived, covered only by the very inadequate fig-leaf of their engaging manners. True to type, they revert in panic to the qualities which, in normal theory, they most deplore. When they are frightened, the high priests of toleration lead the cult of intolerance, and their "pietistic" atrocities rival, and often surpass in squalid brutality, any deed committed by open advocates of violence.

The "will to power" man[2] is fundamentally a person without a purpose. To dominate is to him an end in itself. If he were a keeper in a zoo he would fulfil the instinct to dominate if he went into the monkey house with a whip and made the inmates obey him. No matter if he despised the material with which he was dealing, and had no hope of obtaining any results from his contact with them, or indeed, of implementing any constructive purpose to secure any higher form of life, he would yet be satisfying the desire to dominate."

(1.10.1947)

"The will to achievement could never be content merely to control and preserve an insufficiency, and thus to frustrate its dynamic purpose toward the attainment of a higher level of existence for humanity. Will to achievement must clearly use power, but only, and always, as a means to an end.

---

2   *In the Adlerian, not the Nietzschean sense.*

This is essentially the character of the creative artist: he does because he must. He is beyond money; that means nothing to such natures, and has never meant anything. He is even beyond power, which only means to him what brush and chisel mean to the artist in plastic arts. Power is the instrument for the great doing: not the deed itself.

Will to achievement combines certain characteristics which are usually dissociated, but must be harmonised for the fulfilment of higher purposes. Such a character unites mind and will, and combines the executive and imaginative qualities. Robustness of physique and will is joined to the sensitive and perceptive qualities of high intellectual attainment. The lost force of the intellect finds again life's purpose in the acquisition of effective will. The final and most difficult of all syntheses is at length achieved, and harmony and dynamism are combined in one nature. For an individual to win harmony with himself, and the world, and yet to retain the striving will toward ever greater purposes and higher forms - to unite harmony and dynamism - is not only to become a near perfect man, but also to be the near perfect instrument of destiny in high achievement.

This was the great vision of Goethe in the prophetic rapture of his Faust. The harmony of Greece - that sublime at oneness with self and nature, which needed no beyond in the ecstasy of a genius for life-fulfilment - was married to the eternally aspiring and heaven reaching Gothic of persisting dynamism, which can know no fulfilment in the ever new becoming of ever higher forms. This has been seen in the highest natures that have yet appeared on earth, which are but the first shows of the thing to come. These are the men who do because they must: the supreme artists of action and of life: the instruments of destiny, and the servants of any people who willed high things. If Europe requires a great service in great new purposes, this continent must devote some attention to hastening the evolution of more such men.

Deliberately we must accelerate evolution. This may well become a root thought of this age; it is plainly a necessity.

It is not only the relationship of states and their rapid enlargement to a wider unity, that we need more speed. We must also accelerate the evolution of man. We must lay before humanity, as a religion, the deliberate striving for a higher form upon this earth."

(1.10.1947)

Then shall come the union of the spirit in the creed which inspires. Like all the great forces of the spirit it must be felt rather than described. I have attempted, elsewhere, some account of this belief which derives from 3,000 years of European culture, and now moves forward in the light of these wonders of new science and of modern thought to fulfil the eventually discernible purpose of the divine in the achievement of ever higher forms. Yet it remains a creed which can and will be felt by millions, but can entirely and finally be described by no one.

It is the challenge to every creed of materialism which seeks to imprison the soul of man in the bonds of earth. It conflicts with no spiritual purpose of church or doctrine which truly seeks to lift man beyond these limitations. It is a creed which fulfils the age-long striving of the European toward an ever finer and nobler life.

Our creed is both a religion and a science, the final synthesis.

(1.10.1947)

Beauty of Life

The present creed of reducing all to the ordinary, or below it, is not merely a denial of normal nature which works slowly to higher forms of the future, through the outstanding of the present. It is a complete negation of the first necessity of this age, which is to accelerate evolution by increasing the numbers, and intensifying the gifts and character, of those who are above the ordinary.

It is even conceivable that in a really civilised community it would be a recognised function of a considerable number of gifted people to be wholly dedicated to the discovery and development of fresh forms of the beautiful. It would be well worth the while of any society animated by the finer values to place great resources at the disposal of such people. Their task would be to show the world how beautiful life could be. The artist in life would be honoured only less than the artist of eternal beauty in music and the plastic arts.

There may be some argument in favour of a society which shows the world how beautiful life can be, but few reasons exist for the maintenance of a society which shows the world how silly life can be. Yet, that is the inevitable effect upon such a society of a system which fails to discard the unfit and unworthy, and only draws to itself reinforcements from the sphere of money.

(1.10.1947)

Synthesis and Original Thought

"I am not particularly interested in debating to what extent our thinking is original, and to what extent it is derived from previous thinking or is a synthesis of prior conceptions. If we had to choose between the power of synthesis and the capacity for original thought, I should be inclined to the view, which Aristotle at least indicated, that the former quality is the more vital attribute. Yet none of these considerations really matter at all. What matters is that our thinking now exists as a conscious and comprehensive European policy.

In part, our thinking is a synthesis of what previously existed and, in part, it is original thought. That is as it should be in the development of a creed which is organic and, therefore, both related to the past and responsible to the future.

In fact we Europeans are part of an organic process which has already 3,000 years of great history and is moving to ever higher forms. It is at one with nature's laws. Nature works not only in a steady progression, but in great leaps after long lethargies; and the greatest of all these forward springs is expressed in modern science. That is why for practical purposes all things are new after the cataclysm which precipitated this great advance. For this reason we must think again; then act most strenuously, and on a greater scale than ever because we have greater possibilities. But we remain in the service of the European spirit in a movement to ever higher forms, which began millennia before us and will continue long after we are gone."

(1.2.1956)

The Problem of Power

"Can we combine the ability to act rapidly, which the people require from their government in a period of change and crisis, with the individual liberty which the people rightly require in their private lives? If we can, we achieve the system of government which we all desire. Let us first try to clear away some confusions. There can never again be any question of dictatorship - in the sense of investing any individual with anything approaching sole power - within a European system. Any form of European government must have the character of an *equipe*, a team which acts together without any pre-eminent individual, in this case without even a captain. As in all other human affairs, where men have to work together, the ablest, whoever they are, tend in time to acquire the influence their qualities deserve. This occurs more rapidly in time of crisis, when decision is difficult and responsibility is heavy. There is always room at the top, when it is a mast-top on a very stormy night; the competition diminishes as the storm mounts.

I pledged myself before the war that, under any government for which I had any responsibility, there would be no imprisonment without trial, and I was not persuaded to ask release from that pledge by later experiencing this outrage for myself. It is not only a crime against the very basis of individual liberty; it is also a public confession of the incompetent which cannot frame, and persuade the people to pass laws giving it all the authority necessary to carry out its duties.

Without power, the modern state cannot survive and, *a fortiori*, any ordered movement to any higher form of existence cannot occur. It is too late to speculate on how agreeable the world might be without power; things have gone too far.

There is much to be said for never leaving the ground in an aeroplane, but there is nothing to be said for going up in the aeroplane and, at a height of ten thousand feet, deciding to strap up the pilot and leave the aeroplane to fly and land itself. It is unwise to do it even if you think the pilot is being too authoritative, even if you have clear reasons to believe he is not very competent, even if you can cite numerous cases of pilots crashing aeroplanes and killing the occupants: when all this is said, and proved, you still have a better chance to land safely if the pilot's hands are free than if he is tied up.

It should be possible for the world of the future to ensure that men are properly trained for power; to define with more precision the terms within which power may be employed, and to devise more effective machinery both for its exercise and its check.

Nothing is more difficult than to devise a system of government which combines the power to act that the modern age requires, with a meticulous regard for individual liberty. It requires the contributions, both critical and constructive, of many minds for its full development. As a basis for discussion I suggest the following summary.

(1) Government should rest on the direct vote of the people given at intervals not longer than three years. Other parties should be free to contest these elections but not to conduct any campaign except in the two months preceding the election. The government in power should be responsible for foreign affairs, defence, order, finance and science. It should also have the power to initiate legislation in Parliament.

(2) Parliaments should be elected on an occupational and not on a geographical franchise, with the object of securing a practical and not a political assembly. Power in all social questions should rest with parliament, subject to the right of government to initiate legislation, and to check legislation by refusal to finance. In the event of the necessary funds being refused, the parliament would have no direct redress against the government. On the other hand, parliament could thoroughly publicise the matter; consequently, any party would be free to take up the point at the next election, and, thereby, to secure the defeat of the government, if the people agreed with it.

(3) The judiciary would be entirely free and independent of government, and would administer laws, which, within their defined spheres, would be passed by government and parliament respectively. Its present position and prestige would not only be preserved but extended and enhanced. I would also suggest that a new branch of the judiciary should be constituted, and invested with powers which do not exist today. The first power would be to examine at any time, and anywhere, any possible corruption in government, and to publish findings if such corruption existed; it would, of course, be possible for the government to reply, and the people could judge between government and judiciary and vote accordingly. The second power would be to continually examine new ideas and to submit findings on them to the government. In the event of the government refusing to implement an approved idea, the judiciary could publish the facts to the public; the government would then be free to reply giving its point of view. Such ides in a technical age of ever-increasing complexity are best discussed by experts in the judicial atmosphere of a law court: the prosper, critic, assessor procedure of my book *The Alternative* might provide some basis for consideration.

(4) The press should be quite free, but anyone attacked - whether individual, institution, or government or party - should have equal space to reply.

(5) The trade unions should have the constructive task of co-operating with government in progressively raising wages over the whole field of industry, as, and when, science increased the power to produce. They would have not a lesser, but a greater, position and status than they have today. Reference to the trade unions as another "estate of the realm", would, in our proposals, cease to be only a phrase and become a fact.

(6) Science and government should become more and more as one. Statesmen and scientists should live and work together in this age as the statesmen of the Renaissance lived and worked with artists. As society develops they should become more and more interchangeable. The men of the future should be part statesmen, part scientists.

The object is clearly to combine the system of rapid action which the present age requires, with the full maintenance of individual liberty and every possible check against the abuse of power. It remains true that the only way to a free individual life, and to the full development of the human personality, is the creation of a system which gives leisure and a higher standard of life; this requires drastic and continuing action by government in modern conditions. It is equally necessary to preserve the right of the individual to use these resources as he wishes, and, by using his vote, to participate in the direction and control of the whole. We believe this system to be the true democracy, because it enables the collective will of the people to be carried out, without the infringement of the individual's liberty. We believe that the mass of the people, if they are not deceived by artifice or confusion, and if they can learn the facts as they are revealed by a calm and ever developing vision of truth, will always will the good."

(1.7.1955)

"I have often found it necessary to criticise the Civil Service. The new inflated bureaucracy is the curse of the period, but the hard core - that lean and muscular professional Civil Service, which is surrounded and impeded by this fatty degeneration - remains a fine instrument on which any creative mind must rely; and he can do so with confidence. I worked for a year in the Treasury as a minister proposing measures with which Treasury officials at that time felt impelled to disagree, but I could never have asked for more loyal or capable colleagues. Whether they agree or disagree with the policy, they will put their whole energy and ability into its operation once a clear decision has been given by a resolute government which knows its own mind. The trouble with the Civil Service is not obstruction but lack of decision from above. The obstructionists are really the small fry who drifted in with the war and bureaucratic socialism, and will find themselves floating out with more than natural speed when a real government takes over. The relief of the real Civil Service will be as great as that of the country.

Such are the principles we believe to be vital. They are possible to apply because they are in accord with nature which loves the energetic and self-reliant; whenever nature is denied, life in the end is lost. But let us never forget what civilisation should add to nature; the strong must be free to create, but they must be kind to the weak."

(1.11.1954)

"When we work within a movement we should go to the extreme of patience, and even of gentle consideration in dealing with colleagues; all our wrath and all our blows should be reserved for the enemy. A character in politics which, for reasons of ambition, vanity, or petulance aids the enemy and betrays friends is generally despised; it is rightly reckoned that if the grounds of disagreement were those of principle an honest man would leave. There are a number of conspicuous examples in both the great established parties of the state; men who fight their own side harder than the enemy; or who backbite in private when they dare not fight in public. They none of them get anywhere, though they often represent well founded discontents within the party. They have neither the loyalty to stay in as good colleagues, nor the courage to go out as good enemies, therefore, they are rightly held in contempt. The world is character; and, in present politics, character is more than ever needed."

(1.12.1955)

"Let us then quite simply recognise and face the worst, but ever strive for the best; even if it should sometimes seem that all were lost. Nothing so paralyses as hopeless pessimism, nothing so jeopardises as thoughtless optimism. True balance of mind surely realises that the worst can often be turned to the best by intellect and will; in fact, through the worst can come the best which, otherwise, would be smothered beneath the slow degeneracy of mediocrity."

(1.1.1956)

"If, for instance, we had been adult in 1910 we might have been as liberal as the best of them, gradual in politics and comfortable in life, broad in the precedent and broad in the beam. Preventable poverty certainly existed in a considerable section of the population, but a minimum of sympathy, sense and energy could have put it right. That was not a situation to turn a sensible man to revolution.

There is nothing more finally impracticable than to be outside the rhythm of your age; and that was the tempo of that period. But the rhythm of this age is profoundly different, or our whole thesis of present existence is wrong. If this is a period which can be fitted by these measures and these men we shall be greatly mistaken. We could then withdraw to the relative felicity of a private life which would certainly be more agreeable than our present struggle and, at least, more distinguished than the squalid competition for the small prizes of current politics."

(1.1.1956)

"It is the age of decision in which the long striving of the European soul will reach to fulfilment, or plunge to final death. Great it is to live in this moment of fate."

(1.10.1947)

"All things are possible: that is the fascination of this great age.

Great things are never easy: they seldom, if ever, come in the best and easiest way that mind can devise.

A great new birth of the spirit comes usually like a new birth of nature, with long pain and deep striving."

(1.10.1947)

"I have read too much of history, lived too much in the field of action, and seen too much of human nature to believe in an easy perfectionism. Our idealism toward that which shall come must ever be tempered by a certain cynicism in relation to that which is. A high idealism in relation to posterity is perfectly compatible with a measure of cynicism in regard to much contemporary humanity."

(1.10.1947)

"Only cowards surrender their beliefs when they are true; only fools cling to their beliefs when new facts render them no longer true. To live in the world a lifetime without learning anything is a waste of time, even when circumstances do not greatly alter. To live in the world without learning anything during years in which all things change, is simply to be a fool."

(1.10.1947)

"This idea was born of new facts in the long opportunity for intensive reading, reflection and creation, which was afforded first by imprisonment and, later, by a complete withdrawal from the world."

(1.10.1947)

"To state an idea, which contains the force of truth and of the spirit, is finally to implement it. Nothing, in the end, can resist such an idea; if it be true.

This idea could not come before: we had not thought enough,

and mankind had not seen enough."

(1.10.1947)

"Just as pure mind, in the shape of science and a new type of political intellect which is competent to work with it to mould new forms from its discoveries, emerges as entirely dominant in terms of power realities, strange figures of the chattering "left" run to and fro announcing that the day of "the common man" has at last begun. It is, of course, obvious that the day of the uncommon man is about to begin. At last mind prevails over mass, and brain replaces brawn; quality will be everything and quantity next to nothing. The people will only be able to realise their desires through the service of exceptional men. These are the terms of reality in a new age, and neither talk nor desire can alter them."

(1.10.1947)

"In essence the better human situation depends on the return of faith; at least faith in something. Compulsion is becoming necessary, because faith lacking; our English situation provides the prime example. For years political and industrial leaders have exhorted the workers to produce more; and exhortation without faith has not been enough. Now they fall back on compulsion. That is the real meaning of deflation; sufficient unemployment is created to compel men to work harder by the spectre of the unemployed man standing at each worker's elbow, wanting his job. They can give men nothing to work for; higher wages are proved to be not enough. So they now turn again to compulsion; that is what this new policy means. It is true that men only work for faith or compulsion; men are only moved by love or fear. But it is only those who can give no faith who need no fear. We have faith - faith in union of a people of genius, who will then reach out to the highest civilisation the world has yet seen. Brotherhood and patriotism - the two strongest appeals of Left and Right in the past - combine in a new faith, which inspires but is also practical. We can show men how to live better, and to move higher. They will know what they strive for and love what they know. That love will do more than the fear to which the old world turns again in its despair."

(1.11.1955)

"History confronts us now with the same classic tragedy on a far larger scale. When the best are divided, no one can benefit except the worst. The division of the classic world could only entail the final triumph of the barbarian. The division of Europe today brings the victory of the two-headed barbarian of the modern age, who can be named - mob and money. Communism and finance are the only beneficiaries.

In this definition mob is a vertical and not a horizontal separation. It is not a question of wealth or of that artificiality which is now called social class, but of fundamental values.

Mob is disintegration; only at a later stage does integration occur into the positive evil of communism. Before that can happen the abiding values of the European must be undermined and destroyed; and a rich man can contribute more to that process by a spiritual adherence to mob, in a silliness of attitude and frivolity of life, than any poor man will effect by a bitter agitation, which at least contains a dynamism toward better things.

By money, we do not mean the reward which energy and ability have secured. Money in this modern sense is neither the wage earned by the worker, nor the deserved profit of the productive individual. It is rather the force which exploits, and, ultimately, destroys them both through the operations of speculative finance. The interests of the producer whether employer, manager or worker, stand in sharp opposition to the interests of the speculator.

Mob and money only prevail when every higher expression of the people's will is denied; they are triumphant only when no real government exists which can implement that will."

(1.10.1947)

"To make finance the servant instead of the master of the state is beyond the wildest ambitions of social democracy.

The circumstances which assist both finance and communism are flux and chaos. The profit of finance depends, in broad terms, on buying at the bottom and selling at the top. Continual flux is, therefore, essential to finance; the opposite condition of stability provides neither a bottom nor a top and, therefore, no speculative profit. The advance of communism depends also on continual flux which destroys social stability and leads to ultimate chaos. It is unnecessary to accept the thesis of a conscious conspiracy between these forces in order to observe their effective interaction.

Mind and soul must prevail over mob and money. The change of the spirit must ever precede the change of material things: the attempt to reverse this natural order is responsible for many present failures and troubles."

(1.10.1947)

"The most important thing in life is to know what matters, and the next is to know what does not matter.

A great people confronts its enemies and supports its friends; a dying people abandons its friends and seeks the favour of its foes.

A great country does not fall so far and so fast without defeat in war unless a deep moral rot has first occurred; the immense mistakes of recent policy could not have happened in a society which was free from an organic disease of the mind and spirit."

(1.7.1953)

"It has indeed been well said "dead fish rot from the head down." Fortunately, in politics, an operation which removes the head is not fatal to the body."

(1.7.1954)

"Muddle is a much greater factor than wickedness in the affairs of mankind; particularly in politics. There are more Falstaffs than Macchiavellis among statesmen of the world; the great disasters are more often the work of clowns than of villains.

Hemlock was always the response of a ruling class beaten in argument. We shall dare to question everything and we are not afraid to answer any question. When civilisation rocks, its foundations are open to question; and it is only the discovery of facts which can enable a firmer foundation to be built. Let all things be discussed, and let the truth prevail."

(1.3.1953)

We want more great men: and greater. This fact is much resisted at present, but the necessity will soon be proved by the rule of the small.

The Union of Intellect and Will

"We require the union of intellect and will. The main trouble in the contemporary scene is the divorce between intellect and will. How familiar is both the man of intellect without energy, or will to act, and the man of action without the intellect or vision to act rightly. The rare combination of intellect, and will in one nature can be, and has been, a turning point in history.

The genius of Greek civilisation consciously sought that balance and harmony between mind and body, which is the essential basis for the union of intellect and will. We must give robustness to the intellect and reflection to the will.

We must build a chassis of the will strong enough to lend effective purpose to the engine of the intellect. How often we observe the busy, mental engine of the intellectual, knocking to pieces the weak chassis of an almost physically defective will power directly the flimsy machine is taken out on the rough road of action.

How often we see a chassis of physical will strong enough to drop over a precipice without much hurt, but motived only by an engine of the intellect just strong enough to convey it to the edge of the nearest cliff."

(1:10:1947)

"To this end it is necessary to produce men who are beyond childish things: who are adult, in the true sense of the word.

To live forever is a dream: to evolve a higher type has become a practical aim. Once again we postulate that the prime necessity of our age is to accelerate evolution. This generation must play the midwife to destiny in hastening a new birth."

(1:10:1947)

"The question is how to restore liberty to the people and meaning to the vote, which expresses their will. To do this we have first to relate the system of government to reality and truth."

(1:10:1947)

"All crimes are permitted in a bureaucracy, provided they are not great. Everything is forgiven on condition that it creates nothing, either good or evil."

(1:10:1947)

"Outside a subject which we understand discussion becomes meaningless for any of us, and our opinion carries no weight. If our verdict be given on such matters it merely brings confusion. In spheres outside our own knowledge we cannot effectively shape events; we can only give our verdict upon the results achieved by others who possess specialised knowledge."

(1:10:1947)

"Let us return to the basic principles of service to the people. The way to serve the people is to carry out their will: and the way to carry out their will is to improve their conditions. This can only be done by creating a machinery of government which is

179

capable of action. To these ultimate simplicities the controversy of our day can be reduced."

(1:10:1947).

"The people must always know what the government are doing, and the government must always know what the people are thinking.

What matters now in terms of power reality are not the numbers of a country's population but the decisive weapons which it possesses. In all spheres quality will be nearly everything and quantity almost nothing."

(1:10:1947)

"It is a difficult and dangerous task for any government to restore reality to these crowded isles. Success depends on two things; a government capable of explaining to the mass of the workers what it is doing, and of convincing them of its justice; a government with the clear objective of a great policy such as Europe-Africa, which can evoke the enthusiasm of the mass of the people, and persuade them to effort and, if necessary, temporary sacrifice to attain it."

(1:3:1956)

Imprisonment Without Trial

"Every kind of abuse is possible once law and trial yield to the arbitrary power to arrest opponents and hold them without even the suggestion of a charge that they may have broken any law. Long before I suffered from such experience, I pledged myself, for those reasons, never to be associated with the establishment of any system of government in Great Britain which included imprisonment without trial. I stand by this pledge.

Let Europe on the march leave behind retrospective law, and all the vile trickery whereby sly rogues can do in the dark things they dare not do in the cleansing sunlight."

(1:10:1947)

"The idea of "function" does not traverse any cherished belief of religion and the state on which the modern world is founded. If it be true that "God created men equal" and that they are "equal in his sight", it is at least very evident that he equipped them very differently, for the only discernible purpose of performing different functions.

If we are to recognise fact, we must admit that differences exist between diverse men and diverse races, which suggest that they must perform different functions in life. We can set aside the sterile argument whether one function is "higher" and another "lower": it is enough to establish that they are different.

(1:10:1947)

"This is the type on whose lips is ever the most familiar slogan of contemporary English life: "I'm as good as him"; to which the answer is quite simply "Yes, when you have done as much."

Disaster is the ossification of a revolution of thought into a new bureaucracy."

(1:10:1947)

"It is much easier to make systems than to make men.

It is not enough to change the system of selecting men: any new system must fail unless we can produce new men."

(1:10:1947)

"Before our eyes must ever be the eternal words of Aristotle: *"The process of evolution is for the sake of the thing finally evolved and not for the sake of the process."*

(1:10:1947)

"Authority must never be divided and responsibility must always be clear. The executive, therefore, should be subject only to the will of the people as expressed by direct vote."

(1:10:1947)

"The time may come, and we must do all we can to hasten it, when statesman and scientist will be combined in one form. Until then the world requires a union between statesmen who understand enough of science, and scientists who understand enough of politics, to make their co-operation effective in this strife with chaos to win a new world order."

(1:10:1947)

"The idea rests on two premises: the first that it is always necessary to allocate administrative responsibility to a definite individual: the second, that it is vitally necessary to synthesise the many branches of national life and activity which are now uncoordinated."

(1:10:1947)

"No man, any longer, can "take all knowledge for his province"; but we must organise to make the whole province of a far greater knowledge still available to man. It cannot be left to the haphazard, or the methods of chance: life has become too big and too serious."

(1:10:1947)

"The old cliché is ever on their lips: all power corrupts, and absolute power corrupts absolutely. To this the first answer is - if power corrupts a great man, how much more will it corrupt a small man. If a statesman, carrying open responsibility for power, is corrupted by it, how much more will a civil servant, who evades all overt responsibility, be corrupted by power?"

(1:10:1947)

Would anyone now, in theory deny the principles: - "*All shall work and thus enrich their country and themselves; opportunity shall be open to all, but privilege to none; great position shall only be conceded to great talent; reward shall be accorded only to service.*" The reader must be warned against accepting such principles as plain commonsense, for they are extracted from the objects of British Union, which were first published in 1932 under a storm of denunciation."

(1:10:1947)

"Would not thought-deed men have lived in the company and inspiration of scientists, as a Medici lived in the company and inspiration of artists? By their life with, and understanding of, the artist, and their genius for organising and co-ordinating his work, these men of the renaissance left to posterity works of art which are the glory of the ages. By a similar companionship, understanding and co-ordinating executive genius, the thought-deed men of politics could work with the scientist to achieve a new world."

(1:10:1947)

"The future of the world depends on rapid action by those who are capable of achievement. The nations possessing that capacity are those which have produced great science."

(1:10:1947)

"The state should be concerned with great things; not with small things! The task of the state is to create, not merely to appropriate what others have created. The mission of the state is to be a leader in new enterprise, not just a parasite on old enterprise. The work of the state is to construct, not to restrict. The true function of the state is to create new things; not just to take over old things.

In short, our idea of state action is the exact opposite of the present idea of state action."

(1:10:1947)

"We suggest that executive government should direct the general policy of industry, but not interfere in daily business.

The more complicated life becomes the more difficult the theory that everyone understands everything.

Everyone is supposed to understand everything in a period when it is becoming truer to say that nobody understands anything."

(1:10:1947)

"This is not to argue that the people should not have power over their own destiny and that of their country. On the contrary, I suggest that this right should be restored to them: they are now deprived of it by an elaborate swindle. It is necessary to create a system by which the will of the people can be carried out and the people can be served by statesmanship."

(1:10:1947)

The True Democracy

"If we define democracy as service of the people, I claim that the view expressed in these pages is the only true democracy. My point is that the people cannot be served by the form now called "democracy" because it inhibits the action by which alone the will of the people can be implemented."

(1:10:1947)

"The interest of the people is to find men fit to serve them. On that discovery depends the future of the peoples of the world."

(1:10:1947)

"Is it mistaken, then, to suggest that the people should do in public life precisely what they would do in similar circumstances in private life?

In circumstances which become ever more extraordinary they must find instruments beyond the ordinary. The attempt to reduce everything to the ordinary, or below it, has failed. We must go beyond the ordinary or succumb."

(1:10:1947)

"Already appears less fantastic my view in 1947. To win a war, the first essential may be to present no target; to conduct a government, the first necessity may be to avoid being seen or located."

(1:3:1950)

"Vast possibilities loom of hope and of menace: all things are possible except that life will stand still."

(1:10:1947)

"This is not an age of middle ways: the illusion of easy paths may be left to those politicians whose plans are always so much duller than what happens in real life."

(1:10:1947)

"The constitution of such countries as America and Britain will permit them to change rapidly and peacefully to a new order of things by vote of the people once the peoples are convinced of the danger and the necessity: our duty is to persuade them to move in time. But will they be left to themselves and will they have time?"

(1:10:1947)

Health, Strength and Power

"The health of prime ministers is a serious matter, and the subject merits serious consideration. What are the fair principles to apply in this matter? Is it just to say that a man must be fit enough to see a crisis through, when crisis arises? If he cannot, should he not go for good? A nation simply cannot afford a leader who collapses through strain during a crisis. If a man stops a bullet or a knock on the head, he is, of course, out of action for the time being through fair cause. But we cannot have men going to bed because things get rough. They must keep going until a particular crisis is over; in the interval between crises they can rest as much as they think fit, provided they can keep on top of the ordinary routine of business. Are these not fair rules for general guidance in these matters? - if not, what are they? In fact, the whole manner of life of leading statesmen, as well as their administrative method, needs a radical overhaul. A man cannot be at his best if he plays the fool with his life to the usual degree of politicians.

The first thing, of course, is to develop a proper administrative method which depends on knowing what matters and what does not matter. The man in the lead should be the initiator of new policies for which he needs time to reflect, and he should be the breakdown gang when the smash is so bad that no one else can manage the job, for which he needs a carefully conserved health and energy. Most prime ministers occupy their days with much interference in a lot of small things which other people can perfectly well do, because they love the sense of the small exercise of power. The psychological explanation, of course, is that such characters shrink from the responsibility of doing big things and escape into small things. Shaw, with his wide experience and his unerring instinct in such matters, depicted the type in several plays which were so near to the facts of high office that they are scarcely even caricatures.

A man capable of great action, on the contrary, is impatient of doing anything but his supreme task. When he is not doing his particular work, he would rather sleep to conserve his energy, or reflect to develop and preserve his mind, rather than dissipate the river of his vitality in the sands of the trivial. For any man who really wants to do anything serious, it is incredible to spend time in high office playing bridge or reading detective novels; the distraction idea is the greatest nonsense, for it does the tired system no good to fill it with garbage. If a man wants to change the rhythm, he should read something which lifts the mind from the diurnal and inspires to fresh thoughts; the trouble for the creative mind in good reading is that it sparks off so many new ideas that it is difficult to get on with the reading.

Statesmen require not only a selective and concentrated administrative method, but an entirely different way of life. The acme of nonsense is reached when a statesman in responsible office runs round a lot of dinner parties; it is just another form of escapism, and disastrous for the health both physical and mental. He should not even attend the Lord Mayor's banquet. Let him confer with expert bodies by all means and keep touch with the mass of the people through their representative institutions (also directly in informal ways) as well as using television, screen and occasional great meetings to explain to them what the government is doing. But apart from his work, the private life of a prime minister - his feeding, resting and way of living - should be as carefully secluded and considered as that of a Derby winner. After all, more depends upon the race, and even the British will be convinced of this before long. And, of course, long before he has reached this position he should have trained himself to sleep when he can; in crisis snatching sleep for a few minutes at a time, at intervals throughout the twenty-four hours, and at all times sleeping twice during that period, which is the best conserver of energy for those under great strain. And, of course, he should also have trained himself to remain still, to reflect, and to think out his decisions in calm whenever he has a chance, rather than to run round in circles performing small tasks which are simply an escape from the reality to which he feels inadequate.

This attitude is not Puritanism; it is simply an athleticism of mind and spirit. On the contrary, we believe an innate Puritanism is the root cause of many breakdowns. Men should enjoy themselves to the full whenever they have the chance, but that opportunity is not during time of crisis. It is no paradox to say that you are less likely to go to Jamaica beach as prime minister in a crisis, if you have previously visited certain agreeable beaches on more appropriate occasions. Relax when you can, and relax good and proper, provided always, of course, that relaxation is not exhausting. The classic Greek with his life of moderate asceticism relieved by feasts, was nearer to the formula for a crisis-proof character than the puritan with his regular life of fussy little rules and superfluous tasks. The man who has been trained as a racehorse can pull out the extra pace, when it is needed, more easily than the man who has been trained as a donkey.

Away with Puritanism, and let statesmen in their training subject themselves, in accord with Plato's high advice, to every reasonable test of pleasure, as well as to the test of pain, which the modern age imposes in any case on any true man. The steel will be all the more resilient after such experiences for the great stretching and testing of crisis. But when real men come to their task, for which all life should be a preparation, they must become completely concentrated and entirely dedicated beings. We need new men as well as a new policy. We cannot afford men who crack; they must go.

But where can the Tory Party find new men to replace them? - or, for that matter, where can Labour find them? Most of those available appear to have cracked already on lesser occasions. What is the matter with British politicians? Why do politicians nowadays succumb so much more easily than men in other walks of life, e.g., soldiers, lawyers, businessmen, etc.; they, too, have their strains in this world the politicians have created? The answer is, surely, that something exists in present political life which softens men through and through, which rots the very fibre of a man. Many of these men began with very good war records in the first world war, which was certainly by test of casualty figures or by any other criterion the hardest proof of will and character men have yet had to endure; they were clearly once reasonably strong types. But after long years of the political life, the virtue has entirely gone out of them. Yet history clearly indicates that really strong characters are stronger in age than in youth. It is the disease of current politics which destroys them; the eternal compromise, the humbug, the jollying, the junketing and bogus good fellowship in all the great racket of mass deception for small ends.

Only the men who conform to the Establishment are so vulnerable. Those who arrive *contra mundum* do not crack. In their various climes and languages they are more apt to echo the reply of Lord Randolph Churchill, when asked if he was finding it very hard work being Chancellor of the Exchequer: "Not nearly such hard work as becoming Chancellor of the Exchequer."

Much has been said from many and very diverse points of view about Stalin, Mussolini and Hitler, but no one has yet suggested that they cracked under tests somewhat more exacting than a clash with Egypt over Suez. It is these stall-fed, hand-groomed and pampered animals of the Establishment who catch cold directly they go out in the wind. After a few decades of this treatment, they are sure to get a chill when Suez begins to flow through the drawing rooms.

Perhaps Sir Winston Churchill was saved from this particular disability by having the Establishment so violently against him for so much of his life. As one of his early intimates observed the other day: "the secret of ultimate success is to live long enough for all the men who hate you to be dead." Yet it must be recognised that character, as well as experience, has much to do with it; toughness, the power to endure, also a natural inclination towards a hard way of life. But the Establishment cannot normally tolerate characters like that; it only accepts them because it must when all else-has failed, e.g., Churchill in the war. And by then they may-no longer be available.

The most likely choices now to head a government of either
established party are men who happen never to have undergone
any hard, difficult or dangerous experience in their whole lives:
men who give a more marked impression of real softness than
any statesman England has yet experienced. And we have already
observed nature's rule; it is not enough to begin hard, you have to
keep hard. We shall now experience the men who began soft and
have inevitably become softer. At the end of it all must come a
government by men who have not spent their lives in orthodox
politics, but in contact with some forms of reality however diverse.
During the war, and on other brief and particular occasions,
many such men have acquired some experience of government
and administration, but have not been long enough in current
politics to suffer the great rot. The age requires men. The dolls
have had their day."

(1:1:1957)

Europe-Africa Economy

"May I postulate, at once, two necessities of the future? The
first is that Europe should unite, and the second is that Europe
should develop Africa to secure the foodstuffs and raw materials
which the home continent lacks.

Africa is the key to all, for the following reasons: (1) It can
produce any foodstuffs and raw materials we require; (2) In
our African colonial possessions local industrialisation so far
scarcely exists; (3) We control these regions and can thus plan
a permanent economy by which their primary products are
developed in exchange for our manufactures. We start with a
clean slate, in our own possession, and can write on it the plan
of the future."

(1:10:1947)

"Each European country is in too small a box for modern
conditions. The solution is to create the viable economic unit of
Europe/Africa. Within it they could combine high wages and

low prices through the high rate of production made possible by modern science. The revival of Europe alone could restore stability and progress to a world which had so long been guided by its thought and action, and inspired by its art and culture."

(1:3:1956)

"A market of two hundred and seventy million Europeans awaits us in which our economic life need not be destroyed by the competition of sweated oriental labour supplied by finance with modern machines, nor by the dumped surplus of great industrial powers in the final rigor mortis of nineteenth-century capitalism. The combined manpower of the Europeans and their pre-eminent science can rapidly wrest from the neighbouring continent of Africa a wealth of raw materials which will make them as independent of world supplies as they will be free from the chaos of world markets."

(1:4:1955)

"The supreme opportunity of this period is the Union of Europe and the joint development of Africa by all Europeans. Europe a Nation would pool and commonly possess the African colonies. Ample living space would be found for the coloured population in rich and fertile territory which is unsuitable to white occupation.

The combined manpower of Europe would develop a living room containing our own supply of raw materials and our own markets, within which the European genius could speedily build the highest civilisation the world has yet seen. The sufficiency of raw materials would be clearly assured. We come back to the question of markets as the central problem of the industrial revolution.

It is necessary for government, by deliberate policy to equate production and consumption; apart from that, the less government intervention in economic matters the better. For this purpose it is necessary to operate within an area large enough to be independent of outside supplies, and consequently independent of outside disturbance. The task is then greatly to raise the purchasing power of the people until their demand as consumers can equal their production, after the requirements of capital outlay for new developments have been satisfied. Government and trade unions must act together to raise wages equally through comparable industries over the whole field of industry. The sum total of purchasing power thus created must be sufficient to evoke and maintain the full productive-power of industry. As science increases the power to produce, consumptive power must be increased proportionately.

The basic necessity is an area large enough to contain all necessary raw materials and to provide a full market for the production of its own industries, coupled with the complete control of imports from outside. In the early days, imports from outside will be virtually excluded; when the system is functioning smoothly an exchange of specialities from various climes will be permitted and encouraged. It is the control of imports and not the control of exchanges that is the key. It would not make the slightest difference if a man in Europe-Africa exchanged purchasing power in that area for another man's purchasing power in America; it would not even make any difference today if an Englishman in London exchanged his right to drink a glass of beer for a Belgian's right to drink a glass of red wine in Brussels, if we are not blinded by all the mumbo-jumbo of exchange control and the financial sorcery of all the wizards who make profits from obscurantism. It is the movement of goods in and out of countries which matters in terms of economic reality, not the movement of money."

(1:11:1954)

Economic Leadership

"The pioneer state will go in front like a bulldozer over forest land; private enterprise will follow behind like a plough and cultivator of agriculture in the culture of varied products, when the ground is cleared."

(1:10:1947)

"The state should direct not by control but by leadership, not by bureaucracy but by wage-price mechanism.[3] It is possible to guide the industrial state in the necessary, and in the desired direction, by fixing wages in comparable fields of industry, and, when necessary because competition does not exist, by fixing prices. Over the whole great field of competitive industry where both private enterprise and syndicalised industry will exist side by side it will only be necessary to fix wages; when no monopoly or combine exists prices will look after themselves, if a reasonably sound monetary policy is pursued. But in monopoly conditions prices as well as wages will have to be fixed by the state or exploitation can occur, and, conversely, when a great increase of productive power is evoked by such factors as automation in productive industry, wages, and consequently, in some degree prices, must be fixed in the basic services, which are virtually monopolies, in order to provide the enlarged market which productive industry cannot secure in sufficient degree by raising its own wages.

It is at least arguable that the state should plan further in advance, and should consciously guide the development of industry by deliberately making wages more attractive in the area to which it desires to draw labour; thus introducing a flexibility often lacking to present capitalism, and forestalling the problems of obsolescence and redundancy.

At this point we break new territory in examining the possibilities of a wage-price mechanism, and certainly enter

---

3   Mosley's theory of wage-price mechanism can be studied in his writing on European Socialism and Automation.

highly debatable ground. These are problems which will sooner or later have to be faced as the revolutionary development of science imposes them on statesmanship. We must devise methods in every sphere for moving far quicker than any system can move today, or any present principle can suggest. What I want here to propose is one simple principle; within an insulated economy the wage-price mechanism can give government the power of leadership and action without bureaucratic control. If that contention be valid we can be at the beginning of a certain revolution in economic thinking.

In principle we must have a system which leads free men by a method of rapid action to meet the revolution of science; I believe the wage-price mechanism can supply that method. When capitalism abdicates to chaos throughout the West, such leadership alone can meet and defeat the cumbersome machine of the Soviet system, which is enforced by the brutal tyranny of the Communist Party."

(1:5:1956) .

The Economic Situation

"What is now beginning slowly to develop is precisely the crisis of the system which some of us have long foretold; it has hitherto been postponed by a war and two armament booms. As a relic of our original monopoly of world markets and our long neglect to develop our own resources, the country is abnormally dependent upon export markets. The slightest change in world conditions affects us to a far greater extent than any other nation; a serious change can at any time now bring a disaster. The Conservative Government has been living in a fool's paradise of post-war sellers' markets and an American armament boom."

(1:4:1955)

"Before the war, we suggested that an insulated system could be constructed within the British Empire: it could have been. At that time we possessed great financial resources which dated from our previous period of monopoly in world trade and could have enabled us to purchase any capital equipment that we could not produce with sufficient speed and in sufficient quantity in Britain. We also had unlimited manpower.

Since the war we have thrown away all hope of such assistance in Empire development. We ourselves have not even sufficient manpower for our own mines and agriculture in these islands. How can it any longer be argued that we can now find men and resources to develop what is left of the Empire - and with sufficient speed? It could have been done over a considerable period of years with our pre-war resources which were thrown away in the late war."

(1:11:1954)

"How was the crisis overcome for the time being? Not by a constructive policy for the development of British Empire, which our Movement wanted, but by the fighting of an unnecessary war. Unemployment was overcome by the armament demands, and by sending men out of industry to die in foreign fields. After the war there was still employment in repairing the war damage.

But in the end the escape of the politicians into war only made things worse for their system. British Empire and all our great resources were thrown away and we face the same problem with far less strength to meet it. Soon we shall have to compete not only with the surplus production of America and the sweated coolie products of the East dumped on every market of the world, but also with the cheap production of the defeated countries like Germany who are now again forced to live and compete within the old capitalist system.

So we are heading straight for the biggest economic crash in British economic history."

(12:7:1952)

"America was making up the great lag in home demand caused by the war, and has since been devoting much of her yet greater productive power to rearmament. When Americans armament demand is satisfied she must return, under her capitalist system, to world markets; and with her greatly increased productive power will become the greatest competitor we have ever known.

What prospect have we of maintaining our present level of exports, and of increasing them sufficiently to become independent of the American dole, when Germany, Japan and America return as more active competitors than ever to world markets? Yet on this fantasy, that Britain can not only maintain but increase her present inflated exports, rests the whole policy, not only of the present Chancellor, but of both Tory and Labour parties. What a disaster for Britain, if at the end of all this restriction and suffering our people find that the terms of trade have again moved against them by reason of new competition."

(9:2:1952)

"It is true, of course, that the inherent difficulties of Britain's present position have been increased by an unsound monetary policy which was not only unnecessary but dishonest. In brief, present inflation is due to two main causes: a hand-out budget and an easy credit policy, during a precarious period, in order to win an election - coupled with the chronic weakness of the present administration in always giving way to the wage demands of the big trade union battalions of the unskilled; instead of government giving a firm and decisive lead with a clearly defined wage, salary and general remuneration policy which affords differential reward for skill and full production. Contributory causes are, of course, the cowardly failure to face unpopular decisions in policy affecting the swollen rate of government expenditure; issues such as the artificial and unhealthy system of subsidies and the purely wasteful elements in the welfare state, which need a radical and fearless overhaul. In short, the present difficulty is really gratuitous, just home-made; the product of dishonest electioneering and recurrent weakness of character in facing a series of relatively small social and industrial problems.

The first slight phase of crisis has been caused by irresponsibility in government, by sheer folly.

They have neither the mind nor the will to devise a wage and salary policy which gives reward solely for effort and, consequently, gives incentive to skill and high production; nor have they the courage to put it through even if they had the mind and the will to devise it. So the first phase of crisis, which is the purely domestic malady of a muddled inflation, is likely to endure in some degree, unless the Chancellor's fiddling with monetary measures precipitates, more by accident than design, the old Tory remedy of a real deflation, with consequent unemployment and industrial strife. At present, there is no need for any trouble at all if we had a government that could govern; this first phase of crisis is home-made by weakness and confusion, despite ideally favourable world conditions. It is in the second phase of crisis that real trouble will begin, and that has not yet occurred.

Here we are up against something which is not entirely of our own making, it is partly inherited; the fault of our generation is not to have recognised changed facts in time. [This was the main theme of Sir Oswald Mosley's speech in the House of Commons following his resignation from the Government twenty-five years ago.] Our industrial system is completely out of date, it is a dinosaur in the modern age, monstrously enlarged in some respects but mortally vulnerable at the points that matter. As it happened, we were the first industrial nation of the world, and we still behave as if we were the only one.

We inherit as a relic of that period a far larger population than these islands would normally support, and an unnaturally swollen export trade which dates from our period of world monopoly but remains necessary, under present conditions, in order to buy the food and raw materials we cannot produce at home. The maintenance of that export trade became progressively more difficult as other competitors entered the field, all with the avowed object of exporting more than they imported, of selling more than they bought; a quaint paradox of the present system is that the orthodox aim of a favourable "balance of trade" for all is quite plainly a mathematical impossibility. We passed beyond the sphere of difficulty in export trade to the region of the impossible when two developments occurred: great countries with assured home markets reached a position in which it was easy for them to dump abroad their surplus production at low prices, and cheap labour countries were supplied by Western finance with modern simplified machinery to produce at costs which were out of the question for us. The doom of these new facts has stared Britain in the face throughout our lifetime, without any recognition from our generation as a whole.

The second phase of crisis is the British phase, our particular malady from which others are more or less immune; we can even suffer a disastrous depression while others are enjoying a boom. Our abnormal dependence on export trade and the fickle movements of world markets already begin to make us the sick man of Europe. We shudder into crisis at the slightest draught from across the Atlantic; we watch with neurotic anxiety the temperature chart of world prices on which the sale of our vital exports and the cost of our essential imports entirely depend. What will happen when the draught becomes a storm wind in the third phase of crisis; the American depression and the consequent world crisis?"

(1:12:1955)

"We have long talked about the coming crisis. Perhaps too long; we incur the danger of those who cry wolf. For it is impossible to determine the chronology of crisis. The only thing certain is that crisis will come; it is a mathematical certainty. It may be a matter of months or years, but it will come. The whole structure of the present system has long been obsolete, and recently has also become rotten; it must crash.

The obsolescence of the system begins to be admitted; even a conservative Chancellor of the Exchequer recently spoke of economic difficulties which have been developing for the last fifty years. My own speech of resignation from the Government drawing attention to these facts was made twenty-four years ago: in the accelerating pace of events conservatism catches up with less than its old time lag. In the interval a war and two armament booms have postponed, but will in the end accentuate, the operation of these economic facts."

(1:10:1954)

"The situation, of course, was aggravated long before the last war by the equipment of the oriental with modern machinery at the hands of international finance, for the sake of more profits; the modern Labour Party seeks to complete the process with its Colombo Plan, etc., for the sake of socialism. The effect in either case is the same; the industries of the West are undercut on world markets by coolie labour which is paid a fraction of our wages. The transfer from a capitalist to a socialist system in an individual country which is still tied to the international trading system makes not the slightest difference to the result; the only effect is probably to reduce the competitive efficiency of its industries and to make disaster more certain.

The lack of markets is always the root problem of modern industry in normal conditions, and the lack of markets is simply the lack of purchasing power in the hands of the peoples. That basic deficiency is of course accentuated by the fierce competition on international markets which is inherent in the present trading system. In a rational system it would only be necessary to sell abroad sufficient to purchase anything that cannot be produced at home. In an area of raw material supply and finished product market as large as Europe-Africa external trade would be entirely superfluous; a possible luxury but never a necessity. But in the present system it is obvious that a ferocity of competition is inevitable when all are striving to export more than they import in order to secure a favourable balance of trade. Wages tend then always to be driven down in order to undercut competitors, and as wages decrease the home market of each country contracts.

We began with a crazy system which could only work while the world was young, and clung to it long after it was completely out of date. Our subsequent follies have done everything possible to make it collapse quicker than it would anyhow have done; the measures, or rather the accidents, which are now postponing that collapse will in the end make the disaster worse.

Is our situation then desperate? Not in the least. The troubles which the follies of some men created can be repaired by the minds and wills of other men. Statesmanship must grow up."

(1:10:1954)

"In this article we will try to discover what the old parties will do in the coming crisis in the light of their proved character, capacity and tradition. Broadly speaking they have only two choices within the limits their nature imposes upon them:

(1) To force down wages and reduce the standard of life. They did this before in lesser crises by the weapon of deflation and unemployment to bring down wages, and by other instruments such as the Geddes and May committees to cut social services and reduce expenditure. The effect of this was to force down production costs, and place Britain again in a competitive position in the financiers' game of international trade. On the last occasion, in 1931, the operation was headed by the leaders of the Labour Party in coalition with the Conservatives.

(2) To inflate their way out of trouble. This is to do the same thing, but to do it more painlessly in the first phase, though with even greater chaos in the later stages. By letting the price level rise, weak governments reduce both the real wages of the workers and the burden of every fixed charge upon industry. The

rise of internal costs is then offset by a sharp devaluation of the external value of the currency. If the devaluation is greater than the internal rise in prices, the competitive position on world markets is improved, until other nations do the same thing, or until internal costs rise in proportion to the devaluation.

The governments who adopt this course usually indulge in successive devaluations which are chased by the ever increasing internal costs. As prices, of course, rise faster than wages, the purchasing power of the people is progressively reduced. In fact such governments restore the trade balance at the cost of the people. The result of the second choice is the same as the first; it is, however, harder to resist in that the people are not directly asked for a reduction in wages, but their purchasing power is filched away by rising costs. Therefore strong governments of the old gang prefer the first policy, and weak governments of the old gang prefer the second."

(18:6:1949)

"The Chancellor of the Exchequer stated: "By increasing production and increasing productivity we can hold the situation." He thus repeated the familiar cliché of all incompetent ministers from the unhappy days of Mr. J. H. Thomas onwards. He did not explain what was the point of increasing production for markets which exclude our goods by impossible tariffs or expose us to the competition of coolie labour with simplified modern machinery. If he had any serious hope, after recent experience of this system, that costs would be lowered by a great increase in the rate of production, he might be aware that nations with the assured base of a great home market are in a far better position to lower costs by increasing the rate of production; he should also know that they are ready to dump abroad below production costs directly that market begins to fail them."

(1:4:1955)

"Europe to America is economically nothing but a headache; either Europe lives on American charity, or sends goods in exchange which dislocate American economy. Economically they are better apart as soon as possible, when America has given the primary assistance necessary to set Europe on her feet and on the road to self-help in the African solution. Such measure of assistance is commonsense, because America cannot afford to have a vacuum where Europe was. The subsequent division of the two economies will, ultimately, render easier the union of the two policies."

(1:10:1947)

"Why has America far more machinery? - because America is richer and invests more in machinery; that is the first answer. But how did America become richer? We can be sure, anyhow, not by working three times harder. America became richer by mass production for a large and assured home market. It is worth installing the latest machinery if you are certain of full production for such a market; and if it is worth while you get the necessary investment to pay for the machinery because it is certain of a good return on the money. Mass production is cheap production; cost is determined far more by the rate of production than by the rate of wage.

The American worker produces three times as much as the British worker for one reason alone: he has the tools and the British worker has not. And the American worker has the tools because he has a certain market for which to produce, and the British worker has not.

In Europe, a market of three hundred million people, with a relatively high standard of life, is immediately available, if England will take the lead in European Union instead of obstructing it. How long would it take to develop a comparable market in the Empire? The Empire should have been developed long before the war in a long, steady effort; that development should have absorbed our energies rather than the war. There is now no time to make an Empire market to replace our traditional world markets, even if we had the men and money to do it. But the European market is ready-made. Once we have the will to unite and to act the economic solution is comparatively easy. A market of three hundred million people is there, and it can be a fair market if, by a combination of government and trade union action, we at once level up the lower paid labour areas to the highest standards prevailing in our continent. The process of levelling up is, naturally, always easier than that of levelling, down. The increase of living standards in these areas could be put through very quickly. It need not entail increased cost, because a greater rate of production would be possible and profitable for the larger market.

To find the manpower for the job from these small islands is difficult; to find it from all Europe is easy. It will not take a very large proportion of European production to develop in our overseas territories the resources we do not possess in Europe itself. And enough Europeans will be willing to go overseas to develop their own for a good reward.

Our market is three hundred millions, and the American market is one hundred and fifty millions. Our technique is at least equal to their technique, and our workers are at least equal to their workers. All that is lacking is union, which will give both the market and the will to develop it."

(1:11:1955)

"We want a national mobilisation of national resources to house the people; we want the best brains in the country to direct the plan and every available expert to serve it on a national scale; we want every available means of production, public or private, to execute the plan, with complete priority for this Number One problem; we all want practice and no theory.

We want, housing treated as a matter of war-time urgency."

(15:11:1946)

"In economic problems several solutions nearly always exist, any one of which may succeed if resolutely pursued. What matters is to get anything done; what is difficult is not to find a paper plan, but to get any plan put through.

The really safe, established industries, now verging on the obsolescent, are selected for the first experiments in nationalisation.

If wages and salaries, as well as the profits of industrialists whose enterprise and energies deserve reward, are not increased in proportion to the growth of productive potential, trade fails for lack of a market and collapse ensues.

The basic principle must be that reward is directly related to result. It must prevail in every sphere, ranging from the highest grade of management and technical abilities to the unskilled manual worker.

The industrial policy of the old parties rests as surely on the industrial conditions of the last century as their system of training for the next war is always based on the conditions of the last war. All their efforts to persuade advanced countries, whether dominions or foreign, to check the development of manufacturing industries in order to provide a balance for our unbalanced economy can be reduced to a simple absurdity - we are asking them to ruin themselves for our benefit."

(1:10:1947)

The H-Bomb

The following quotations make it quite clear that Mosley was nearly four years ahead of anyone (March 1950) in recognising the effect of the H-bomb on political and military strategy. For instance, Sir Winston Churchill said in the House of Commons on November 3rd, 1953:

"It may be that the annihilating character of new weapons may bring an utterly unforeseeable security to mankind. When the advance of destructive weapons enables everyone to kill everyone else, no-one will want to kill anyone at all."

And Mr. Walter Lippmann, the outstanding American journalist, commented in the *New York Herald Tribune* on the 21st May, 1956:

"Thanks to Churchill's genius, the West was ahead of the Soviets in realising the political consequences of the second military revolution, that of the hydrogen bomb.

This second revolution has led us to the acknowledgement at the summit meeting in Geneva that the great nuclear powers themselves are in military stalemate and that they cannot contemplate war as an instrument of their policies."

Mosley had said the same thing as Churchill with more detail in March and February 1950:

"It has often been said that wars would end because they would become too dangerous. That prophecy has never yet proved true. It would be a delusion of optimism to believe that it is now true. But it is possible, and even probable, that wars in the old style will now end for this reason. What state will declare war, or attack and destroy another state, if it is certain, also, to be destroyed? A fight in which both participants are certain to be killed is unlikely to take place. Has the world reached this point? From the evidence it appears to be so. It seems that any concentration of industry or life itself can now be destroyed by any state which has the technical means to produce sufficient hydrogen bombs and to ensure their delivery. The protection even of space and the power of dispersal begins to disappear in face of such weapons.

The life of any modern state, or even of a substantial community, becomes impossible under this attack. Do these weapons, therefore, encourage such attack? On the contrary, a weapon which can destroy everything may be a deterrent, but it is not a winner of wars. The attacker may destroy his opponent, but the counter-blow can still be delivered, and he himself will be destroyed.

At present this is the only answer, but it is effective. The Soviets cannot impose communism on the rest of the world with this weapon, even if they can obtain it. They can only make the rest of the world a desert with the certainty that Russia, too, will become a desert. That is why wars between states in the old style may come to an end. Neither of the great power groups will dare to move because that would mean death to both. We are reaching the period of the paralysed giants."

(1:3:1950)

"Mosley also wrote just previously: What does the hydrogen bomb mean? The answer is, more security. The truth is nearly always the opposite of the first reaction of panic. Why do I hold this exceptional view? Because the arrival of the hydrogen bomb changes completely the power potential. It is changed in favour of the West and of this country in particular. That change means that war is not more likely but less likely.

Consider the facts. The Soviet is reported now to possess the atom bomb. That is a weapon which might possibly be used with decisive effect against a small island or against any of the restricted spaces which are the living room of the chief European nations. It is improbable that it could be used with the same decisive effects against nations with the space of Russia or America. Also, it is a terror weapon, which can be used more effectively against a democracy than a totalitarian state for reasons I analysed in some detail in *The Alternative*. Once they had the atom bomb the Soviets had the chance of gaining an advantage both by reason of their own defensive room and of the structure of their government.

At some point in the future they might reasonably have hoped nearly to catch up with the West in the number of these bombs and to some extent in the facilities for their delivery. The Soviets would then have considered using the actual advantage which technical equality would give them for the imposition of communism on the rest of the world. That was why it was of such great importance that the West should have a showdown and compel inspection to prevent the manufacture of these weapons before the Soviet had reached that point. The western democracies were content to lose that opportunity and, therefore, might have lost the world. Once again they have been saved by science from the consequences of their ineptitude.

They have been saved because the new weapon is so powerful that it even reduces to the negligible the room of Russia. That is the new and decisive factor. Any country, however large, can be knocked out by this weapon if the claims made for it are at all true. No dispersal of industry could be sufficient to enable the industrial life of a nation to continue in the face of an attack by a power which is capable of manufacturing a large number of these bombs and of delivering them with adequate aircraft.

Will all wars then be settled by him who gets his blow in first? The answer is NO - if proper preparations are made. If aeroplanes carrying sufficient of these bombs are ready in relatively remote places, which cannot be located and therefore cannot be attacked, the counterblow can always be delivered. The aggressor, therefore, will know that even if he destroys every industrial centre of his opponents, he will himself quickly suffer a similar fate. The Soviets cannot impose communism on the world with this weapon. They can only make the rest of the world a desert with the certainty that Russia, too, will become a desert.

So the "final horror" may yet herald the dawn of some degree of reason. War may, at least temporarily, have become too dangerous. That event has often been wrongly prophesied; it may at length occur. Let us not, therefore, fall into complacency. A state of equilibrium never rules for long in human affairs."

(11:2:1950)

"Disarmament in the sphere of the hydrogen and atom-bomb may now be outside the practical question. So many H-bombs and A-bombs exist in the world today that they can be hidden all over the place; inspection could never now be effective. We missed the chance to stop their production when we had the A-bomb and the Russians had not. H- and A-bomb disarmament is now out of the question; it does not matter, because neither side will dare to use them. If they are used, it will mean the world has gone mad and the world will end. Once both sides have sufficient H-bombs to secure mutual suicide if they are used, they will not in fact be used; this point will very shortly be reached."

(1:3:1955)

"In summary, the situation in a few years' time is likely to be this. The Russian armies will again be free to march when neither side dares to use the H-bomb in the strategic bombing of cities. We shall also be free to use nuclear weapons for tactical purposes at a fighting front when neither side dare to use H-bombs against cities. The Russians may calculate that their armies can march because we will not destroy the world with H-bombs in retaliation. We may calculate that we can use local nuclear weapons to stop that march because the Russians will not destroy the world with H-bombs in retaliation. By energetic measures now we can even then produce another deadlock, which is, anyhow, preferable to war, if we cannot get peace and disarmament.

All these thinkers ignore the question: What happens when the Russians also have the H-bomb in sufficient quantity to make a mutual bombardment with these weapons a matter of world destruction? At this point we depart from the clearly military region and enter the sphere of high politics and deep psychology. Will the Russians then gamble that no one will take action to blow the world up, not even to stop the invasion of Europe by Russian armies? It is, surely, just the gamble that a fanatic or a fool might take; and, in fact, it might even succeed. If the Soviets begin with a long softening up process through the political and industrial action of strong Communist parties, and follow it up with a deluge of propaganda about a temporary and peaceful movement of their armies for the purposes of restoring order and serving humanity, etc., etc., there may well be a considerable body of opinion within the democracies which will be strongly against blowing the world up to stop their action.

The operation will naturally be done in piecemeal fashion, and relatively few are ever prepared to face certain death to save others. Is it quite certain that the American democracy would use the H-bomb to save, or avenge, Europe after years of horrifying statements by eminent scientists about the end of the world if the H-bomb were ever used, and a few words of very strong warning from the Soviet leaders that the H-bomb will be used against Americans if their government declare war against Russia as Soviet armies march through Europe?

We must have something to stop the Russian armies at the point when neither side dares to use the H-bomb. It should be possible before very long to stop the Russians with ground to ground atomic rockets, atomic artillery and the tactical use of an air force carrying atom bombs; all should be manned and supported by relatively few highly specialised troops. Anyhow, in the very near future (we believe already) it should be an absurdity to think of spending money on short term national service men instead of on highly trained regulars. We need an army of technicians with technicians' training and pay, and with honourable conditions of life that will attract to the services the flower of our people."

(1:4:1955)

New Science and Old Strategy

Mosley has made many other references to the effect of the new science on old politics and strategy. A few selections are as follows:

"Realists in the Soviets must avoid open war in the West. It is now fairly plain that they are trying to do so. Their game is obviously to avoid a military decision and to fall back on their well-tried political measures of agitation and concealed violence. It is lucky for the present rulers of the West that Soviet policy since the death of Lenin lacks all real grip and decision. Otherwise a spectacular retreat by the Soviets in the West, with consequent relaxation of war tension, would precipitate an unparalleled economic collapse in the democracies. During the resulting confusion a far stronger idea and firmer spirit than that of the old parties would be necessary to combat communism. We are faced in fact with the paradox that the present system of the West is only maintained by the indecision of communism, which creates the perpetual mild crises on which financial capitalism thrives and continues.

The new factor is that the advance of modern science, in terms of power, begins to make quality nearly everything and quantity nearly nothing. It is clear that the point of push-button warfare has not yet been reached, because men will not push buttons that blow up everything. Decisions in future wars are more likely to rest with bands of highly-trained specialists using other methods which I have elsewhere described.

At this point the perhaps premature aphorism of the brilliant English tank expert begins to come true: "the greater the mass of the opposing infantry, the greater the victory."

(21:6:1952)

"The hydrogen bomb can stop war, but it cannot stop politics. The Russians cannot use the hydrogen bomb against political demonstrations within their own territory, because they would kill too many of their own people and would destroy their own state. The hydrogen bomb is all powerful - except against political masses. Exit war and enter politics.

This will no longer be a game of make-belief in which two rows of smooth, smug men have a sham fight for a fat prize. It will be a political struggle for a desperate and decisive historical decision, conducted by real men and women of passionate belief and dedicated spirit.

The future will belong to those who can swim in rough seas. Fate has given us some training. Be ready."

(22:8:1953)

"There is at present a real danger that the diplomatic initiative will pass to the Soviets; the prime cause is the costive ineptitude of the Foreign Office, because the Americans are still just a little lost in Europe. The Soviets bang loudly the drum of disarmament, which everyone can hear. The answer should be - "Certainly - real disarmament and real freedom - now let us get down to it in conference; the Soviets dare not couple freedom and disarmament - we dare, and will."

(1:1:1954)

"Free elections and general disarmament are the only way out of the world danger. Hitherto, free elections have been the card played by the West in the ceaseless game of diplomatic manoeuvre, and disarmament the card played by the East. No serious effort has been made to drop the game and bring the two policies together in a constructive achievement. It is true that the West has formulated various disarmament proposals in the obscurity of interminable committees. But Mr. Eden has steadily refused to emerge from behind his barricades of red tape and to wrestle with the Soviets in the open arena until he can turn their propaganda move into a reality of achieved disarmament by pressure of world opinion. So he has lost disarmament and left the Soviets with a propaganda victory.

Those of our opinion have striven for the entry of Britain into Europe and the consequent creation of an effective European defence during the years when Mr. Eden, in the words of one of his chief press supporters, was a "sulky bystander." The first necessity was to defend Europe from a possible Russian invasion, and this could only be done through the entry of Britain. Mr. Eden more than any other man alive was responsible for holding Britain out of Europe; at that time he "felt in his bones" he should not do what he has now done. As a result, four vital years were lost in beginning the defence of Europe."

(1:11:1954)

"Europe should long ago have re-armed, and should then have called a disarmament conference with the Soviets to negotiate from strength. A dynamic diplomacy backed by real strength could have won disarmament, or have exposed the Soviets, in public debate before world opinion, as the real opponents of peace and disarmament. The result would either have relieved mankind from a heavy burden, and a deep fear, or have destroyed the moral position and propaganda appeal of every communist party in Europe, and of many in the East. These things did not occur because Sir Anthony Eden and his friends "felt in their bones" that England should not enter Europe. England's leadership was therefore lacking, years were wasted, we had neither security nor disarmament; the only positive results of this lotus period were that Britain lost the Middle East, America lost the Far East, and Eden gained the Garter."

(1:1:1955)

"Even when the blunders of the British Foreign Office do everything to ensure that Germany shall fight on the side of the Soviets if war comes in a few years' time, the pinchbeck, bureaucratic idiocy of the Soviet leadership produces a countervailing stupidity. We are spectators at a strange game of destiny in which each side seems only capable of scoring against itself; the balance of imbecility replaces the balance of power."

(1:7:1953)

"In Europe arise the gravest questions since the war. Are the Russians really offering the serious disarmament for which we have so long pressed as a western initiative? Are they ready to evacuate the occupied lands in order to place a buffer between themselves and American power? Are they at last playing the card which we anticipated some years ago? Is the object economic crisis and a great industrial-political clash in the West? Will these dangers, nevertheless, give us a great opportunity? Could we then hope, in the words of our article of some four years ago, that there would be "no return to old national divisions within the evacuated areas" and that "a united European state in that region would be the beginning of the European experiment"? Could a "united Germany within that buffer area . . . remove some of the main obstacles to European Union"? These are the subjects now being discussed by the same writer in the German press. Is it safe to accept such a policy provided Germany remains free to enter a full "political, economic and cultural union with the rest of Europe," and provided that Russia is "not free to march back into the evacuated areas any day she wishes"? - which means that the "Russians disarm in some measure, or Germany and the West must rearm in some measure." Can we by a dynamic western policy wrest from the manoeuvres of the enemy and the dangers they present a new life for Europe?"

(1:7:1955)

"One thing alone can render unnecessary the armament of Germany within the western system. It is Russian disarmament within general disarmament. How gladly would the German people then accept the union of their country in exchange for the burden of arms. We have long advocated energetic measures in policy and propaganda to obtain a general disarmament conference and compel its success, while the Labour Party was playing about with their initial contribution to the present armament muddle. General disarmament is the only safety, but it must include the disarmament of the Russian land forces. Will the Russians join us all in general disarmament, or will they stand exposed as the enemies of peace? That is the dilemma with which a vigorous western policy can confront the Soviets and they must yield in the end to our drive to peace."

(1:4:1955)

Basic Requirements of Western Safety

"If we cannot have general disarmament made effective by inspection, we must have the four basic requirements of western safety.

1. We must always match the Soviets in the main nuclear weapons. It is true they are the "great deterrent," even if further analysis suggests the deterrent is not decisive. In this sphere it is almost certain that we still lead. General disarmament is the most desirable thing on earth, but we must always retain that lead unless some really effective system of mutual inspection in this matter can be devised and accepted; this is technically very improbable at present.

2. We must have sufficient strength in modern conventional weapons to check a Russian invasion of Europe within an H-bomb paralysis. When both protagonists possess the H-weapon in sufficient degree to make it clear that its use will virtually destroy the world, neither will dare to use it. But this situation will at best only last a very short time. We may reach a point where the American use of the H-bomb and a Russian reprisal will clearly mean the end of civilisation. It will gradually become a basic and justified assumption of life that neither side will dare to use it. Russia will then be in a position to march with impunity. Nothing could then save Europe from the Russian land mass except a western force with adequate fire power. Science provides us with the means.

3. We need a highly mobile force trained in the use of the most effective light weapons which are now available for air transport. This should be an army of the combined West, ready instantly to defend the vital interests of us all wherever they are threatened.

214

Let us decide what we want, and hold it firmly - and together. The world will accept more readily the will of a united and determined Europe for a limited period than the present vague muddle of the old colonialism conducted by separate and feeble powers in indefinite menace of the human future.

4. We need something more, and something in no way yet foreseen and discussed within the old world; here enters the fourth factor. The fourth factor is guerrilla warfare.

A good deal of preliminary work will be done by the Soviets before we enter the last phase. The general softening up of the West must go much further, and Europe must be persuaded to disarm as much as possible, without the Soviets abandoning any of their really vital weapons. It will be reckoned that the relaxation, of military tension will restore the inherent "internal contradictions of capitalism" and that the economic disintegration of the West will thus be accelerated. The process will be actively assisted by using the men the Soviets can afford to demobilise - since massed land armies became obsolete - in the production of competitive industrial goods. This increased production will not be much used, as the simpleton might suppose, for increasing in any degree the standard of life of the Russian mass, who have long been accustomed to a way of living which would not be tolerated for five minutes in western countries. It will be used, on the contrary, to accelerate the victory of communism by dumping on world markets competitive industrial goods below any prices which highly paid western labour can match; there is already evidence that Russian industry merely enquires what is the lowest western tender in any market and then quotes below it. In their new strategy, this is the secret weapon - scarcely secret, because they have virtually declared their intentions - and it is much the most practical yet devised. With this combination of new methods, the Soviets have real hope of success; the only surprise is that they have been so long in thinking of it.

This success must develop according to plan before the fourth man enters: he is the guerrilla. When a large measure of industrial collapse has occurred in the West, the Soviets hope that the consequent disorder will provide his opportunity. Half-soldier, half-politician, he will be the most highly trained combatant who has yet appeared. The Soviets are past masters of this technique; in this sphere the professional soldier is paralysed and our present politicians are babes in arms. More than at any moment we shall need men in command who will know what to do when the fourth man enters. He is not here yet, but it is time to think about him."

(1:7:1956)

"The question still arises whether Europe will continue to exist at all. The only reason for this doubt is the extraordinary inability of the combined West - three hundred million Europeans plus one hundred and fifty million Americans - to produce the few hundred thousand regular soldiers, highly trained specialists in the use of the new weapons which science now makes available, who could not only guard with certainty the life of our continent but could preserve the vital interests of the western peoples throughout the world. Their absence involves two risks; the first, that we shall be compelled to use the H-bomb at the risk of world destruction even on minor occasions when it should not be used at all, in order to avoid being squeezed out of existence by a carefully planned series of communist guerrilla operations; the second, that Europe will eventually be over-run by Russian armies when both sides are so evenly matched in the H-weapon that neither side will dare to use it for fear of global disaster. Both these very serious risks could be averted if the four hundred and fifty millions of the most advanced and vital peoples in the world could find the sense or energy to put a few hundred thousand men in the field, armed with decisive tactical weapons which our outstanding science can supply in a degree and quantity that no other power can match. The failure to do this may well be regarded by history as the strangest aberration of mind, or spirit, in the long record of human failures. Surely we can raise, pay (what does the trivial sum of any necessary price matter in relation to the combined resources of the West?) and honour with the status and respect appropriate to a high mission, a sufficient number of young men who will give this service to preserve their own countries and the human future; it is so few that are required, but so much is at stake."

(1:5:1956)

How To Deal With The Russians

"The rulers of Russia are assassins, but that should in no way deter the rulers of the West from reaching an understanding with them; the word understanding is preferable to the word agreement, because it is the habit of the Soviets to break agreements when it suits them. An understanding is something which rests on a realistic appraisal of relative strengths and practical political possibilities; agreement is something which rests on honour; understanding with the Soviets is, therefore, possible, but effective agreement is impossible. Realist rulers of England in the past have often reached such understanding with the most bloodthirsty and dishonourable villains, and have thereby served both the interests of their country and of peace."

(1:2:1954)

"So, understanding with bolshevism in the traditional gangster form of a simultaneous laying down of guns is possible and practicable; but an agreement with Russia not to attack each other when opportunity offers, or to fight on the same side in an agreed contingency, is merely to invite a shot in the back. Even after a long experience these plain facts do not yet seem to be grasped by the eminent protagonists of another Locarno, which might well turn the farce of the first such treaty into the tragedy of the second."

(1:6:1954)

"Let us by all means accept the fact that the H-bomb is too dangerous for either side to use. But let us face the corollary that we cannot then have safety without either building an army and air force ourselves, or inducing the Russians to reduce their army and air force to a reasonable level by universal disarmament. This alternative remains a Russian choice, so long as we have governments without initiative. Worse still, at present we have neither army nor disarmament.

Vigorous governments under the dynamic leadership of men who combined executive capacity with the power of mass oratory would so swing world opinion against a Russian refusal to disarm that the position of every Communist party in Europe would be destroyed; unless Russia agreed to join us in establishing this only sure basis of peace. By this drive we should win effective peace; H-bomb paralysis and the disarmament of conventional weapons. Until the present situation is so gripped and resolved, we shall live on the edge of the nuclear abyss, because the H-bomb is at the moment the only answer to slavery."

(1:3:1956)

"In any event it is surely the business of western governments to make contact with the Russians - to find out what is happening, and to influence events; we have no time for an inverted Marxism, which sits aloof and waits for the internal contradictions of bolshevism to throw life's prizes into the lap. The need of the hour is for a continual striving, a spiritual athleticism and sustained toughness of effort to get results; we must begin to wrestle with the Russians for decision in the coming political struggle. Sir Winston Churchill has done his best deed in standing firm for the principle of conference, through illness and much opposition. Will any answering wisdom on the Soviet side discern that all Europe, in a free but disarmed world, might be a more effective buffer, between West and East, than a Potsdamned Germany."

(1:8:1953)

"There is only one way to get peace, disarmament and the political initiative. It is to face the Soviets in open debate before world opinion until we win the safety and freedom we want for the European peoples, or the Soviets lose the moral and political position of every Communist Party in Europe. To reach that position we need men who are capable of the clear thought which can formulate a firm policy, and who possess the ability, will and character to face the Soviet leaders in this debate of destiny with calm judgment. We must steer between the death of the world in modern war and the surrender of Europe to communist infiltration in the final dissolution of western society, which a continuance of the present decadence will make inevitable. Like many plain truths, this seems an exaggeration today, but will seem a platitude to-morrow.

It is so clearly in the Soviet interests that the economic system of the West should not be sustained forever by an artificial armaments boom. The Russians must now realise that if the West takes precautions elementary to its own safety, the hopes of communist victory by military measures are finally frustrated: Soviet policy is bound, therefore, in the end, to promote disarmament, in the hopes of assisting the economic disintegration of the West, which is their other means of victory."

(1:7:1956)

"Why do these fissures continually recur in the structure of the Soviet state? Although they evidently require some drastic action, only communists would take action so brutal accompanied by hypocrisy so loathsome. Is it that a regime of discipline and effort throws such stress on individual participants that the weaker characters dissolve in a hysteria of disloyalty? - some evidence of this is available from other sources. But the final answer to any such determinism of human weakness is surely provided by the experience of all great armies engaged in desperate struggles from the dawn of history; both their ordeals and their discipline have often been much more severe than any political struggle, but such degrees of disloyalty and depravity have so far been outside human experience in any great enterprise. The answer seems rather to lie in the character and teaching of communism; the early Bolsheviks taught dishonour and disloyalty as the most effective means of action; they erected the negation of honour into a principle of government. They have now reaped what they have sown in the progressive disintegration of their own revolution."

(1:9:1954)

The Final Soviet Tactic

"The Russians will finally advance with a political-military method of industrial infiltration and revolutionary action which neither atom bombs nor regular armies can answer; it can only be met, and overcome, by a superior idea and a stronger faith. The age of the paralysed giants will mean not only the passing of the weapons of destruction but also of the men of destruction; they will be replaced in government by men of creative realism who can command the heart of the West in crisis, and can master with a stronger grasp the hand of communism."

(1:9:1954)

"It is probable that we are entering a period of almost completely new forms of struggle for which the past has only slight and partial lessons. In deep character the coming struggle will be a battle of ideas. It is clearly possible only for those who have an idea to take effective part in such a contest. As this struggle deepens our idea will appeal victoriously to the mind and soul of Europe. Communism will lose the battle of ideas because a European idea must prevail in the end over an oriental idea in the lands of the West. Communism will, therefore, once again react with violence - but with new forms of force. The Soviet dare not risk a war between states, because such a war would release the new weapons, provided by the great industrial machines, which would destroy Russia and, possibly, the world. So the Soviets will launch not a war of states but a war of politics reinforced by violence. They will support their losing idea with concealed force.

Their Marxist creed teaches them that they can afford to wait because their opponents will collapse through their inner

220

contradictions and the general rottenness of their civilisation. When Marxists regard the present condition of the money-democracies they will find much evidence to support this view; although, in fact, it is produced by moral rather than material factors.

Realists in Moscow will ask why they should climb trees to pick apples which will fall into their hands in any case: particularly if climbing this tall tree at present means almost certainly a broken neck, and the fruit will be all the riper for waiting. In short, a war in the old style is now very unlikely. Does this mean that the Soviets will wait passively on events, and thus possibly give Europe time to unite and recover? This too, is very improbable.

At some point in the future the Soviets are, therefore, certain to carry the battle of ideas beyond the ordinary political struggle into the sphere of political violence. They believe they will win on this territory because they have a long experience in various forms of political violence, and have a long start in training for this struggle. They are wrong: when the peoples of Europe decide to save themselves and to release for this struggle the vital forces now held in chains - we shall win, and win quickly.

The world has so far had only a slight experience of the new technique. We are familiar with the wrecking tactics of communism, through which the Soviets seek to destroy from within the system of their opponents. The methods of the strike and the mobilisation of mobs for the cruder forms of political violence are well known; also, the use of their agents in all lands both for the theft of secrets and the sabotage of vital industries. They have tried in this way to break down the system of their enemies and to integrate their own; to turn all other countries into a mob and Russia into an army; to impose order at home but to export chaos; to dissolve others, but to unify themselves, under an oriental despotism. Their previous tactics will be intensified, but quite new methods will be added to them. At a certain point the Soviets will make a decisive advance into active political war. It will be a war of infiltration conducted by the political guerrillas who are now being trained, either under the guise of police forces or entirely in secret, within those zones of Eastern Europe which are under Soviet Control. The struggle will then traverse the political-military border line.

At this stage new tactics will be introduced to warfare, and, later, new types of weapons. In 1947 I wrote: "Does any reason exist to suppose that decisive weapons will, always require such immense industrial apparatus to produce them? Talent and invention, when hard enough driven, might, at any time, replace mere weight of industrial power. Some new sling, fashioned by genius from slight resources, would soon fling the stone that brought down the goliath of triumphant materialism".

"The political-guerrilla tactics which the Soviets will introduce in the period of the paralysed giants will clearly give a great incentive to the production of such weapons. Science will search feverishly for these new principles because the military decision will rest with light weapons. If hydrogen bombs are too dangerous for either side to use, interest will be concentrated on new light weapons which can bring the decision within the military paralysis which hydrogen bombs have brought. The future rests not with the greater industrial apparatus and the overwhelming explosives, but with a much more individual inventiveness; with weapons which are conceived and produced by pure intelligence. There is no doubt concerning the decision if all the genius of Europe is at the service of Europe and not of the East.

In the coming period national states cannot enter open war, because that event would bring into action the hydrogen bomb, whose use none can risk. In such warfare, all will operate through political-guerrilla bands in a war which has no front lines. The political and ideological character of the struggle will assist these methods. It will be a war without bases and without supplies; without front and without rear. In all the decisive areas of Europe conditions will be similar to the guerrilla war launched and encouraged by the allies in the later stages of the last war. But that method will be greatly intensified and developed, because it will be the whole war. The tactic will be to hit without being hit. It will be a fight between invisible foes who cannot strike without being located and, therefore, cannot be struck. The weapons will be capable of easy concealment but also of destructive action. The aim will be the nerve centres of the opposing government. The object will be not to destroy, but to win the support of the civilian population. The mass of the people will probably be less affected than by the ordinary wars of the past. But their political support will be ardently sought during a struggle of ideas in which the enthusiasm of the people will be finally decisive.

This war will be begun by the Soviets; in fact, they have already begun it in the cruder forms. The struggle will end with the passing of the Soviets from Europe. They seek to infiltrate their opponents and to destroy their power. In the development of the struggle, which they began, the Soviets can find themselves infiltrated and their own power destroyed.

It may well be that the advance of the trained bands of the Soviet to sabotage, or to actual conflict in a bid for world mastery, will coincide with a resumption of the Moscow banquets for democratic statesmen. The morality which rules Russia has a profoundly different sense of honour to that of European man. Further, the essence of the new war is that it will be disclaimed and its methods concealed.

It is vital to realise that we are living in the greatest revolution of all time, not only in military but also in political thought. The future will belong to those who first understand the new facts. Already appears less fantastic my view in 1947 "To win a war, the first essential may be to present no target: to conduct a government, the first necessity may be to avoid being seen or located." *(The Alternative,* page 301). Such views may soon seem commonplace. When living in a revolution it is important quickly to grasp new facts. But it is, also, necessary firmly to hold the principles on which all action is based."

(1.3.1950)

"It is probable that Russian strategy remains precisely the same as it has been since their decisive reappraisal of the strategic situation. War has become too dangerous, and war is off; they must, therefore, win by other means, for men who have been through so much for their cause are unlikely to abandon it when success seems nearer than ever before.

The other means are clearly political; they begin with the relaxation of tension, a return to normality which, in their belief, will renew the internal contradictions of capitalism. The inevitable economic crash will be accelerated by a reduction of armaments which have distorted the western economies; it is easier to overcome a man if you have first compelled him to a habit of life which deforms him. This crude calculation, for different and often stated reasons, we believe to be precisely true if the Soviets are only confronted by the measures now prevailing and the men now commanding in the West.

The Soviets have a far better chance to take us over from within than they ever had to take us over from without. It is the economic collapse of the western democracies which can give communism its real chance. In conditions of internal conflict we are disarmed; in conditions threatening external war we can very quickly become armed with the aid of our superior science. The giant of the West can be taken in more easily sleeping than he can be awake.

Meanwhile the anaesthetic to the whole resistant will of the West must be assiduously applied "at the summit" during a series of Arcadian banquets beside rippling streams of vodka in which every lion frisks with every lamb to the delectation of the multi-million circulation.

For our part we were against being taken over from without, and we are equally against being taken over from within; we believe it to be the greater risk. One remaining danger of war can be eliminated by land forces in the West armed by science with the modern weapons which can check Russian mass. The alternative is Russian disarmament as well as western disarmament, either we must arm or they must disarm. We believe that one of these two things will now happen. Europe will then face the final reality; the battle of ideas and the clash of systems. We must have an idea stronger than communism and a system effective enough to change the conditions which make communism possible."

(1:6:1955)

"The whole process[4] rests on the grotesque assumption that communists can be beguiled by charm from being communists. It is of course, a thesis that is as insulting to the intelligence as it is to the character of the Soviet leaders. Why should they abandon without adequate reason the cause for which they have suffered so much, just when its prospects appear to be so bright?

So the Russians get away with their posture as the angel of peace, and can still denounce the democracies as the champions of reaction and aggressive war while retaining in their free hands an overwhelming military superiority which might one day face the West with a challenge to surrender or death. Such are the results of substituting dinner parties for realist diplomacy, and private vanity for public capacity."

(1:7:1956)

"In sport and athletics, the Englishman studies "form" meticulously from the very earliest days of a racehorse or a boxer; in politics, which affect his whole future existence, he seldom gives a moment of serious study to the corresponding "form" of an opponent who may be aiming at his life."

(1:10:1947)

---

4   Dining and wining with the Soviet leaders.

225

"In the best reasoned article which has yet appeared denouncing spy mania and advocating complete freedom for scientists, Sir Francis Simon of Oxford argued that the technical knowledge of the relevant matters is now so widespread among scientists that more harm can be done by the precautions of America than by the leakage of facts which are already known. But he answers himself in one passing sentence which he compresses into a bracket: " saboteurs may play a very important role in or just before a future war." In delicate and complex processes it is clear that a few well placed saboteurs may paralyse the defensive mechanism of a nation and prostrate it before its foes. We are the last to shackle scientists because we believe that free and intimate co-operation between scientists and statesmen is the best hope for the future. But we cannot place our life in the hands of communists; that is why we must know what scientists are. In a wider sphere, too, the unchecked penetration of communists into the whole machinery of western government - Dexter White in the key position of the American Treasury, Alger Hiss alone with the President at Yalta, Maclean in charge of the American Department of the Foreign Office, Burgess at Washington - can in full development practically take over the state from within. This is a real world; Englishmen must grow up, even the most eminent."

(1:9:1954)

Results of the War

"Lord Chatham opposed the war against America in violent language; Charles James Fox opposed the war with France, and most of the Whig leaders hurried to Paris to dine with Napoleon during the brief Peace of Amiens. No one thought of arresting them or suggesting that they might help the enemy. We were still living in the tradition of the great Elizabeth, who appointed a Catholic to command her fleet against Catholic Spain; dago values were not yet in command of England. In our own time Mr. Lloyd George opposed the South African war to the point of a bitter personal unpopularity, and defended himself with the well known words: "Is every politician who opposes a war during its progress of necessity a traitor?" If so, Chatham was a traitor and Burke and Fox especially; and in later times Cobden and Bright and even Mr. Chamberlain (Joseph), all these were traitors." Finally Mr. MacDonald became Prime Minister within a few years of opposing the first world war.

It was left to our rulers to throw men (and women with their children) into gaol without charge or possibility of trial for expressing their political opposition to an unnecessary war, on the excuse that they were a security risk. Meanwhile they ushered Fuchs and Pontecorvo into the inner laboratories of our atomic secrets, and Eden's eclectic Foreign Office assiduously promoted the careers of Burgess and Maclean.

When such men add the claim of prophetic vision to their record - Europe divided and ruined; the enslavement of Eastern Germany, Austria, Hungary, Czechoslovakia, Bulgaria, Rumania and the Baltic states, added to the encouragement and subsequent betrayal of Poland; the phosphorus bomb during the war, and the atom bomb after the war was effectively over; Nuremberg and the peace of vengeance, which poisons the air of Europe for a generation; all not to the greater glory but to the destruction of the British Empire - it is time that the late occupants of their gaols should turn aside from more creative tasks once again to challenge their pretensions."

(1:8:1954)

"They found British Empire the mightiest and wealthiest power on earth. We possessed between a fifth and a quarter of the globe; we maintained a two-power naval standard which made us twice as strong as any other country in our vital defence sphere; our industries were so vigorous, and our position was so influential, that our exports steadily exceeded our imports and commanded the international markets of that trading system; the resulting favourable balance provided us with at least four thousand million pounds' worth of foreign possessions, on which interest was paid as an annual tribute which could considerably have raised the English standard of life above the general level of mankind; our Empire contained extensive mineral and raw material supplies, which only awaited direction, energy and a fraction of our great resources for development; the diverse manpower and the wealth which British Empire then possessed could have moulded from that superb heritage the highest level of material well-being and the finest form of civilisation the world had yet seen. One thousand years of genius and heroism created it - the genius of inspired leadership and the heroism of a great people; four decades of petulant vanity and puerile folly have thrown it away.

The loss of a large part of the British Empire as a result of war has reduced the area of British Empire by fifteen per cent, and the population by seventy-three per cent. The American Navy controls the sea and British ships are commanded by American admirals for defence of our homeland, Britain; American aeroplanes with their atom bombs also occupy England to save the English people from the same Soviet power which was recently used for the destruction of Europe; the dominions are protected by special arrangements with America from which Britain, is excluded; our old favourable balance of trade is lost and, instead, a precarious and temporary equilibrium trembles on the brink of catastrophe whenever the lightest breeze blows across the Atlantic; our old foreign investments are nearly all gone and the very few remaining are in pawn to the exchange control as security against the next crisis; the resources which could have developed the Empire are scattered by the winds of war; the manpower of the Colonial Empire, which would once have joined so willingly in a great development of mutual benefit is also gone or is seething with unrest beneath the weakening grasp of the wavering giant. British Empire has lost confidence in itself and has gained confidence in nothing else, neither idea nor hope. England - the land of genius, of daring, of energy, of eternal leadership and creative inspiration - stands humbly hat in hand to beg the support of its American children, and mumbles tired excuses as it shuffles out of Empire, Europe, leadership and history. Has so much greatness ever before been brought so low in so short a space of time by the errors of so few men, without defeat of its people in war?

I have opposed these men throughout my political life, since I entered Parliament as the youngest member. This led to a long and bitter quarrel with most of the class into which I was born. My argument was that they were ruining my country. The argument is over; they have done it.

The argument about the war, too, can now be reduced to its final simplicity. The first test of every policy is whether its object is achieved. The avowed object of the war was to save Poland and to protect all Europe from the threat of tyranny. Neither object was achieved; Poland is enslaved and all Europe is threatened by Britain's ally in the war.

The war was fought to prevent Germans joining with Germans; Danzig was a German city and the Polish Corridor had been regarded for twenty years as the greatest scandal in an iniquitous treaty by every opinion in Europe and America that was worth recording. The result of a war fought in the name of freedom was to subject ten non-Russian peoples to the Soviets, at least seven of them not even Slavonic peoples.

It is true that Britain entered the war without knowing on which side Russia would fight; that makes the conduct of the responsible statesmen the more reckless. It is now clear that if Russia had entered the struggle on the other side, the war, and the whole of the British Empire, would have been lost. As the Soviets came into the battle on our side only part of Europe and part of the British Empire were lost. The point is that to start the war on that issue and in that balance of forces made disaster inevitable, whatever happened.

The rise everywhere of the disruptive Left, is, of course, not just the consequence of Russian victory, but a devil directly inspired and controlled by a vigorous and triumphant Soviet policy. The result is already the breakup of everything. A good thing - some may say - it was out-of-date and bound to go. It is true that the old order must pass and give way to new forms, but it should yield only to some new form of order, in accord with coherent ideas. The flinging of primitive populations to anarchy in the service of communism is a process which neither Churchill nor any sane men of other opinion can approve. Yet this has been the result of England's weakness and of Europe's prostration.

The last devil released by the war now invades the very heart of the West in the upsurge within Europe of the chaotic and, in recent experience, murderous Left. Goethe's final horror is realised; Silenus and his long-eared band trample through the temples of three millennia of European beauty; the sustained order of centuries topples in derisive disintegration.

Attitudes to War

There are three possible attitudes in time of war for men who disagree with the policy of the government of their country. The first is to say: my country, right or wrong, we are at war and I will shut my mouth and obey orders. Many brave and honourable men took this course, and all members of Union Movement who were in the forces or other national employment were advised to do so. All who have fought in one war and been imprisoned for their opposition to the next will have no doubt about which was the easier choice to make. The second course is to aid the enemy and become a traitor, and, if you run away to the enemy at a moment when he looks like winning, that also appears, in terms of personal convenience, a course which is not difficult for a man who is capable of assassinating his mother because he believes her to be wrong. The third course is to say I may sacrifice myself but not my country; I will do my utmost openly and publicly to persuade my fellow countrymen to stop this madness and make peace, at whatever cost to myself; but I will do nothing in any way to aid the enemy, and, if he lands on these shores, I will fight him as I fought before. It was that third course which we adopted and we will always be proud of having done so. It is clear cut in principle and of honourable precedent; it was previously adopted by Lord Chatham, Charles James Fox, David Lloyd George, and a long line of famous English patriots in similar circumstances. They did not suffer similar consequences of imprisonment and persecution, because England at that time was ruled by Englishmen who understood something of the English spirit. But if any swordsman of malice seriously imagines that he can permanently eliminate an opponent by denouncing his adversary for his opposition to an unnecessary war, he will find the quickest cure for his delusion in a short reading of history."

(1:3:1956)

"Early in life the young Englishman of the ruling class is assiduously taught to work at play, and to play at work. Surely, there is nothing so dangerous as to create complacent illusion while deadly reality still remains, or to make the people merely laugh when it is still a matter of life and death to think. Clowns have their place in the world, but not beside the deathbed of mankind; if we cannot solve these problems, they can be our end. Let us face this looming doom like calm, serious and determined men, not like fugitive boys tittering and twittering to keep up their spirits in the dark. It becomes more and more remarkable that our present governing class can take nothing seriously except a war; they can blow up anything, but build nothing (that requires a constant purpose and enduring will)."

(1:9:1955)

"These gentlemen (journalists who complain of existing leadership) should not complain, for it is the long advocacy of such journalism that has enthroned mediocrity to maintain orthodoxy, and the static oligarchy. They played safe in a world without safety. They willed the means; now they have the end. The smoothies enter rough waters."

(1:10:55)

"Nothing is more destructive of moral character in the long run than a public morality which has no relation to private practice.

The great negation operated both at home and abroad; in this respect it was quite impartial. It was not based merely on a hatred of great foreigners; it entertained at least an equal spite against great Englishmen."

(1:10:1947)

"Just conceive the energy that Britain evinced during the last two wars against Germany applied to the development of Africa by the direct action of a united nation, bent on the achievement of a higher standard of life.

The "doers" at home could find employment only in frustrating and defeating "doers" abroad. Such were the uses of high talent and character in the service of Oedipus-Puritan mediocrity; Siegfried in the bondage of the dwarfs. Pity the strange enthralment of the English genius, rather than envy it or blame it."

(1:10:1947)

Morality in War

"The greater good cannot always be achieved without the lesser evil. Will that be denied by those who justified the dropping of an atom bomb on civilian populations with the plea that the war would be shortened and the lives of soldiers would be saved? That argument could only mean that it was more important to save the lives of British and American soldiers, which would have been lost in the invasion of Japan, than the lives of the relatively few Japanese children who perished in the agony of Hiroshima. The argument that the end justifies the means, that national necessity overrides the suffering of individuals, and that the few must be sacrificed to the many, could scarcely be pushed to a further extreme of moral dubiety. It is not for us here to judge these things, and no attempt is made to do so. The purpose of this writing is rather to eliminate an hypocrisy which poisons the soul of the world. In the light of recent history a little humility is not amiss in judging others: not even those who profess the creed which makes humility the chief virtue, but refuse with arrogance even to contemplate the possibility that they have constantly committed the crimes of which they accuse others. Such types in daily life are merely laughable: in the seats of power they are a world fatality. The wounds of Europe must be healed before the work of construction can begin. They are wounds of the spirit, and they are kept open by these animosities and memories of atavistic savagery. These old things have no interest to the creative mind, but they impede our work. That is why we ask Europe not to look back, but to stride forward."

(1:10:1947)

Nuremberg

A Man - a real man in victory has but one thought- to prevent the necessity of further strife. The elimination of the opponent is enough - preferably not by death if he is a brave and manly figure. Can we conceive a real man - in victory dancing round a manacled enemy - shrieking insults in the face of death - laughing at the suffering of the women - frightened of his victim's last words - frightened even of his ashes - terrified of his 'legend'? What strange dark spirit of some remote underworld has possessed our virile England?

With courts, judges and gaolers we are not concerned. They loyally and faithfully execute the laws which political forces lay down; they can do no other. These words are addressed to some of those political forces, and to some only among them:

Are you yet satisfied? Or will you permit the slow murder of a whole people by mass starvation? Even the finer spirits among the war leaders revolt against that; only the small - the incredibly small - demand still further vengeance. The large of mind and spirit have more than had enough; is it not now enough even for the lesser?

The principle of retroactive law has been firmly established in Europe. By that principle an opponent can, at any time, be eliminated by a new retrospective law made to fit this particular case. Do you not yet feel safe? You have not merely killed political opponents in cold blood; that was a commonplace at certain periods of history - we thought they were past. You have also killed brave soldiers who obeyed orders. You have made a zoo and peep-show of your victims for the gloating joy of everything that is lowest in human or beast. You have mocked and derided the sufferings of the women who loved them.

Even now is it not enough? Must you also destroy the million masses of ordinary people? Surely it is only the outstanding whom your natural character leads you to hate. Cannot you spare the ordinary, the poor, the humble, the suffering? Is vengeance not yet slaked? Can you not even now leave the past to history? Or do you fear, too, the cold contempt in the eyes of posterity?

It was well said within our time that the "grass grows green over the battlefields, but over the scaffold, never." This grass will not grow green, revenge will follow vengeance until some generation is found great enough to disrupt the circle of fatality, and to break this "Bondage of the Gods."

Europe must forget and forgive, if the continent is to live, in which resided our history, and on which rests the hope of mankind."

(1:10:1947)

"Can any serious thinker condemn a man of thirty, because there was a mess in the bedroom when he was born? To adopt this attitude is to show a lack both of the historic sense and of any realistic appreciation of the way of nature and of life."

(1:10:1947)

Fate of the Middle Classes

"Will the middle classes die? or will they fight and live? As crisis approaches, first one section and then another is affected. It is now becoming clear that the middle classes are likely to be the first who are hard hit, and to some extent they are suffering already.

The question who is hit first is determined by the nature of the efforts made by government to avoid crisis, or by its inertia in face of the threat, rather than by any cause in the crisis itself. In short, an attempt to escape by the easy way of inflation hits the middle class, while the harder way of deflation affects first the working class.

The identity of policy between the two great parties becomes even closer when they both choose the easy course of inflation rather than the harder pre-war method of deflation. Consequently the middle classes become the first victim of both. This will continue until the middle classes organise themselves, or, better still, enter effectively into a national movement that secures even justice to all sections, which means reward in proportion to skill, effort and responsibility."

(1:3:1956)

Tweedledum and Tweedledee on Economics

"So modern conservatism turns its back completely on the traditional policy of all that was vital in the Party - Joe Chamberlain, Amery, Beaverbrook. The view is finally excluded that Britain can find its supply and its market anywhere except in the free-for-all dog-fight of world markets. Once again Butler adduced the quintessence of the old liberalism in arguing that to think otherwise must entail "a catastrophic fall in our standard of living." He had read in the text books that, if production does not occur under the most suitable conditions, and is not exchanged with other goods similarly produced under the most suitable conditions, an all round fall in the standard of living must be suffered. But these were the text books of liberalism, not of conservatism. They were written before science enabled almost anything to be produced anywhere.

In fact, these text books are quite out of date; yet Mr. Butler is not the type that can think beyond them. It would also, of course, be yet further beyond his compass to think, and still more to act, in terms of an area so large as Europe-Africa, and South America, where production of everything could occur, in conditions of maximum suitability, within an area containing only corresponding standards of living, which would, consequently, be free from the modern dilemma that has torn up the old liberal text books; sweated labour working the simplified machinery of rationalised production at wage rates that can undercut the European on every market of the world.

But Mr. Gaitskell was not arguing with Mr. Butler concerning these premises of the coming fatality, as they are equally accepted by both; while Mr. Wilson has similarly instructed Mr. Bevan, who has as much concept what this discussion is about as he has idea what the Russians would do, if on our side alone, we substituted bows and arrows, or a bottle of champagne, for the H-bomb. Mr. Gaitskell has accepted equally with Mr. Butler the main tenets of liberalism; Mr. Gaitskell is an essentially liberal figure. The only quarrel between the chancellors of the rival parties concerned the method by which they can implement their common principles. In the gathering storm that threatens our balance of payments on international markets, Mr. Butler believes in monetary measures to cut down imports and stimulate exports, while Mr. Gaitskell believes in direct controls.

So we come back always to the choice between the slimming diet and the strait jacket. Neither Tweedledum nor Tweedledee has any idea how to meet crisis, outside the padded cell or starvation. In basic principle, the policy of the parties is identical."

(1:7:1955)

Wanted in Politics: the Adult Mind

"It is characteristic of the child not to foresee the consequences of an act; education and training are largely devoted to showing the connection between deed and result.

The first necessity is to eliminate the causes of the present danger; the prime cause is that light-headed silliness in statesmanship which plunges into foolish action on impulse of vanity, or of anger, without any serious consideration of the consequences. In great affairs we suffer from the lack of adult minds. We are ruled by the type of mind which launched the war in 1939 without any thought that victory would place Russia in supreme power; which floated on the resulting wave of pro-Soviet sentiment in 1945 until the vitals of Europe were gripped by the eastern conquerors; which scrapped the western armies in face of this Soviet advance because democracy "wanted to go home" while communism stood fast and went on with its task; which accelerated by at least a generation the release of science's final horrors (long before the moral nature of mankind was ready) in unnecessary and fratricidal war; which then experimented with these horrors on a civilian population without excuse, when the war was effectively over; which finally worked up in an hysteria of alarm and despair when it discovered the explosion of the world may shortly send some denizens of Downing Street and Whitehall to the extra hot hell of those who have added frivolity to crime.

We need adults, even in politics. The idea is as old as Plato, but for the first time becomes a necessity. We need men who are fit for power; we need in politics men of adult mind. We must find them now."

(1:5:1954)

"The most effective humbugs in British public life appear usually to adopt the preliminary precaution of deceiving themselves before they deceive the people; it works better like that."

(1:10:1947)

"Psalm singing and religious precept used to be kept for Sundays: now party policy is kept for party conferences."

(1:10:1947)

"The part of government is direction not management. The former requires the highest political talent: the latter can only be done through a bureaucracy. When the former is lacking, the latter tends to run the state."

(1:10:1947)

"Individual members of that strangely assorted miscellany of politicians, money-men and press-men, which constitutes the present ruling class of Britain, may have started in cottage or castle. Once they have attained their position as members of this class they rapidly assume the character, and assimilate the vices, which belong to a society that is well content with the present position, and determined to resist any fundamental change which challenges their comfort.

We are faced with the fact that we cannot do without power: the only remedy, therefore, is to make men fit for power. What was desirable in the time of Plato, becomes a necessity in our time.

Plato was not against power: he was preoccupied with finding methods to make men fit for power."

(1:10:1947)

Mosley has written a good deal on analytical psychology, which he studied intensively in his prison years in both English and German. His general attitude welcomes a new science of great future potentiality, but warns against its use in the hands of political quacks for the maintenance of the *status quo* by suggesting that all reformers are "maladjusted."

"The attempt to base an analysis of the supernormal on a knowledge which was largely confined to the subnormal soon became an absurdity.

They may be fair judges of the neurotics who pass through their consulting rooms, but very poor judges of statesmen whom they have not even seen. Their experience has been concerned with disease, not with the problem of abounding vitality.

A powerful and vital man receives a heavy blow, and it leaves, at worst, a bruise: the strong body resists, and works its own cure. A weak body, which is predisposed to disease, may receive the same blow and succumb to it. In the case of the weak body such a blow may lead to the surgeon's operating table: in the case of the weak mind some early adverse circumstance may lead to the psychologist's consulting room.

It is interesting to observe how a technique may be developed in the sphere of psychology, which serves well the propaganda purposes of those who are concerned to preserve the *status quo*. Certain catch-words can be purloined which, in science, denote various well-known manias: they can be applied in a general broadside of loose terminology to anyone whom a particular set of political interests happens to dislike. The broad category of their displeasure, of course, includes anyone who wants, for any reason, to change things as they now exist.

The whole process can become a simple and beautifully conceived expedient to prevent anything being changed. It could have been used against all the great teachers and doers of history from Christ to Mahomet, and from Caesar to Napoleon. Even Mr. Gladstone was obviously 'maladjusted' when he upset, landlord society by wanting settlement instead of shooting in Ireland; Lord Shaftesbury was a sad "misfit" when he checked the criminal sadism of the treatment of child labour in the early Victorian age.

If such men had not been "maladjusted" they would have been quite contented to let the grouse follow the London season in the usual social ritual of their class and epoch. By such a line of argument it would be possible to shout down any man who wants any reform. If he does not like the smell of your cess-pit, it is clear evidence that he requires an operation on his nose: if that does not cure him, he must be insane."

(1:10:1947)

Labour Party and its Programme

"The Labour Party's programme *Challenge to Britain*, is, in effect, an elaborate device to get the best of both worlds. This is true in two respects; it combines the disadvantages of autarchy's closely controlled system with international capitalism's exposure of the producer to a chaos of free competition in world markets; it also combines the disadvantages of nationalisation, which abandons the incentive of private enterprise, with a denial to the workers of any effective share in management which might replace individual initiative with collective initiative. This remarkable combination of all possible errors would, in itself, be sufficient to destroy any country which was foolish enough to adopt the programme. If such a policy is added to the present difficulties of Britain, a disaster can occur very quickly.

The very first sentence of *Challenge to Britain* summarises the problem which the programme does nothing to remedy: "our standard of living is based on foreign trade to an extent unknown by any other major country. Here lies our wealth and our weakness." Yet, after publishing this striking fact of which Labour was first informed over twenty years ago in the debates which preceded the downfall of MacDonald's second government, the concrete proposal of the party is to intensify the evil of which it complains: "we shall therefore have to export more and more in years ahead. At the same time we can expect increasing difficulties in selling more of our traditional exports." When the trouble is at length recognised, after the lapse of a generation spent in slow-moving reflection and quick-moving experience, an attempt to deal with the root of the problem might reasonably be expected, rather than advice to sell yet more goods abroad in conditions of even greater difficulty.

We are told that in the first place there must be a guarantee of raw materials - but how? Our supply of raw materials is threatened because we have difficulty in selling exports on world markets to pay for them. Labour would remedy this situation by bulk buying. But, leaving aside the proved inefficiency of bulk buying under Labour, how can we buy in bulk unless we have the means of payment - and how can we have the means of payment unless we can sell exports abroad? At this point the gay circuit of the mulberry bush becomes a vicious circle."

(1:10:1953)

"How do they know that these dollar earners - the Gold Coast for instance - will remain in the Commonwealth, or even in the sterling area, when they are thus equipped by British money? They have been given full political freedom by a Tory Government under Labour pressure, and they may well consider it will pay them better to leave an Empire for which they have no great regard, and to make direct arrangements with the United States, or with Russia - for whose propaganda they are now "ripe." Is it conceivable that Labour would then intervene to win back by force what reason had led them to abandon?

All this talk of British equipment - what, in hard fact, does it amount to? In the most optimistic statements of the Labour leaders (optimistic for the overseas recipients, but pessimistic for the British donors) a surplus of some three hundred million pounds per annum of production over a meagre and restricted home consumption is set as the target for investment abroad; has this sum any more relation to the size of the problem than a flea to the back of an elephant?

In the plain language of reality it means that America pays: and, in the very plain language of a Republican Congress, which has had more than enough of paying for the upkeep of people who have not yet learnt how to help themselves - America won't pay. Labour may suggest, beg and pray - until the flag turns from pink to purple; America will not damage her own industries

241

by admitting to her markets goods that Britain cannot sell elsewhere, and will not burden her budget to provide for every coolie in Asia the wherewithal to buy goods from Lancashire.

The alternative to persuading the Republican senators to injure their constituents for British benefit is shown to be the "siege" economy with which Mr. Harold Wilson and, in politer language, Mr. Gaitskell, have long threatened an unshaken America. "We must restrict imports which cost us dollars or gold to the minimum requirements for full production". But what happens if we fail to sell America sufficient exports to obtain that "minimum" requirement for full production? *The Economist* reminded us not long ago that this can very easily occur."

(1:10:1953)

"Mr. Bevan is able to remain in the party because he differs only on the single point that he wishes the traditional policies of Labour to be more thoroughly applied. He wants more nationalisation, not less; more militancy against the Tory "vermin" at home but less armament against the Soviet danger abroad; more criticism of American policy, but more cash from the American Treasury; more money to spend on charity, disguised as health, but less freedom to earn it. He wants a third block of nations on the quaint condition that they must be weak; his fear of Germany and of all vital elements in Europe precludes his co-operation with any third force that might be effective. He wants to intensify the policy of the welfare state until nature itself is denied; his ambition is always to make two false teeth appear where only one real tooth grew before. He possesses in high degree the pathology of the underdog, which well equips him for the present Labour leadership but incapacitates him for future statesmanship. He knows well how to play on every chord of vague socialist sentiment and pacifist tradition; his music is effective as propaganda within the Socialist Party because it is familiar, but it is out of date in a rapidly changing age precisely because it is so familiar; every idea of Bevanism belongs to the nineteenth century.

It is more serious to observe how his ex-university professor and Chancellor of the Exchequer designate, Mr. Harold Wilson, labours to reconcile the traditional international socialism of Bevanism with the hard realities of an island position in a competitive capitalist world. The first answer is indeed remarkable for Mr. Wilson believes in a return to the classic capitalism of the nineteenth century.

The only contact of that policy with any form of socialism is that the programme is entirely according to Marx: in the sense that it is precisely what Marx prophesied capitalism at this stage would become. Paradox is piled on paradox, and, in the name of socialism, the Bevanites attempt to restore capitalism in precisely the manner which Marx foretold would prelude capitalist collapse. Every socialist knows that Karl Marx prophesied exactly this; the internal contradictions of capitalism would always lead to the dumping of surplus production in backward lands, the process of dumping the surplus would then lead to the rule of finance and the imperialism of the wealthiest capitalist powers. We need not elaborate because the classic sequence of that thought is familiar to all who know anything of socialist theory; the only surprise is that the causative chain should again be set in motion by the two economic experts of the Labour Party (Messrs. Gaitskell and Wilson).

So they propose that American capital shall develop the backward areas of the world with immense investments of money (surplus production) in order that these regions shall acquire the purchasing power to buy British goods. The renewed capacity to sell British goods abroad will enable Britain in turn to buy either from these areas or from America the goods she cannot produce herself. America is to be in part requited by the raw materials thus developed; but unlike Britain in the nineteenth century America must permanently divest herself of a large proportion of her total production in the thankless role of the world's greatest moneylender (Marxian, all too Marxian).

Mr. Wilson speaking over the B.B.C as reported in the *Listener*, March 6, 1952, said:

"America .... has still to learn the full duties of a creditor nation. In the nineteenth century Britain was the creditor nation; we recognised our responsibilities in two ways. We kept an open door, in the shape of free trade, to products of the rest of the world, and we invested capital abroad on a prodigious scale without always seeking the security that it would be repaid."

To make the whole position quite clear Mr. Wilson added in the same oration: "... the most important economic effects of the war were just those which disrupted the economies of Western Europe and made them more dependent on North America, not just for a year or two after the war, but it is now clear, for a generation to come."

The two best, economic authorities of Labour, orthodox and unorthodox, official and Bevanite, are therefore completely agreed on the fundamental problem and remedy. They could not have described in plainer language the system of nineteenth-century capitalism, and they both want it, restored. They both want America to take Britain's place as chief moneylender of the world; in their view that is to be the only difference between the nineteenth and twentieth centuries.

America may not know much of classic Marxism, but that hard commonsense is unlikely to use its surplus wealth either to equip its trade competitors or to assist Russia. America thinks pragmatically, and, in a situation without precedent, which changes continually under the impact of modern science, it is not a bad thing to do. The feeble wishes of Left wing fantasy have little chance in the power house of Wall Street realism; and, in this respect, who can deny that hard heads hold some sense?

But if we leave behind the first fresh innocence which suggests that America should equip Russia's present allies, what is the next proposal? Their favourite scheme is the pet idea of Labour's late Foreign Secretary, Mr. Ernest Bevin, and is known as the Colombo Plan. This scheme relates to the Commonwealth countries of South East Asia, and the plan would require the sum of £1,868,000,000. Again, do we really think that America is going to spend this money in equipping territories contiguous to the Soviet power, particularly if Labour will insist on a reduction of the armaments by which alone they can be defended? It is significant that the proposals for the largest expenditure are always in territories either now controlled by the Soviet or very vulnerable to Soviet attack if they are not strongly defended.

Bevanism in hard practice is bound to be driven back on the siege economy which they used so light heartedly as one of their rhetorical threats to America; what then? Their only chance of making it work, even to the extent of the physical survival of the people of Britain, is the vigorous development of the Colonies.

To promise the salvation of Britain by colonial development while promising colonial self-government is another contradiction in terms; and with it vanishes the last serious hope of Bevanism (and we might, add, of present conservatism).

The inevitable doom of Bevanism arises from a simple sequence of errors; they sought the restoration of nineteenth-century socialism in the conditions of the twentieth-century; in practice their thinkers found it easier to conceive nineteenth-century capitalism than any form of international socialism in an island which now lives by open competition on the markets of world capitalism; this process depended on a close co-operation with America which the basic psychology of their movement makes impossible; their only remaining hope was then the development of African colonies, but they have pledged themselves to throw these colonies away; so they will end, whether they like it or not, as the dependants of Russia, because they have renounced all means of independence; but even this is the last wish dream of fatality because Russia has not got the means to support them but only the means to destroy them.

So passes Bevanism; it is the duty of all Englishmen and of all Europeans to ensure that England and Europe do not participate in a farce which may become a tragedy. This movement aspired to be an American pensioner in the greatest and most improbable charity the world has yet seen, but in practice can only become a Russian satellite with starvation as the reward of shame. Mr. Bevan is the last of the Socialist leaders really to believe in international socialism; the futile attempt to reconcile an obsolete but still popular faith with the hard and unpopular facts of an island position in the twentieth-century has made his doctrine Britain's contradiction in terms."

(1:10:1953)

"Labour's programme is truly a design to get the worst of both worlds. They get rid of individual initiative without securing instead the collective initiative of the workers. They tie us up at home, not to give us freedom from chaos abroad, but to tie us more securely to it. England might tolerate a period of autarchic regulations in order to create a new system, which is free from dumping, undercutting and cheap labour competition that world finance brings to the present international markets; the country might welcome also some curtailment of private enterprise in order to engage the eager participation of the workers in their own industries; but to be tied up and handed over, as a helpless bundle of a plaything, to present world anarchy, is a fate which few in the end will be prepared to suffer for the pleasure of the busy little bureaucrats, who derive interest, if not profit, from the aimless sadism of the modern state.

There we can leave this plan to free us from the dollar system by binding us more tightly to it. How long will it survive in a world of reality, which is ready to listen to doctrines of reality? Smooth little men are now drifting on smooth waters, in the gentle sunshine of continual make-believe; the storm clouds which have been slowly gathering over the British economy for the last fifty years (even Mr. Butler admits it now) have been held back by the winds of two wars, and two armament booms; the accumulated force of the tempest will in the end be the worse for this respite. When it strikes unreality will vanish in an hour; the doctrines, and the men of reality, will then enter in a real challenge. How long, and how successfully will such policies as a *Challenge to Britain* then struggle against such doctrines as European Socialism; a post-war creed which has been born of experience, both real and hard? When international socialism, leaning on international capitalism and claiming a difference by giving another name, is challenged by European Socialism; which seeks to unite all Europe into one nation, to pool all African possessions for common development by the European peoples, to link both with the European overseas empires and with South America, as the only escape into a system large and strong enough to be free of world chaos: - when bureaucratic socialism is challenged by this new syndicalism; which combines a system of complete workers' ownership for developed industries with entire freedom for the creative pioneer in industry and science to work for the full reward he is now denied - will this argument between the old and the new last long; particularly when the door to a fresh popular appeal, now closed by artificial prosperity and the still intact money power of vested interests and of trade unions, is burst open by a tornado - which sweeps away most things that are? We shall see: and, possibly, soon."

(1:10:1953)

"Bureaucratic socialism is now irrevocably the policy of Labour; the Webbs triumphed over the guild socialists when it was still early enough to take another turning, and the bureaucrat has finally frustrated the worker owner in the policy of Labour and in the outlook of the present trade union leaders.

The policy of nationalisation has been applied for years with results that are now too well known, and the question arises whether it can usefully be pursued any further. Even if nationalisation had been a glittering success, there is a clear limit to the number of industries that can be so treated, and there must be ever increasing strength in the argument of the right wing that the limit has been reached.

But the policy of nationalisation is not merely out of date; it does not affect in any way the main problem of the age. Export or die is the slogan of both the old parties; no one can begin to suggest that nationalising a key industry in Britain can assist us to sell goods in foreign markets; if anything, it reduces our competitive efficiency. A party is in a bad way when the main plank of its policy has nothing to do with the main problem of the period.

Can we envisage an eternally recurrent process of one Parliament nationalising three or four industries and the next Parliament denationalising them? If both parties are sincere, and neither is in a permanent minority, this is bound to happen. In fact, it is the prospect which is introducing complete insincerity to the serious leaders of Labour, and increasing disillusion to the rank and file who have been taught to believe what they say. No sane man believes that a constitution can exist on the perpetual scrambling and unscrambling of eggs: the result would be another and even more deadly starvation diet.

The frustration of Labour will be complete when the rank and file realise that the Tories have so arranged the exchange position that financial panic, or manipulation, will immediately remove any Labour Government which arrives in power with sincere intentions, just as Blum was soon overthrown in France in similar conditions. In fact, it will require a party and a government different in whole character and structure to face any such storm, whether natural or artificial.

(1:7:1955)

"No wonder a flood of resolutions is reported to be reaching the party conference agenda, in favour of a greater measure of worker's participation in management, control and profit. But this last echo of working class opinion within the Labour Party will agitate in vain; they are up against new bosses - the bureaucrats - the boys with jobs, and the jobs made for the boys - the whole great apparatus and paraphernalia of the Labour "state." The Webbs have won, except that their great disinterest has been stifled in the great vested interest which their party has created. Cole, Hobson, Orage, and the earlier guild socialists have lost - hopelessly, so far as the Labour Party is concerned. Cole in his later years writes timid, but still lucid, little articles in the *New Statesman and Nation*, warning Labour to be careful how it monkeys with capitalism. He once said of the Webbs that at least they had "the courage of their obsolescence"; what a pity that he has not had the courage of his own prematurity.

The Labour Party, so misconceived in whole structure, and so perverted in every value of life, can only in the ultimate analysis of crisis perform one of two roles: the first is to be a sycophant of conservatism and the second is to be a pace-maker for communism."

(1:10:1947)

"In time of crisis that dynamism of the mass breaks through to true expression in some creed of reality, and the quaint, small figures of gilded straw and painted cardboard vanish overnight, as the great wind blows through the little places that once knew them - in search of truth."

(1:10:1947)

"The Labour Party alternates between snobbism and Spartacism."

(1:10:1947)

"Labour's brand of socialism merely takes over what capitalism has done as the latter is ready to move on to new fields of greater interest and far more profit."

(1:10:1947)

"State-enterprise should not play the role of liquidator to the obsolescent, but pioneer in new and greater enterprises too large in scope, and even too imaginative in concept, for ordinary private enterprise to undertake."

(1:10:1947)

The point was put, with its usual naive clarity, by the *New Statesman and Nation,* which is revelling in the political Buchmanism of publicly confessing Britain's weaknesses. But not unexpectedly there is some profit for the Left in this self-abasement; it means peace with Russia at any price - even an Eden price.

The New Statesman and Nation

"But is all this true? - Is our situation so desperate? The *New Statesman and Nation* ran up the white flag with the following words: "Whenever and wherever an imminent danger of general war emerges, any British Government is bound to exercise restraint of the U.S. even at the risk of being denounced as an appeaser. For no British politician of any party can condone belligerent actions by an ally which could result within a week in the total destruction of civilised life on these islands. Our uniquely exposed position forces us to behave as a nation of 'appeasers' whenever an international crisis is permitted to develop to the point where appeasement is manifestly the only alternative to annihilation."

(10:7:1954 article entitled "Adenauer Agonistes").

"It is true, as those of our opinion pointed out after the war for some years without much effect, that Britain's sheltered position has gone forever; the Channel no longer exists in strategic terms. But is our position so much worse than everybody else's that we alone must grovel? - apart from the question whether some Englishmen might still not prefer dying in an upright position to following Messrs. Eden and Kingsley Martin round the Soviet compound on all fours. The answer is surely that our position is serious, but no more serious than that of everybody else. We shall, however, certainly be the first casualty if we are the first to lose our nerve. It is true that these crowded islands could probably be finished off quicker by atom bombs than the countries of the great open spaces like Russia, China and America. A year or two back our position was rather more exposed in this respect than any other, but as usual the Left shoots behind the bird; today the position of everyone is just as dangerous. "Dry" hydrogen bombs, with various additional devices of suicidal human destruction, can do as much, or more, damage to America and Russia as atom bombs can do to us. The facts of life have changed before Mr. Kingsley Martin had time to wake up and get frightened; in the present pace of things he is giving himself hysterics in last week. The simple fact is that if the new weapons are developed and used with full resolution by each side, all civilisation will be wiped out. This small island might be a little flatter than the rest, but when everyone is dead it does not matter if your grave is rather smoother than the others. These are the facts which are going to prevent another world wide war unless everyone goes mad. But there are two ways of going mad; one is to start using these weapons and the other is to break the line and start running. In this situation it is the usual experience of those accustomed to real events, and dangerous lives, that the first man to run is the first man to get shot or lose his life even more unpleasantly. The runaway is in mortal danger because anything can be exacted from him. Mr. Kingsley Martin is proving the validity of his bete noire's most dubious thesis: it was Spengler who observed that in a pacifist world ten thousand armed men could dominate mankind. In a world of Kingsley Martins, the one-eyed man with a bomb would be a king.

We can at least agree with the *New Statesman and Nation* to the extent of admitting that a future clash of nations will not be like the nice, safe old wars in which socialist politicians signed on as conscientious objectors when they were young, and sent younger men abroad to fight in their political quarrels when they were old."

(1:4:1954)

Age and Youth

"The result of it all is that a few young men with old ideas replace a few old men with old ideas; the new wine is not very new, and the bottles remain very old. On the whole, it is more natural for an old man than a young man to have old ideas; a young man who lives in the past is likely to be an even bigger fool than an old man who cannot bring his ideas up to date. The real question for Labour to decide is not whether it selects its leaders from Chelsea Hospital or the kindergarten, but whether it can change its nineteenth-century idea into a twentieth-century idea. In the light of historic experience, even more nonsense is addressed to the subject of age and youth than to most topics in this epoch. In fact, it seems that a good man is good at any age; when he succeeds depends on whether he gets his chance early or late, and that depends on the age in which he lives. In able men the mind improves and the will hardens with age, until the final decay of faculties begins, and that moment is being constantly postponed by modern science. The mind is very like a muscle which improves with use and practice. It also atrophies without hard and regular exercise; hence the oft-observed phenomenon of old at thirty and young at eighty. Experience also counts for something, though it is very far from being everything; Mr. Disraeli perhaps rather overstated the case in his aphorism: "to the creative mind experience is less than nothing" (curious how unconservative, in many respects, was this tribal totem which the conservatives imported from the sunny shores of Sicily and beyond). On the whole it is probably true that a good old 'un is better than a good young 'un, but a discussion which may touch on the topic of genius is the last in which we should be dogmatic. The one thing certain is that it is always wrong in weighty matters to replace an old heavyweight by a younger lightweight."

(1:8:1955)

"Bernard Shaw summed up the subject most aptly, with the remark that whether a man was at his best young or old depended on what he wanted to do. A man is getting old to be a pingpong champion in his twenties, a record breaking runner in his thirties, a boxing champion in his forties; while in the sixties he might find it difficult to lead an army in the field, at any rate in the days when it involved long hours on horseback or on the march. (Against this view stands Lord Wavell's analysis

in *The Times* a few years back concerning the age of great
commanders, which showed that they were about evenly divided
between the old and the young at the summit of their power;
also were not von Moltke and his two chief colleagues all over
seventy years old in the most decisive of all German campaigns?)
Shaw, characteristically, concluded his enquiry with the remark
that a man was too young at eighty to be a statesman; the only
way to give him sense enough for such responsibilities was his
Methuselah remedy.

If we look beyond the statesmen to the prophets and the seers, the
golden hair of Billy Graham, in the thirties, does not necessarily
make him a greater teacher than Goethe, in the eighties, when he
finished *Faust*. Altogether this is a subject which at various times
has engaged grave minds without any emergence of the trite
conclusion that all difficulties can be resolved by ever younger
statesmen, until the cabinet room of Downing Street is filled
with cradles. It is only when to all thoughtful and vital minds a
system is rotten with age and the corruption of senescence and
only the deeply decadent are content to conduct it without any
attempt of the radical change which time makes necessary - in
effect to profit by its decay in conditions of personal ease - that
new men are continually required by government, for the sole
reason that they are still too young to have had opportunity of
proving their inevitable failure. It is more than possible -it is
probable - that the present hectic advertisement of youth is a
symptom not of vitality but of degeneracy; when the present
government proudly announced a reduction in the average age
of the cabinet it may well have been a sign of neurosis rather
than an access of vigour."

(1:8:1955)

"In each civilisation the epoch of *gravitas* stressed government
by the elders rather than by youth. It is the age of decline and
disillusion in which Peter Pansy enters with his flight from
responsibility, his frivolity, his pathetic dependence on the all-
pervading matriarchy.

The observable fact seems to be that the youth cult at this stage of civilisation can often mean a flight from life, a back-to-the-womb complex, an escape from gathering difficulty and menacing danger by means of a light head, a fluttering hand and a nimble foot. When, above all, we need to be men, we escape to childhood, if we find that life is too much for us to face; and in no period has the temptation to fly, to evade, been so great as at present. Man seeks the womb not to create, but to escape. The age of pure fantasy, the triumph of nonsense returns in the second childhood of humanity; "youth has its day." These can be, and have been, apocalyptic symptoms. The task of a movement of renaissance is not to teach men to behave like boys, but boys to behave like men. What matters is to have a new idea in a new epoch, and to find the real men of each generation who are prepared to face the steel test of standing for a new truth. More than ever are they needed in this greatest of all ages of decision."

(1:8:1955)

The British People

"The British never move before they must: then they move fast. They possess the ultimate realism.

I turn to my own countrymen - to the real people of England whom I have known in real things, in agriculture, in the great professions, in the back streets of East London, in the industries of the North, in the Army and Royal Flying Corps of the 1914 war, to whom are now added a new war generation of similar ideal - and I ask them this question: Will your genius live again and in time to make its unique contribution? Too long has it been enchained to serve purposes the opposite of those you desired. . . . Their politics persuaded you that you were a knight errant going to the aid of the oppressed. Your fine and generous instinct to help the "under-dog" was exploited to make you the instrument of European frustration.

Mob and money laugh and dance on your generous ideals. The finest and best in a new war generation sink beneath the wave of bitter cynicism which submerged our few companions, who still lived in 1918. Deceit was the end, but yet the means were noble. You gave all for high purposes and, in so doing, you made your own high character. That remains, when the ends for which you fought dissolve in dust and ashes. Nothing matters now except that you should use the character you gained in the hard experience of that great illusion to serve now ends of reality and truth.

Such has been the character of the English in their sunlit, creative periods, and that nature still lives in the real England. The great river still flows in deep and calm, if latent, purpose; but the scum on the top is thick. Beneath, are still the great qualities of the English; your kindness, your toleration, your open-minded sanity, your practical sense, your adaptability in plan, your flexibility in action, your steadiness of spirit in adversity, your power to endure, your final realism, even your ultimate dynamism; all the great qualities are still there, which took you out from the northern mists to see with the Hellenic vision of the Elizabethan bright lands which you held and moulded with firm, Roman hands."

(1:10:1947)

"It was not always so in England. Profoundly different was the Elizabethan spirit; almost Greek in its hard Hellenic gaiety and passionate admiration of the great and vital qualities in nature and in men. What came afterwards to change so deeply the whole character? The answer is, broadly, a relaxation of outside pressure - and Puritanism!

From the depth of their vital spirit surged up, in response to the life challenge, a great outburst not only of life action, but also of triumphant music, drama and poetry, which was the genius of the Elizabethan mind and the illumination of Europe. The warrior land was also "a land of singing birds."

The Elizabethans had no modern science with which to abolish poverty - while we have. They could not use a science which they did not possess; but we can use a science which we do possess to remedy misery rather than to cause it.

They were the beginning of a civilisation of genius, not the maturity. They were the dawn, the tragedy is the absence of high noon.

Why was that continuity of the Hellenic tradition, which is the soul of Europe, driven from the place of rebirth, in the soil of England, to live again and to live forever in the German genius of Goethe and Schiller - which was both precluded and followed by all that is finest in the spirit of France - and was reflected again in the revolt of Byron, Shelley and Swinburne? The answer to all these questions is Puritanism - that cold, dark sickness of the mind and soul. Puritanism bent, twisted and deformed for generations the gay, vigorous and manly spirit of the English. Puritanism turned even the Empire, which their invincible energy and courage won, from what might have been a Parthenon of human achievement and constructive beauty into a counting house concealed in a monastery. Puritanism turned a natural friend and early leader of European culture, who might later have participated harmoniously in the building of ever higher forms of civilisation, into the persistent and malignant enemy of all striving and aspiring spirits who served purposes of great construction. In short, Puritanism has been not only the tragedy of England, but the disaster of Europe."

(1:10:1947)

"The fear of a German revival prevents European Union; the lack of that union inhibits the action by which alone Europe can survive.

A united and active West could afford to ignore in large degree the threat of Russian communism, provided inspection eliminated the risk of attack by certain weapons. But it cannot be united while

German territory and population are under the heel of a tyranny which is saluted by the remainder of the West as an ally.

The worst imbecility of history is to divide the West in order to provide the barbarian with the decisive talents which he so conspicuously lacks.

What other effect can be produced by the present treatment of Germany?

My constructive suggestion for the German problem is that for the first time Germany should be given equal opportunity both in membership of the European Union and in African development.

Would England rest tranquil while a Mongol horde was bullying and ravishing in Kent and Norfolk and an assorted mixture of pettifogging bureaucrats was bossing them about in the streets of London.

It has been charged against the writer, as a reproach, that he is pro-German. I reply that anyone who wants either to save Europe from destruction or to get things done in a new Europe must be pro-German, because if Germany is not brought into European Union, the West will be divided and the East will triumph. But Germany can only be brought finally and securely into European Union as a united and satisfied people in full possession of their own land.

The reasons for my attitude are simple and clear. All my life I have striven to do something in my time to improve the lot of man and raise his fortune; my life has, at least, proved a certain dynamism. In the Germans I see a people with an energy and capacity which can contribute greatly to large construction and high design. Whether the world likes it or not, they are a force for good or evil - for construction or destruction: like all great elemental forces they will either find an outlet or explode, they will either greatly serve mankind, or, in the end wreck the world in the bitterness of their frustration. The spirit of the doer, in eternal opposition to that of the denier, reaches out to Germany the hand of a comrade in high endeavour."

(1:10:1947)

The German People

"No less vital to great achievement than political and technical skill is a people that wills great ends, and can stand in union through long endurance to achieve them. Not even the most bitter enemy can deny to the German people that quality. They have been, and ever will remain, a factor in world history which cannot be ignored. From their own character and historic experience, derived from geographical facts, they have drawn these qualities. For centuries they have stood sentinel on the eastern marches of Europe against the oriental invader. The barbarian was ever at the gate. If they had not possessed great character, they would have succumbed centuries ago; if they had not suffered these experiences they would never have acquired the mighty instinct to cohere into a granite column and not to splinter into soft fragments. Their great quality contains a natural urge to unite and not to divide, a longing for great leadership and a desire to lift it when found to a place where it can greatly serve their great ends; in short, a solidarity, a conscious and deliberate self-discipline to secure high things, which their intelligence and industry enable them very clearly to understand. These qualities are the result of experience imprinted on a character which has been rendered harder and more definite and effective by the experience. *"Was uns nicht umbringt, macht uns härter."*

Such are the supreme qualities of the German people which have lifted them to the heights where they belong. What defects, then, have cast them again to the depths? What errors of character or judgment have robbed them of everything which their immense abilities and energies deserved? No people could plan, organise or execute so well in detail; or bring to the task a greater power to endure in combination with a superb energy and fiery idealism. But few people have suffered from greater errors in the profound judgment and long planning of future action which were necessary to use these great qualities to the best advantage and bring them to material triumph. Their policy lacked lucidity in design and finesse in application. Industry and knowledge were never lacking; only clarity in great decision. "Intellect, proportion and clarity" exclaimed Schiller - "There is Hellas." The supreme direction of Germany has often lacked that combination of qualities which, in the world of action, was also the guiding genius of imperial Rome. That calm, cold clarity in far plan; that power of flexible adaptability to fresh circumstance combined with rigid inflexibility in root principle; that deep realism in harmonious union with high mysticism; that perfect balance and control of character superimposed on fierce but persistent energy; that still regard for nothing but facts combined with the passionate onrush of a nature wholly dedicated to a higher purpose; that mind of ice but will of fire ... The absence of these eternally indispensible factors in great achievement has been the tragedy of Germany, which brought to dust all her supreme attributes. The presence of some of these qualities on occasion in the war statesmanship of the British people has often brought them extraordinary fortune, despite the intermittent energy and incredible frivolity of the British ruling class. In strange repetition of Bonapartist history the immense energies and capabilities of the German people were twice defeated by the great political skill of a rare but recurrent type in British statesmanship, which is only permitted to attain effective power in Britain for such a purpose. Men of genius have thus frustrated a people of genius.

The world pays the penalty when artificial division overcomes a natural union. History indicates that Germany requires some of the finest qualities which England has produced in order to reap that great harvest which is deserved by the character and capacity of the German people. No less does every fact of this age prove that the English need the complementary qualities of the

Germans in an equal partnership which can only be denied at the cost of further and, probably, irretrievable disaster. The qualities of Germany may be regarded by the rest of the world as a menace or a merit - judgment depends very largely on the question whether you want to get things done or to keep things as they are - but they must be recognised as a fact. The affirmative mind says: - here is something great with which great things may be done; the negative mind says: - here is something dangerous which may destroy our comfort and complacency. The ruling mind of Britain was negative because Britain was ruled by the comfortable and complacent. When the mind of Britain changes from a great negation to a decisive positive, Britain and Germany will come together as naturally complementary and related peoples. When America and France, too, under the creative necessity of this age move from a negative to a positive, we shall be within reach of a new harmony, leading to a new dynamic of achievement, in which German qualities will be regarded not as a danger, but as an essential of world survival and advance. In one way or another the Germans will come back; and, in the end, no power on earth will keep them apart or hold them down."

(1:10:1947)

Britain and America

"We have always stood and will always stand for close friendship with America, but for the equal friendship of men, not the dependence of vassals. We have in common the profound interest of resistance to Russian communism. Together we stand, divided we fall - we both know it. The equal friendship of men means that we are possessed neither by their money nor by their civilisation. They helped us in need and we should never forget it, but a united Europe can stand on its own feet and repay that help with a steady and reliable friendship in the issue which matters most to America. With America we have a common interest but a different civilisation. In this we differ from those who would give us the same civilisation but conflicting interests."

(1:11:1955)

"At a certain point of development does it not become illusory to say: "I like Englishmen and do not like Americans," or vice versa? It has long seemed to us nonsense to take such an attitude within the European family, e.g., for Englishmen to say: "I like Germans and do not like Frenchmen," or vice versa. Once we overcome the inhibition of language we do not any longer see things like that. We feel, rather, that we like some Frenchmen and like some Germans, but do not like other Frenchmen and other Germans; and so on throughout the European family. Some Europeans in all nations we learn to love like brothers; for others our feelings are the very reverse of fraternal."

(1:12:1955)

"American support is now a necessary evil; it is better to live under America, until Europe is free, than to die first under Russia. It is a dirty dog that bites the hand which feeds him and protects him. I will neither join now in the pack which turns on America nor in the hour of our triumph will I forget the friend of our adversity. But I do not forget also those who put England in the position of a dog and a dependent; they were not Americans but Englishmen. We shall work for European independence and strength, but remain friends with Americans who helped us in the moment of mortal weakness and danger."

(1:8:1954)

European Common Market and Question of Sovereignty

"A far bigger question is whether the economic approach is the right beginning. It is hoped to avoid the question of sovereignty, at least until a much later stage. Very soon, of course, any form of economic union or free trade area will bump right into the question of sovereignty. We shall then find ourselves in a far worse position than if we had faced the problem in advance, thought out all the implications and planned to meet them. If we never dare to think of any difficulty until it hits us on the head, life will become a series of bigger and better Suezes.

A common trade, or free trade, area presents immediate problems if the question of sovereignty is not faced from the outset. Within Europe we have different wage rates, different hours of labour, different taxation and rating systems, different systems of welfare, social and industrial insurance, etc., which impose varying charges on industry. All these things make an immense difference to the competitive capacity of the various peoples in a common market.

These great variations in rewards and conditions must create much competition that is unfair and can be disastrous to many well established industries. How can these problems be overcome except by a common sovereignty? The first act of union should clearly include power to some common authority under government at least to secure sufficient uniformity of conditions to ensure that competition is fair between comparable industries; there must be a deliberate levelling up of the lower standards of life by active co-operation between European Government and European trade unionism. How else can it be done? And if it be not done, how can economic union work? Without such action, should we not risk such a failure that the whole European idea would be discredited?

Will not our leaders then once again fulfil the only historic purpose they have so far evinced - the capacity to take an institution bequeathed by others (e.g. British Empire) or an idea conceived by others and resisted until the last moment by themselves (e.g. European Union) and very thoroughly destroy or discredit it by the weakness of their character and the ineptitude of their conduct?"

(1:11:1956)

Britain and Africa

"When a man seems bent on suicide he may at least be asked to consider what he is doing. We ask the English people to face the facts in Africa. Present policy can only end in evacuation of the whites; already that possibility is being canvassed by the journalism of the Left, and so far conservatism has merely followed Left wing opinion at a steadily increasing pace. This event will mean the suicide of the English as a great people, because Africa offers us the only remaining opportunity to become again a great power; in fact, within our present trading system, our only hope to live at all is the sale of African products in a particularly vicious form of Colonial exploitation. It is, therefore, well to think a little before we take the final step.

Any attempt to check, let alone reverse, present policy is greeted with execration; all the familiar clichés of abuse come at once into play. The English have talked themselves into such a fit on this subject, in the course of their war propaganda against German *Lebensraum,* that they suffer agonies of guilt at any thought of modifying the haste to discard their imperial heritage. So let us quickly make clear that this is no plea to save the old Empire; that is too late. This is not a plan for returning to the past which is dead, but for entering into a wide life of the future.

It will appear a paradox to some that I should claim to have advanced the most liberal policies in relation to the negro yet put forward from any quarter.

The first plan was formulated in 1948 with my friend Mr. Oswald Pirow; his knowledge and experience in this matter is far greater than mine, because he has occupied several of the chief executive positions in South African government.

The second plan I defined in 1953 as an extension of our general European policy. It will appear another paradox to orthodox opinion that it is not only an alternative to the first plan but in some ways the extreme opposite to it. This is not an inconsistency in our thinking, because it is a consistency of our thought to believe that there are usually several ways of solving a problem, often different from, and even opposite to each other. Our dogma is effective action rather than restrictive formulae; to think of several ways of doing a thing is of course very suspect among people who cannot think of one.

The first idea is genuine apartheid, a real separation of the two peoples into two nations which enjoy equal opportunity and status. This is in strong contradistinction to the bogus apartheid which seeks to keep the negro within white territory but segregated into black ghettos, which are reserves of sweated labour living in wretched conditions. It is confusion about what is meant by the word apartheid which has made it so unpopular among humanitarians, who give more emotion than thought to this problem. They are right to condemn slums of black pariahs, but they are wrong to condemn the two nation proposal; hysterical propaganda has made the term apartheid cover both concepts, although they are entirely opposed. The clear mind of the present Archbishop of Canterbury discerned the difference when he said: "If it were entire separation - two separate countries with separate cultures and governments there would be much to be said for it"; this is precisely what we mean.

For my part I would like to travel with the utmost possible speed to a complete division of the white and black peoples of Africa into two separate and entirely independent nations. Admittedly there must be an interim period before the black labour can be entirely replaced by white labour in the white territory, and before black government can do without white assistance and technicians in the black territory. But there is no reason why two self-governing states should not be constituted in the quite near future; the basic problem of national dignity and human rights for the negro population would thereby be solved. During the necessary interim period black labour would then travel freely to our territory for the relatively high reward it would there command, and white technicians would doubtless be tempted by substantial inducements to work in reasonable numbers for black government in the constitution of their state. Once the two nations exist the rest is a matter of simple economics and straight bargaining. As rapidly as possible black labour should be replaced in white territory by European emigration, and the white technicians who have been hired by black government should be replaced by the negro personnel they have trained; it is probable that the former process will be completed long before the latter, but time will show."

(1:4:1954)

"It is with feelings of warm sympathy rather than hostility that we approach the negro problem; my alternative plan makes this clear. I suggest that the Nation of Europe, as I should call it, or the United States of Europe, as others would prefer, should give to the negro of Africa complete equality of citizenship within Europe/Africa. It is impossible to grant that equality of citizenship within an area so limited that it would finally produce a black majority. The whites who have lived up against this problem simply will not stand for it. Either they will leave altogether, or they will fight to the death; the first means that Africa will revert to jungle and savagery, the second means civil war. Are Europe and America prepared to lose from western civilisation the wealth of Africa (including the uranium which Russia in those circumstances would probably seize through some black communist movement) or to send troops to shoot down white settlers in the interests of negro domination? If they are not in the end to be faced with this dire choice, the way out is either to divide the peoples or to grant equal citizenship in a territory so large that it will contain a permanent white majority. As usual the practical plan of tomorrow is the fantasy of today.

How long would it be before Russia took a hand if Africa became a vacuum of civilisation? Communism alone has mastered the technique of mass agitation with crude symbolism among backward peoples. Communism will enter the vacuum left by Britain, and Russia will lift the sceptre which has fallen from tired old hands. It will then be a matter of life and death for America to forestall her, and English "humanitarianism" may finally add full scale war in Africa to the other blessings it is showering on mankind.

At the end of this dream policy, as at the end of all dreams, we shall meet reality; and a small trick cannot always defeat reality, at least not in a great age of historic decision.

The small trick, of course, is to govern behind pliant African politicians, and in the process to exploit the masses of the negro population very thoroughly.

The one thing certain is that present policy makes England the ultimate loser; it is a weak and squalid way out for a great imperial people. It is also a world disaster, because Europe with English inspiration could hold the balance of mankind. In coming years the English people must decide whether to pass from history or to increase their greatness."

(1:4:1954)

Chapter 9

Speeches: Post-War

Speaking at a conference in London on Saturday, February 7th, 1948, Sir Oswald Mosley announced that the organisation of Union Movement would begin from that day. It had been formed at the desire of 51 groups which were represented at the conference and would now be merged in one large organisation.

Oswald Mosley said Union Movement stood for a complete change of system, a new way of life and a new civilisation. The need for that great change would in time be made all too clear to the British people by the facts of their daily life.

It was already becoming clear to those who studied history and serious politics. Let men be judged not by their words, but by their deeds; not by their promises or programmes, but by the results they achieved. The old parties must be judged by the facts of their rule. Their government during the lifetime of this generation had brought only two things. The first was the loss of British Empire, and the second was the communist menace to the very life of western civilisation They had built nothing: their record was destruction.

If anyone doubted that statement let them judge by contrasting the position of Britain in 1914 with her position in 1949: it was a short interval covered by the adult life of a man of 50 who was just old enough to fight in the first world war. In 1914, Great Britain still had her Empire intact; it was won by the exertions and genius of our fathers and covered a quarter of the globe. She had a two-power naval standard which gave her a defence force in her vital sphere equal to that of any other two nations in the world. She had a trading position so strong that our favourable balance of trade was steadily piling up credits in our favour all over the world; she had thousands of millions of foreign assets created by the surplus production which our ancestors had exported: she had a steady stream of tribute from all over the world in the shape of interest on those assets; that wealth was often collected by finance in a manner which injured industries like agriculture, but it enabled many people to live on a standard of life which was created not by their own exertions, but by those who had gone before.

In 1914, Britain was a colossus bestriding the world with a material wealth, physical power and moral force which dwarfed any rival on earth.

Such was the position inherited by the small clique of politicians who ruled the old parties by virtue of the great interests of money power, press power and industrial power which they controlled - or which controlled them. What had they done with that high trust, which was the greatest heritage mankind had known? Again, let them judge the results. Thirty-five years later - in 1949 - this was the position. The Empire was gone or going. India was lost; Ceylon was lost; Burma lost; South Africa was on her way out; Ireland, also, on her way out: both by reason of past crimes and follies of old gang governments in Britain. Canada was being drawn irresistibly into the sphere of the almighty dollar, because the pound was too weak to hold anything; Australia and New Zealand were attracted in the same direction. What was left? Nothing but the colonial Empire in Africa and that, too, was scheduled for demolition; because both Labour and Tory Party said we were only there as trustees for the negroes, and would move out when the "juju men" were ready to take over. It is, therefore, no over-statement to say that the Empire is gone or going.

As for physical power, Britain had not merely lost the position of being twice as strong as any other power; she was now barely half as strong as America either on sea or in the air. In defence, the once all-powerful Britain had been reduced to a base or outpost of the American system.

As for material wealth, we had been reduced from a universal creditor to a nearly universal debtor. The proud Briton, who once received his tribute from all mankind, now went cap in hand to the American Congress to beg his next crust. In fact, old party rule had brought Britain from the heights to the depths; from a pinnacle of power and glory to the mud of defeat and despair in which the supporters of the old parties seemed all too content to lie. When they saw what the small ruling clique, of politicians and financiers had inherited from the past, and what they had left to the present - well might they say - never has so much been thrown away in so short a time by so few people and for so little - for so little either in terms of material gain or spiritual purpose.

At this point I ask England only one question. Were I and my friends, after all, such unreasonable people to have spent our political lives in fighting this iniquity? We have fought these men and their system throughout. In peace we fought their stupid and inhuman policies, which brought poverty, unemployment and disaster in an age in which science had solved the problem of production and could have brought an age of plenty if it were allowed to work in a world organised for peace and happiness. In war, we opposed a policy of unnecessary war which was in no way vital to the defence, life or interest of Britain. In particular, we opposed the crime of the Brothers' War, which divided Europe, slaughtered its sons, destroyed its wealth and erected on its ruins the tyranny of oriental communism. After the war, we opposed the policy of revenge pursued by small men in spite and fear, instead of that classic policy of greatness which in victory seeks reconciliation and a new union on a higher plane.

It was a bitter thing to face these facts. But, until they were faced Britain would not be great again. Not until the British understood the degree of the disaster, and the measure of the necessity, would they make the effort. When they understood, a great people would react in a great way; if they did not they would pass from history. In the language of modern history, they had to see the challenge before they could make the response. Therefore, the worst service to the British people was to conceal the fact. That was, of course, the principal occupation of these politicians who were responsible.

It is the task of a new movement to build where the old parties have destroyed. We will create a third Empire after they have lost two Empires.

The same types in power lost us a western Empire in America and have now lost us an eastern Empire in Asia. The same ruling clique in different forms and guises has ruled the country for generations. Their wooden obstinacy, wicked folly, short-sighted self-interest, and violent crimes have lost us two Empires - one in the West and one in the East - one in America and one in Asia.

After the loss of two Empires by the follies of the few it is the heroic task of our generation to create a third by the will of our people and the genius of the new science which can serve them.

Africa will be the Empire of Europe. This is the way out of present disaster to a finer life both for the British and for our brother Europeans with whom our fate is now for ever united. Whatever politicians may do or say we have been united with Europe by science. You must agree with that basic statement unless you are prepared to see all Europe under Russian communism with rocket missiles carrying atomic explosives from the Channel coast to blast every city in Britain.

Science has left but one choice and that is Union with Europe. What policy can unite Europe? There is only one, and the completion of it can never be achieved by the old parties. How can they unite Europe; it was they who divided Europe. They have missed their moment of greatness because they lacked the qualities of greatness. They preferred revenge to reconciliation, and party triumph to the Union of Europe. The true policy of Europe will declare - Europeans shall never be slaves either of West or East, either of finance or of bolshevism. We will neither be bought by Wall Street nor conquered by the Kremlin. We will neither serve beneath the yoke of usury nor suffer beneath the knout of communism. We in Europe have deeper roots, a higher culture, a greater tradition, a longer and more tested strength, a hardier vitality, a finer purpose and a further vision than any other power on earth. By reason of our past greatness, our present knowledge and our future capacity to produce great works and great thoughts, we in Europe have the right to a free and independent life. Europe shall be free and in Union shall be great.

This is our declaration of European right. It is made in hostility to no other people. To America we extend the hand of a friend and an ally against the menace of communism which threatens us both. We will grasp the hand of a comrade in danger, but not the hand of a master in bondage. We extend our hand, too, to the Russian people and to any government which they freely elect but not to the small clique of a bloodstained tyranny, which denies them freedom and oppresses half Europe. We seek no war, but we are on guard against attack. We will secure the liberation of the enslaved lands of Eastern Europe, the union of the German people and restoration of their territory, freedom, too, for the Baltic, Balkan and Polish people. We will win the liberty of Europe without war when we are strong enough to demand it from a position of strength instead of weakness. Till Europe has freedom there can be no final peace.

The way to the strength, peace, prosperity and happiness of the Europeans is the development of Africa. Europe a Nation and Africa the Empire of Europe.

Let us now pass from the right and policy of Europe to some detail of practical application. We British possess more in Africa than any other nation. What should we do about it? There is a lot we should have done long ago. The old parties have shamefully neglected Africa. Now, time presses; the old system breaks to pieces and we must build rapidly to replace it with something better. If we had unlimited time, or if past opportunities had not been neglected, we could do it ourselves without any aid. But any man would be a charlatan who told the British people that we could do the whole job ourselves with the war-exhausted resources of one single nation in the time at our disposal. Any man of realism and honesty must say we cannot. To do the job available in the time before the final crash we must take others into partnership. Just as an established firm which desires a new and quick development in business takes others into partnership, and thus acquires additional resources, so we British should take others into partnership in the development of Africa. And other nations with African possessions should do the same.

I propose that those nations who now possess African colonies should invite to full and equal partnership in the development of that continent those nations who have no such possessions. I suggest that nations like Britain, France, Belgium and Portugal should invite in partnership such nations as Germany and Italy. I propose that the combined energy of a United Europe should thus develop the immense resources of Africa in the shortest possible time for the good of all. Together they will fight the war against nature to build a new civilisation with the same energy in which they fought against each other during the Brothers' War, which destroyed the old civilisation. The only basis for such an achievement is equality between all great nations. If they can make equal contribution to the work they should have equal share in the direction and proceeds of the work. Thus will be born the future government of Europe in the practical task of developing Africa. Union will come from building together. The practice of reality will thus replace the emptiness of theory. Africa will be developed under the equal direction of all the great European peoples. The future position of the peoples in the European family will be decided in the end by their work and ability as in all human affairs. Opportunity of service will be equal to all. The effort of each will decide their future.

What is the alternative for Britain? We have the choice in Africa of partnership with Europe, or being bought up by America. Which do you prefer? That is the only practical choice. We cannot be told by supporters of the old parties - whose chief concern at the moment is whether or not America will throw them their Sunday dinner through the bars of the dungeon state which bureaucratic socialism has made in Britain - that we can do the job single-handed. It is their policy which has brought the ruin which makes that impossible in the time available. It is up to them at least, to find the means to buy the next dinner before they start bragging about developing a new continent without assistance. It is they who made us beggars - not we. Now we propose to beg no longer but to enter into partnership with all other Europeans to do a job together which will give us back the means to live in freedom, independence and dignity. Just think what could be done, and in how short a time, if the energies of Englishmen, Frenchmen, Germans and Italians, and all the other European peoples great and small, were pooled and directed by common consent and purpose to win wealth from the richest continent on earth. What material happiness could be achieved and what spiritual satisfaction. The plough would replace the sword; sweat would pour but not blood; construction would rise above destruction; and union above vendetta; new civilisation will be born in that achievement Within it will continue and develop the endless diversity and invention of the European genius in measureless contribution to the future welfare of mankind. How trivial and artificial seem the disputes of the moment beside any conception of reality. The politicians are always quarrelling about the share each will get before they have created anything to share.

One guarantee we can give - and our system ensures the method. The new wealth of Africa will go to those who produce it and not to the moneylenders. The workers by hand and brain shall have that wealth - those who plan, give the energy and take the risk - not those who use the credit others have created to get their hands on industries to which they have contributed nothing. Rewards shall go to producers not to moneylenders - to creators not usurers. Once wealth has been created there will be no limit to the amount by which wages can be raised except the amount of the wealth created.

We must give people something to work for. It is no use asking the workers to sweat and toil to bolster up a system which is falling to pieces before their eyes; no use asking the workers to supply goods for markets which will not receive them; no use asking them to export in exchange for raw materials which cannot be obtained at any reasonable price or condition. But show the people a new system, and a new and practical method - a new hope - and you give them something to work for. They can be shown in Africa a steady market which will absorb our machinery and manufactured goods and send in exchange raw materials of industry at a price far below that prevailing today. In the end, Africa can send us everything America can send us at prices far below anything the Americans can touch. That will mean sending less goods in exchange from Britain, keeping a bigger proportion of our production for our own use, and thus greatly increasing our standard of life. All this, too, without counting the greater production evoked by a new system, a new method, and a new social spirit.

The new movement conceived an ideal patriotism on a higher plane than even Englishman had known before. They suggested not only a practical plan to meet disaster and a new system of government - they further believed in a new way of life which led to ever higher forms of human existence. Programmes must always meet the existing facts in a clear and decisive, fashion. They must continually be adapted, flexibly and quickly to meet new situations. Programmes must never become doctrines which freeze the life and thought out of men. But beliefs and creeds reach out to a higher sphere of immutable truth, and seek contact with that Infinite which governs all things mortal and immortal. It is a changeless creed and eternal belief which inspires the finest of the Europeans to march as an elite, tested by destiny, through every disaster and vicissitude to achieve the final glory of the European spirit.

I made some attempt to describe that belief in the closing pages of *The Alternative*. It can never be entirely described because like all the great spiritual forces it can be felt more fully than it can ever be expressed. But it is a movement of the soul of man towards ever higher forms on earth in accord with the divine purpose as it appears revealed to man. Once you have felt it you will move away from the low, the ignoble, the destructive, toward the high, the constructive, the creative which reaches forward and upward to ever greater summits. That next great peak which now emerges from the mists of time to enter the vision of man is the union of the family of Europe. They were ever united in blood and history; they will soon be bound together by something stronger than any ties of common government; they will be united by the spirit of Europe which will bring them together in a great creative task. All to-day admit the old landmarks have disappeared - all, who think at all, say the boundaries of man must be enlarged. All say, unite - the people ask - with whom? Some reply: unite with the West - that means with finance. Others reply: unite with the East - that means with bolshevism. We say, unite with Europe. There are our brothers. There is our destiny."

(17:10:1949)

He noted the suggestions coming from unexpected quarters that the Germans should be rearmed to fight in defence of Western Europe. He was scarcely surprised since he had long since told them the day would come when they would rather have the Germans in front of them than the Americans behind them. But he insisted they face the fact that the Germans would never fight as the mercenaries of the West for those politicians who had bombed their women and children when they were last fighting on the Russian steppes.

The Germans would only fight under conditions of honour and complete equality, either in a European army in which all soldiers would have the same right to rise to such command as their qualities deserved. Furthermore, Germany required assurances of future unity and freedom, and he made the following solemn statement: "I declared long ago and I declare again tonight for the Union of the Germans and the restoration of their lands, so that they may enter under conditions of freedom and honour into the Union of Europe."

It was impossible to expect the Germans to fight, as long as they were accused and their leaders condemned on account of "war crimes" five years after the war.

He went on: "I declare on this platform tonight that the greatest of all war crimes was the declaration of war. This was done by the leaders of the Conservative and Labour parties of Great Britain." (This challenging statement was received with one of the loudest and most prolonged cheers of the evening.)

The excuse for war was the German attempt to "liberate" from the Poles the German city of Danzig. Yet today not even a diplomatic protest was sent against the subjection of all Poland by Soviet Russia. They had forgotten their "word of honour" to Poland now.

Who could unite Europe after the war? Not those who had divided Europe. Once again, amid loud and sustained applause, he added: "Those, who will build the world to come, will be those who have no blood on their hands."

He then stated that they had gone beyond fascism and democracy, and, while he did not ask anyone to deny his past, as he certainly had no intention of doing, he called upon all present to rally together to save their country and their civilisation in 1950, whatever their past opinions. The politicians had divided Europe, but they could and would unite Europe. England and Europe shall live together.

(22.4.1950)

A forest of 10,000 hands went up at Ridley Road, Dalston when Oswald Mosley called upon the mass rally of East London workers to demonstrate in favour of European Socialism.

His May Day message to the workers of East London was an appeal to them to end brothers' wars with their fellow workers among the other European peoples and to combine with them for the realisation of European Socialism. This would break the grip of the finance capitalists who were responsible for the horrors of the recent "unnecessary war" and open up the virgin continent of Africa, as a source of wealth which would enable the workers of Britain and of Europe to enjoy a higher standard of life than anything of which they had ever dreamed.

At the end of his speech which was continually interrupted by loud applause, he pointed out that there could be no European Socialism as long as all Europe, including Britain, was menaced by the Soviet tyranny, and Communist Parties were tolerated in the Western European states and were in effect conspiracies against the state in favour of a foreign power.

(6:5:1950)

He was proud to have opposed the last war. He was even more proud of his record in that war than in the first, when he fought in the trenches and in the Air Force. All the three old parties dragged us into the second war. They dragged the Germans off the Russians when they had them down.

Now they want the Germans again to protect them from the Russians. (Applause.)

The last war was the most gratuitous folly and reckless crime in political history. Churchill himself had given the final proof of that, in his speech last week; Churchill admitted that, if the hydrogen bomb were not in the hands of the Americans, all Europe would be a satellite of the Russians.

What an admission! When Churchill went to war - how did he know the hydrogen bomb would be invented, which alone had stopped the Russians? He did not know. He was saved by pure chance from his own follies.

Who can say now the Blackshirts were not right in opposing the war?

And now look at East London after that war. Look at the houses, and the ruins. That was the result of Tories, Liberals, and Labour starting the war. According to one of their own spokesmen they had deliberately sacrificed London.

He first joined Labour in 1924. One of his strongest reasons was the state of housing then. Yet after thirty years and several Labour Governments there were still rotten houses in Glasgow, in Birmingham, in East London even a short distance from where he was speaking. Yet with modern science it was possible to give all the people good houses.

If the old parties had put a fraction of the energy they put into war into building houses, what a paradise Britain could be.

Get rid of the rackets. Make housing a war priority job. Bring in the whole nation. Treat the needs of the people as seriously as fighting a war.

These were the issues on which this fight was being fought. Other fights would come later - the fight of syndicalism, for workers' control of industry, side by side with a really free enterprise. The fight for Europe a Nation.

But now, with this fight, the people would be saying to the old parties - "Wake Up! Change is coming. New movements are on the, march. Wake up, and get on with the job. The British people are on the march—!"

(15:3:1955)

The scandal of Labour rule in London, he said, was their failure to house the people. They never tired of boasting of their achievements: their election address was one long brag.

In fact, he said, their record was disgraceful, and he would prove it from facts and figures they published themselves. Mr. Reginald Stamp, chairman of the L.C.C., said in 1953 that 50,000 families were on their housing lists at the end of the war. Yet 178,000 families were on their housing list eight years later.

In other words, the problem was over three times as bad after eight years of Labour since the war. The figures were much the same today after 10 years. Labour was walking backwards, not forwards.

As for slum clearance, they had not touched the fringe of the problem. Ten years after the war they had no real idea how many slums there were. The Tories, however, "thought" there were one million.

They admitted it would take them ten years at least to clear the slums. Thirty-seven years ago, when he first entered politics, there had been a million slums. Lloyd George won the "khaki election" at the end of the first war on the promise to build a land fit for heroes to live in.

After all these years there were still one million rotten houses. The old parties did not hide the fact. They openly admitted it.

What would he do about it? The answer was he would treat it like a war priority job. He would build houses, as shells and aircraft were produced during the war. He would mobilise resources, all the skilled workers needed for the job.

He would clear whole slum areas, laying them flat, while the people were housed elsewhere in temporary accommodation. When the areas were rebuilt, the people would come back to familiar but modern surroundings and another area would then be dealt with.

Mosley made it clear, however, that he would build not only flats. There were many good and serviceable houses, only needing modernising, but which the old politicians pulled down to make way for jerry-built flats. He would stop that waste: he would make the housing programme cheaper all round by mass-production, where new houses were needed, and modernisation where good houses existed. He would cut rents by making re-housing cheaper.

(22.3.1955)

The Burgess and Maclean affair was not only a great scandal. The infiltration of key posts by Soviet agents menaced the life of the State.

The present Prime Minister was more responsible than any man alive for the present condition of the Foreign Office. In the last 25 years Sir Anthony Eden had been Foreign Secretary for 11 years and a Minister connected with the Foreign Office for an additional five years. In the lifetime of a generation he had been a responsible minister at the Foreign Office for over 60 percent, of the time.

Since the disappearance of Burgess and Maclean he had been Foreign Secretary for four years, which he had spent hushing the matter up instead of cleaning the Foreign Office up.

The plain truth was that Mr. Baldwin had made Mr. Eden and Mr. Eden had made the Foreign Office. His record now proved Sir Anthony unfit to be Prime Minister in a period when the Soviets were fighting for victory through the economic collapse of their opponents, and the infiltration of their failing systems by highly-placed agents. The present inflation in Britain would contribute to that collapse.

Nothing brought revolution so quickly as inflation, and nothing brought inflation so quickly as weak government. We were in the grip of inflation because, at each stage in a series of small difficulties, government had lacked courage and decisive policies.

Courage and sound money went together. In this small home-made crisis both the Government and the Labour Party had shown their incapacity to meet the coming world crisis, which would necessitate the entry of Britain into Europe and the building of a new economic system.

(8.10.1955)

In the security debate the Foreign Office was on trial before the court of public opinion on account of the now proved facts of the Burgess and Maclean case.

In effect, the Government then said to the Foreign Office: "Mr. the accused, will you please examine yourself in private and report to the court on your innocence or guilt. If the evidence of your guilt is so overwhelming that even your best efforts can no longer conceal it, will you please be so good as to arrange for your own reform."

The Government had stated the Foreign Office was still to be in charge of its own security without outside interference. Britannia could sleep quietly in her bed, because some of the same people who had put the last bomb under it could be trusted to look under it again for a security check up.

There were, no doubt, still some admirable and trustworthy people in the Foreign Office, and some of them might be used to this work. But also in the Foreign Office were powerful men who had obtained the protection and promotion of Burgess and Maclean.

This was not only a ridiculous humbug, but also a danger to the state. Needless to say, Labour opposition had joined with the Government in this tragic and dangerous farce which lowered the dignity of Parliament and sacrificed the national interests to shelter incompetent minsters in both parties.

(9.11.1955)

Discussing the situation now arising, he said it was at present inflationary, and would therefore hit the middle class most. Rates were going up, rising prices were hitting fixed incomes and all who could not demand more with the big gun of mass organisation.

Inflation above all factors brought big changes. The middle class would now be most disposed for change. But he was not running a class war; far from it. To do anything effective they must have a national revolution. The best of both classes must unite. That was the difference between Union Movement and the adventurers who would now spring up all over the place.

(18.2.1956)

Two measures were necessary within Britain to meet the coming crisis, apart from external measures.

The first was a showdown on the whole question of wage, salary and reward in this country. A man should take out only what he put in. Men and women must be paid according to what they did and the responsibility they accepted. Reward for skill was disappearing, and those who accepted responsibility were often getting less than those who refused it.

The principles of the old parties were rotting the nation. The men of energy and initiative, the creators, were held down, while the parasites were held up.

The second necessity was to shift taxation from income to expenditure. People should be taxed on what they spent and not on what they earned, on what they paid out and not on what they brought in. The thrifty should be free to develop their businesses and to save. The spendthrift and the luxury buyer should carry the burden of taxation.

The energetic and the hardworking in all classes were being penalised and often ruined. The professional, business and trading classes were the worst hit by the inflation. This had been the first effort of weak government to escape from crisis; because it was the easiest way. The deflation they were now trying would hit the working class, because it would cause the unemployment which Mr. Gaitskell, also, recently recommended. Neither method dealt with the deep cause of crisis which would soon hit all classes alike. That cause was an international trading system which was 50 years out of date.

The middle classes should get together and act if they were to survive. But there were not enough of them to win by themselves. They should join hands with the energetic and the thrifty in the working class who were also suffering. Those who worked should not be divided by false barriers of class in an age when great scientists worked with their hands and most manual workers had to use their brains in their daily jobs. Those in the professions, business and trade should join with the mass of the people in a movement of national action. Together they could build not a class but a national revolution.

The break-up of the old British Empire was caused by our own propaganda, which had been invented for the purpose of winning the last war. The principles then stated had made it inevitable. In the end ideas were the most decisive weapons in the world. This was even more true in this age when science brought military paralysis. Both the old parties had preached doctrines which destroyed the British Empire. As a result, the old colonialism was dead a century before its time, and nothing had been worked out to take its place.

British Government was scuttling everywhere and abandoning backward peoples to communism. All experience showed that these countries would go communist directly we left. But the only thought of the present Government was to clear out quick and let them go red. They had neither the guts to fight nor the brains to think out a new idea. Their only answer to communism was to scuttle. Nothing was thought out and planned in advance. They just moved as far as the last kick sent them.

A fair example was the scuttle from Suez into Cyprus. They had no idea where they were going or what they were doing. They were just hoping for a quiet life. The new quiet spot turned out to be an even hotter spot. Now they are asking themselves whether it was worthwhile to have a civil war with the people of Cyprus and to break up the solidarity of Eastern Europe in the face of Russia. It was not worthwhile for the sake of shutting themselves up in a strategic death-box which one H-bomb could put out of action. It was a policy of folly as well as of cowardice.

The Conservative leaders were the men of betrayal who had rotted English life and lost British Empire. Let a people's revolution chase them from the high places they had so long abused.

Let the British people then join hands with their brother peoples of Europe. Let them decide what was necessary to our existence, and then hold it together. In the end they would need nothing more than Europe and white Africa for a good life. But until these great areas were developed they must hold what was necessary to the life of Britain and Europe. We must have a clear plan and decisive action. A better world could be won from the confusion of these days if Britain would lead again. But before Britain could lead again the British people must wake up and revolt.

(18.2.1956)

The Chancellor spoke as if everyone was responsible for pumping extra money into the system at a greater rate than extra production. But it was the Government alone which was responsible because they alone could do it. They did it through their control of the Bank of England, Treasury bills and their other methods of financing the nationalised industries. Any private person who paid out more than he had went bankrupt.

It was idle for the Government to blame either workers or employers in this matter. They should blame themselves, and mend their ways.

They had used the printing press and handed out cash all round because they were afraid to upset anyone. The result was an inflation which usually occurred only in time of war. They had been so timid because we were now, in effect, a beleaguered island with an abnormal dependence on increasingly difficult export markets. The final remedy was to enter the viable economic system of Europe-Africa, where the balance of payments problem would not exist. They would then no longer be faced with the absurd and tragic paradox of having to throw men into unemployment, and so curtail production, in order to make their system work.

Meantime Britain needed a surgical operation to cure our present disease by taxing expenditure instead of income, and by giving full reward to skill and responsibility. The Chancellor had not helped by spilling the bread and milk over the surgery table. The artificial system of subsidies could only be abolished as part of a great policy. Playing with the problem in a trivial fashion only made matters worse.

The aim of policy should be to let everyone have a tax-free income sufficient to buy the basic necessities of life, which should, also, be free of tax. All spending beyond these necessities should be subject to a graduated expenditure tax which made unnecessary spending bear the burden of taxation and, at present, cut out all extremes of luxury.

The consequent elimination of the considerable tax evasion which now existed, would enable the level at which taxation now began to be substantially raised, and would bring relief to all. That was the quickest way to restore incentive to industry, and it was urgently necessary.

(28.2.1956)

The present Government stumbled from ignominy to shame. Unable to make up their mind on any clear cut and decisive line of action, they had pushed good men into impossible positions and then betrayed them. They had scuttled from Suez without any idea of an alternative plan, and so had abandoned the Middle East to Russia.

(5:3:1956)

The Soviets had decided to win by political and economic war, since full scale war had been made too dangerous by the H-bomb. Their chief weapon in that war was nationalism. They hoped to break up the economic resistance to communism by inciting each people to assert its own nationality and so become divided from the rest. In this they were ably assisted by many members of the Labour Party who had spent their lives in singing the *Internationale*. They had always been against nationalism until it became an instrument for the destruction of their own country in the service of Russia.

Two facts had to be faced. The first was that the present economic system of Britain would crash if we lost the oil of Arabia, the rubber and tin of Malaya, and the dollar earning products of the Gold Coast and Nigeria. The second was that the old colonialism was dead. Neither the Government nor the Labour Party had any answer to these facts. The answer was a clear decision to hold what was vital to us, until we had built an alternative system. We should state what we would hold, and for how long. We should then create a regular army to do the job, not only with the necessary pay but with the honoured status they deserved.

We should invite our fellow Europeans to join with us in a similar policy for the benefit of all Europeans, and ask the Americans to support us in this determined drive against communism. We should use the time, which this clear policy would gain, to build an alternative system of Europe and white Africa, which would make us independent of outside supplies.

Such a policy, which was limited in time and plainly defined, would restore our traditional friendship with the Arabs. If, elsewhere, it was necessary to use force, it would be a limited and local military operation because full scale war was now excluded by science. The choice was between firm action now or slow starvation later, when we lost our only present means of life.

The final and complete humbug came, as usual, from the Labour Party. They contended that the present system could be made to work without colonialism. How could we sell enough of our manufactures in open competition on the markets of the world to buy our necessary imports, if we lost these raw material supplies and special dollar earning areas? How could we hold these areas if we abandoned them to the infiltration or conquest of communism?

Mr. Gaitskell's writings had made it clear that he believed in the main principles of nineteenth century capitalism just as much as the Conservative leaders. That system could no longer work when we had lost the colonial base which alone maintained it. Now we had to earn what we lacked not only in competition with mass production countries like America, but, also, with the cheap labour countries of the East; and that was proving impossible.

Even if the old international trading system could still work, it was a bankers' and not a producers' economy. The real choice now was between an isolated island, giving to the whole world specialised services like banking and insurance, and a producers' economy, which meant entering a larger economic unit like Europe-Africa with our own market and supplies.

The outworn system of international finance was now supported by both the Tory and Labour parties. Mr. Gaitskell had stated publicly as recently as last November that he was prepared to face some unemployment in order to maintain it. It was a paradox that the Labour leader admitted this necessity while the Conservative Chancellor denied it.

The only way to avoid the curtailment of production and the artificial creation of unemployment, which was now actually beginning, was to enter a great economy of mass production for an assured market. Europe-Africa was the only answer to the present attempt to force down the British standard of life in order to drive our exports into world markets.

The opponents of our people are the money lords and the press lords who control the old parties. Britain is now ruled by King Bunk and King Bank.

(5.3.1956)

Governments faced with a balance of payments problem which threatened the life of the nation, should immediately explain the desperate character of the situation to our people and should act as follows:-

1. Cut out all unnecessary imports either by direct control or by the more rapid and flexible instrument of tariffs.

2. Tax all luxuries so heavily that they would mostly be driven out of the home market, and use the resultant revenue to subsidise them as exports.

3. Have a showdown on the whole question of wages and reward to restore incentive for skill and the acceptance of responsibility.

4. Revise the whole fiscal system with the utmost speed in order to shift taxation from income to spending.

5. Raise, pay and honour as saviours of our people a regular army to hold our vital supplies throughout the world until we have built an alternative system; in addition, of course, to the main nuclear weapons which defend us from a major aggression.

6. Invite our fellow Europeans to join with us in holding sources of supply vital to all in a united policy, until we have together built an alternative system.

7. Urge our fellow Europeans - all of whom are also on the danger list - to join with us in building the new system of Europe-Africa.

8. Ask America to support to the utmost our efforts both immediate and ultimate to build these effective bulwarks, against Communism.

Such action would meet the immediate situation, even if we had to act alone, and such leadership by Britain could ensure the future by bringing others together to build with us a greater and more durable civilisation.

(10.3.1956)

Referring to the Russian visit, Mosley said: Anyone at all sane must want peace, since science had provided the means for war to blow the world up. The question was how to get it. He did not believe the way was to deal softly with the Russians. Small trade deals in big cocktail parties would get them nowhere.

It is easy enough to send the Russians machinery which was urgently needed for the re-equipment of our own largely obsolete industrial plant. It is easy enough to get in exchange the wheat which we could, also, get from our own Empire, whose granaries were bulging with unsold wheat.

The question was what the Russians would do when you had thus equipped them, and they needed you no more. You could not trust the word of men who made a principle of dishonour. They would never keep to any agreement as soon as it suited them to break it. As a well known financier was reported once to have said of a famous Labour leader: "It is easy enough to buy Jimmy; the trouble is he does not stay bought".

It was idle to hope you could buy the Russians off, or smile the Russians off. Whenever Britain had had a weak government which tried this method it had always failed, from the days of Danegeld onwards.

We should take a strong line with the Soviets. Our position should be declared and maintained in public debate on neutral ground, not whispered to Communist ears in the scented drawing rooms of London plutocracy.

We should make this debate continuous and relentless, until they had explained why they would not give free elections in the occupied countries, and until they were ready to accept general disarmament. If they said that armaments were the fault of the West, let them prove it to the peoples in debate with men who had clear, strong heads and were experienced in hard controversy. They would have a job.

By this means we would oblige the Soviets in the end to liberate the enslaved peoples. We would, also, oblige the Russians in the end to disarm their great land armies, and save us the burden of arming to meet them. If the Russians continued to refuse free elections and disarmament they would be exposed before world opinion in public debate, and the moral position of every Communist Party in Europe would be destroyed. Either we would gain peace and freedom, or they would lose communism.

(12.3.1956)

Mosley said the Conservative Party abandoned all its principles which might still work, and clung to all its principles which could no longer work. They gave up tariffs which might temporarily save their trade position. But they maintained old-fashioned colonial methods which they themselves had denounced and made unworkable.

The present trading system was doomed. It was deceiving the people to tell them that it could be saved by a few small measures. But it was necessary by effective action to gain time for the building up of a new system.

Goods were flooding into the British market, which could easily be produced here. They were upsetting our balance of payments.

This must be stopped, and tariffs were the most rapid and flexible instrument for this purpose. We also would soon need subsidised exports to enter foreign markets in sufficient quantity to pay for our essential food and raw materials.

It was feared that other countries would retaliate. But we could not always be paralysed by fear of what other countries would do. We could not let our house fall down in case building it up offended our neighbours.

It was quite true this state of affairs could not last. All European countries had now become relatively small powers between the giants of America and Russia. They were all trying to produce the same things and sell them in competition with each other on world markets, where they, also, had to face the competition of America and the East. It was obvious that they could not all succeed at the same time.

Britain was more dependent than any other country on export trade and was, consequently, in the most vulnerable position. Therefore we had the greatest interest in creating a united Europe, which we had so far obstructed. Once we had that market of 300,000,000 consumers with a relatively high standard of life, each people would soon be producing the goods it was best fitted to produce.

Specialised and mass production would replace the present competition of small economic units for the difficult and fluctuating world market. In Europe-Africa they would have a market more than twice the size of America, which contained all its own food and raw materials. The inevitable result would be greater production, lower prices and higher wages. For prices depended on the rate of production far more than on the rate of wage.

We must escape from the small prison which small policies were now making of Great Britain, into the greater life which awaited us in Europe. We could bring European Union quickly in two ways. The first was to give moral leadership which we had refused, or been afraid to give. The second was to adopt a practical way of saving ourselves by reducing imports and subsidising exports.

This would oblige a rapid revision of the present European economic system. Other countries would then see that we would not die quietly, and something must be done about it. We were willing to enter with them into a great co-operation which would save us all. If they were not willing we must defend ourselves, and were still strong enough to do it if we had the will. In fact, a Great Britain which was ready to act and would lead would find all the vital spirits of the continent ready to join in building the new Europe.

The old world was dead. They must make a new world before Britain died with it. The energy and resources of a united Europe under British leadership could make a greater and safer economic system by the development of white Africa. Europe-Africa would rest not on the exploitation of backward peoples but on the science and technical skill of three hundred million Europeans applied to a mass production which would continually raise their standard of life.

In the meantime we had to decide in a clear cut plan what overseas possessions we must hold until the new system was ready. We could carry our fellow Europeans and the Americans along with us if we had such a clear policy to save England and Europe over a defined period of years. The only way to restore Britain's independence and greatness was to take the lead in the Union of Europe.

We could then remain close friends with the Americans, particularly in our common opposition to Communism, but would no longer be dependent upon them. It was contemptible to beg from the Americans one day and abuse them the next. At present we made our teeth meet in nothing except the hand that fed us.

We were insulting our friends and inviting our enemies to dinner. Let us not forget that the men who are behind the shooting of British soldiers all over the world were the chosen guests of British Government next month.

It had needed a thousand years of genius and heroism to create the British Empire, which in a few brief years had been thrown away by a few small men. But the same genius and heroism of the British people could now in a few years create something even greater: the Nation and the Empire of all Europe.

(18.3.1956)

It was now admitted that our war ally Stalin had spent his whole life in murdering his opponents. The Conservative and Labour parties had assisted him to complete the process at Nuremberg.

Stalin's jackals were denouncing him now he was dead, and were coming to Britain as the honoured guests of the British Government. They had been his accomplices in every crime until they found themselves on the danger list.

The Conservative and Labour parties had also joined together and became his accomplices in many crimes until they found Great Britain on the danger list. Even now they were playing the fool in thinking they could buy off men who had the same principles as Stalin. The wolves had just put on the new clothing in order to eat what they believed to be a foolish old woman. Their estimate of present British Government was correct. But their estimate of the British people would be proved very wrong.

(20:3:1956)

No conservatives who were responsible adults during the war were now in a position to attack the Prime Minister for entertaining these assassins. They had used the master murderer Stalin as their war ally, with results that had already ruined Europe and were now beginning to threaten their own country with ruin.

They had sat at his banquets guzzling and swilling - toasting him and grinning their sycophancy - soon after he had deliberately caused the slaughter of hundreds of thousands of the Poles they were pledged to defend.

After the war they had joined with Stalin to kill in cold blood brave soldiers who had committed no crime except to obey orders in time of war. Krushchev now pleaded that he and his colleagues had no choice but to obey orders in time of peace. Yet the soldiers were hung by the British Government and the communists were invited to dinner.

All this pack of conservative politicians - whether they were against the coming Russian visit or not - had licked the boots of murder till it kicked them in the face. They had ratted on Britain when they went pro-Soviet during the wartime popularity of the Russians. Now some of them hoped to clean their record by re-ratting when the Soviet crimes had found them out.

The Labour Party were in an even worse position. For they had once threatened a general strike to save the Soviet Union, and thus made possible the long record of murder. They had threatened the life of their own country in order to save the lives of Soviet assassins. More recent Labour leaders had shown but two natural aptitudes: the first was to drag their country into unnecessary wars, and the second was to avoid fighting in these wars themselves.

Turning to Union Movement policy Mosley then said it was the first task of Union Movement to restore a sense of reality, the means of effective action, and a true patriotism to British politics.

The two ruling parties had betrayed both their principles and their country. The Conservative Party droned away about an Empire which no longer existed. The Labour Party prated of a socialism which, also, no longer existed.

Speeches: Post-War

The war had done away with the Empire because it had left Britain too weak to hold our old colonial position. The peace had now done away with socialism, because the new Labour leaders, whom the war had produced, no longer believed in it. They were bureaucrats and not socialists.

The Labour leaders thought they could make nineteenth century capitalism work a little better than the Tories could. They were wrong because that system was doomed. It had only survived so long owing to the artificial demand created by two world wars and two armament booms.

The escape of the old capitalism into war was no longer possible, because large scale war had been excluded by the H-bomb. War was definitely off when it became more dangerous for politicians, bureaucrats and profiteers, than for soldiers, sailors and airmen.

It was idle for those who believed in the old Empire and the old socialism to dream of the past and all its lost chances, and to think they could turn back the hands of the clock. Their only hope now was to stride forward with resolution into a greater future.

Britain could play the greatest part in all her great history by leading all Europe into union. Europe a Nation, inspired by the new principles of European Socialism, could realise and use the full power of modern science to make the greatest civilisation the world had yet seen.

European Socialism combined a really free private enterprise in the early stages of industry, with workers' ownership, instead of nationalisation, in the later stages of industry. It lifted bureaucratic restraint and the burden of taxation from the creative individual who made the new industries, by shifting taxation from income to expenditure. It placed their own destiny in the hands of the workers in developed industries, and rid them of the bureaucratic tyranny.

Union Movement believed in this policy because they believed in the people of Britain and of Europe. Let them be free to create wealth for all within the boundless possibilities of a new system which gave three hundred million Europeans their own foodstuffs, their own raw materials, and their own market.

Europe-Africa would be twice the size of either America or Russia and would soon become twice as strong. Their strength would enable them to live at peace in a world which gave nothing to the weak.

The hard truth of international affairs was being brought home to the British people by a bitter lesson. The war had so weakened and impoverished Britain that we were temporarily unable ourselves to maintain order and peace in all the areas in which we were interested.

The vanity, petulance and incompetence of the present Prime Minister had made us friendless, because he had divided us first from Europe and now from America. He had prevented us working fully with our fellow Europeans, because he feared entry into Europe. He had now also separated us from America, because he pursued an obsolete policy in the Middle East, where he had made a series of disastrous blunders in the problem he was supposed to understand best.

The Prime Minister had now completed his performance of separating us from our friends, by exposing Britain to the infiltration of our enemies in the recent tour of Malenkov and the coming Russian visit.

The reason why the Americans had now fallen out with the Prime Minister was that they suspected him of employing methods of the old colonialism. It was particularly idiotic to lend colour to that suspicion by the trivial posturing of weak men trying to appear strong, when - in reality - we had long been giving these colonies away with both hands.

The Conservative Party had thus secured for Britain the worst of both worlds. The reason was their total failure to produce a new and effective policy suited to the new conditions. They had to continue living on the backs of the native populations in Malaya, Nigeria, the Gold Coast, etc., because the products of those countries were earning the dollars which alone bolstered up the obsolete economy of the British Isles.

Yet while we were living on their backs, we were promising them independence and handing out free constitutions all round, which would become operative in a year or two. Naturally the first thing these peoples would do when they were free, would be to throw the exploiters off their backs, and if the idea had not already occurred to them, the large Soviet delegations we had admitted to these territories would quickly put the plan into their heads.

Yet the Tory and Labour parties staked the life of Britain on the hope that these countries would always allow us to appropriate the dollars they earned, and to give them instead blocked balances of sterling in London, which the Government had been doing its worst to make worthless by inflation. A government foolish enough to think that trick would work for ever, would believe anything.

The folly and vanity of the Tory leaders had become a menace to the life of Britain. In the Middle East they had muddled away the whole of Britain's old position of strength and popularity. Yet that area contained the oil supplies on which the life of our country at present depended.

This way lay ruin and death. The British people must call a halt to this madness, and demand a real policy. We needed both an immediate and a long term policy of effective action.

The immediate measures were to concentrate our remaining strength on guarding the interests vital to our life, and to raise, pay and honour as saviours of their country a regular army to do it. The long term measures were to join with our fellow Europeans in building a new civilisation in Europe and white Africa which would give us - through fair work and trading - all the vital supplies we could not long continue to obtain by exploiting the old colonies.

The old colonialism was dead. Let the new Europe live.

(16:4:1956)

In practice after the war the resources of Empire could now only be developed with American money, and that meant in reality the Empire would be American-owned. This was just one of those "take-over" operations now so familiar in the City of London. They took the name and goodwill of the old firm but changed the control and management. That would be a financiers' heaven but a people's hell - financiers would be in heaven because they would be at one with Wall Street and the dollar world, which would permit them to make greater profits than ever. But it would be a real hell for a proud people who were accustomed not only to manage their own affairs but to lead in world affairs.

It was not the American people but the trans-Atlantic financiers in our midst who desired to make us the tail of America instead of the head of Europe. They naturally preferred a Wall Street world to a people's economy and a United Europe. If they could finally divide Europe by making Germany the tail of Russia and Britain the tail of America, there would be nothing to stop the immediate rule of finance which would lead in turn to the ultimate triumph of Communism. But the British and German peoples of all Europe would have something to say in this matter.

This was a fight between the money-masters and the spirit of Europe. Three thousand years of great history and the will to live of three hundred million people could not be put down by men such as these. The Europeans would come together in their hour of crisis, and would release the full strength of modern science to achieve in peace a civilisation of plenty and freedom whose ever upward reaching culture would fulfil the age-old destiny of Europe.

(6:5:1956)

It was now becoming as plain as a pikestaff that Britain could not live much longer in the system of international trade. But the only suggestion of the Government was to reduce our defences in order to try and win a trade war which we should lose in any case.

We thus risked losing both wars; the trade war and a real war. For a real war of a new kind was possible within the military paralysis produced by the H-bomb. If neither side dared to use the H-bomb Russian forces could still move if we and the whole West had not got a good army with modern weapons to meet them.

But it was quite clear that all this was beyond the strength of Britain alone. We must join with our fellow Europeans. It was now an absolute necessity to do this in order to build together the market and the supplies which we could no longer obtain by international competition. If three hundred million Europeans came together, they would be the largest market in the world. If we added white Africa to Europe we should have every foodstuff and raw material we could possibly require.

Three hundred millions of the most skilled people on earth, with our own supplies and markets, could be the greatest civilisation in the world. They could insulate themselves from world chaos and raise the standard of life until the people could consume what the people produced. This was the answer to all modern problems, including automation. At present automation meant throwing men into unemployment because costs had to be reduced to compete on world markets.

And it was true that this was the only way to survive at all under the present system. But the real way to meet automation was not to create unemployment and reduce purchasing power but to increase purchasing power in a higher wage system that gave the people power to buy more.

What they needed was not class-war but a national revolution in which all classes joined together in a great, national union. It was a revolution which could be won by the mass of the people just walking down the street and voting when the time came.

But they needed first the leadership of dedicated men and women who would devote themselves to a great cause and ideal. He appealed to all such men and women who were capable of leadership to join with Union Movement. Within that movement such men and women could prove their power to lead. Any man or woman could form a branch anywhere. No bureaucracy would hinder or frustrate them. The principle of Union Movement was: let him lead who can. So any young man or woman, or old man or woman, could prove their mettle and give a service of devotion and sacrifice to their country which would be remembered in days to come.

Communism and all the evils of the day could only be beaten by a stronger idea and a greater faith. Union Movement declared the ideal of Europe a Nation and the creed of European Socialism. The states of Europe could only live between the giants of America and Russia if they came together. They must be the United States of Europe if they were to face the United States of America and the Union of Soviet Socialist Republics.

They must strive for an ever wider union. First the union of the British, then the union of all Europeans. Let the union which was life become ever wider and stronger through the dedicated life of those who gave all to Union Movement.

(1:7:1956)

The Government could never make up their mind whether to develop the Empire or enter Europe. Their permanent state of indecision was represented as a clever balancing act between Europe, the Empire and America in which Britain would get the best of all worlds. The end of present policy would certainly be a fall between all three with the worst of all worlds for the

British people. Slowly but in the end surely Europe was getting on with the task of unification without Britain. They would welcome Britain as a leader at the beginning of the process, but it is doubtful whether they would welcome Britain as a penniless applicant for membership when all British policies had failed and European Union had succeeded. Britain must decide quickly and firmly whether to save herself by developing the Empire, as he and others had advocated before the war, or now to enter Europe and take the lead in developing Europe-Africa. In reality the chance to develop the Empire had been thrown away in the war. Britain was now again an island which at present could not even provide the manpower for its own mines and agriculture or the production necessary to balance its own international payments. What nonsense now to talk of Britain alone and single handed finding the manpower to develop what was left of Empire, and the immense resources necessary for that purpose which could only be secured by a great annual surplus of production over home consumption. Protest as they might, the post-war advocates of that policy would end by making Britain the 49th State of America because the money to finance it could only come from America.

The Government were now talking with many reservations of entering a free trade area in Europe. It was not such a desperate risk, as it would only come into force in twelve to fifteen years' time, and during the intervening period there was a far greater risk of the whole economy of the West breaking into pieces or being broken by Russia. British Government was terribly afraid of impairing what it called its sovereignty. In its relations with Europe, it again risked getting the worst of both worlds. It would get the intensive competition to British industry which would come from entering into a free trade area with hard-working European peoples, some of whom were on a lower standard of life. But it would not get the power in government to level up wages in the underpaid regions, to make competition fair throughout, and to give the freedom and mobility to labour and development capital which could rapidly make Europe the greatest and most prosperous economic area of the world. That required a common sovereignty. That was the policy of Europe a Nation for which he had stood ever since the war. Any lesser policy would secure for Britain all the disadvantages and difficulties but none of the advantages and successes of European Union. Timidity, hesitation and indecision would, as usual, get us the worst of all worlds. We risked ending up as a small, over-populated island clinging to the edges of the American and European systems. We even risked being picked up by Russia in the coming economic crisis with the help of the Soviet's agents in Britain. What a fate for a great people who could lead Europe into a new civilisation which could hold the balance of the world. There was still time. But they must soon decide.

(29:9:1956)

Chapter 10

Literary Essays

In his studies of neo-Hellenism, Mosley has attempted to synthesise classic philosophy and Christian teaching in a new and practical statement of European morality. In his doctrine of higher forms may be discerned an urge towards a fresh religious impulse of the European. He thus follows further the path of many European thinkers who have derived their philosophy from observation of nature, and seeks synthesis between this thinking and the discoveries of modern science, which he believes can support and assist to develop it into a coherent whole of doctrine. He seeks synthesis too with all those who recognise a spiritual basis of life, and thus his thought conflicts in no way with the teaching and work of the churches.

The three essays from which brief extracts are given here are: an introduction Mosley wrote to the Bayard Taylor translation of Goethe's *Faust*, his review of *The Disinherited Mind* by Professor Heller, and a centenary appreciation of Bernard Shaw's book on Wagner.

From An Introduction To Goethe's Faust

"The reading of Faust is an eternal discovery. New meaning and an ever quickening beauty is the reward of every return to one of the original masterpieces of the world. This creation engaged Goethe during 60 years of his life. It carries his accumulated wisdom in furthest flight of the imaginative intellect. Fortunate indeed would be he who could discern the end. For most men the enchantment of the riddles must suffice. They will see in various aspects of the prophetic vision diverse reflections of the modern age. How much does the new writing of history owe to the original inspiration of Goethe's concept of the interaction of good and evil? Can primitive man move beyond the elementary without the stimulus of pain and disaster? Is developed man urged to further exertion by the charm and irritation of the senses which will not let him rest? Is the progress both of individual men and of civilisations achieved in some degree by the challenge of evil which evokes the response of good? Is not, therefore, what men call evil merely an instrument of good?

Faust must learn that beauty cannot be lightly grasped: long labour, as well as fierce effort of mind and spirit must precede that supreme moment. Once again throughout the Walpurgisnacht which preludes the Helena we trace the major theme that ultimate beauty arises from the elemental forces of nature.

In his age Goethe recaptured the horror which repelled him in his first realisation of the stark brutality and looming tragedy which was masked by the hard gaiety and glittering loveliness of the Greek nature. "Das Land der Griechen mit der Seele suchend" was an experience whose fulfilment demanded "Ganzheit": that completeness of knowledge and of character which could comprehend all and embrace all with a great affirmation.

The "Olympian," in the eternal synthesis of his last phase, had passed beyond horror to discover its relationship to beauty. The monsters of the Walpurgisnacht were, in their elemental force, essential to the creation of the miracle of Greek beauty. Faust passes through the Walpurgisnacht to the achievement of Helena, and in final synthesis the romantic north is united with the classic south to conceive the genius of poetry. But this genius of beauty is not content with the loveliness of the world which God has accorded to man. Once again the tear-laden words of Schiller whisper the prologue to another unnecessary tragedy.

"*Die Welt ist volkommen uberall. Wo der Mensch nicht hirikommt mit seiner Qual.*"

"The world is perfect everywhere. Till man comes with his self-torture."

What is lacking to Euphorion? *Verstand und Mass und Klarheit* - again would answer Schiller in his yearning for the union of sanity and beauty in the Second Hellas. What doom is it that works within Euphorion? - the eternally aspiring energy of the Gothic north forever challenging fate, or the *Hubris* which the Greeks believed brought down the wrath of the Gods when man dared to surpass the limit set by the Divine? Both may have been present to the enchanted child, and both echo in the heroic but fateful words:

"Immer höher muss ich steiaen,

Immer weiter muss ich schaun."

"I must clamber ever higher,

Ever further must I see."

So far he is within the bounds allowed to striving man. But his ecstasy increases with the sound of approaching war. He aspires to both beauty and achievement. In his longing for the furthest flight he reaches for the forbidden wings. Disaster strikes down from Heaven.

Once again at the climax of the great drama, beauty is blended with the sense of Faust's supreme striving. All the great motives of the Mothers and the Helena seem to be united with the apotheosis of the aspiring Faust in that mystic mingling of the spheres of beauty and of active life which is inherent in the thought of Goethe.

Often in the story of man poets have anticipated the philosopher and the systematic thinker. Faust is the outstanding example of this most intriguing phenomenon of thought. For example, Homunculus - what is he?

"He has no lack of qualities ideal:

But far too much of palpable and real."

Is this the intellectual whose physical will is inadequate to the urge of the mind? Is he an imprisoned spirit seeking union with something greater than himself? - yearning for that infinite which is symbolised by the vast spaces of the sea? Is his pure mind wishing to escape from the physical into some Nirvana of nothingness - or of beauty? A dozen different answers to several diverse riddles are presented by this single character alone. In every phase of Faust, thought is veiled in mystery.

So the last riddle may remain unanswered - how much in the final phase did the Olympian know? - and how much did he only feel? The answer may possibly be found in this new world of bright achievement and dark terror where the thought and feeling of his sublime perception mingle with a hard and clear reality. Already the great consciousness of Goethe towers into this age. His concept of good and evil and of the purpose of the Divine emerge in clearer outline to the eyes of modern thought. A certainty of knowledge illuminates those heights through all the creative mists of inspiration.

With calm clear sanity he provides some answer in the lines with which Eckermann rightly closes his great work:

"It would have been no entertainment to God to make this coarse world out of simple elements and send it through the ages rolling in the rays of the sun if he had not conceived the plan to establish in this material soil a garden for the culture of spirits."

The true and faithful Eckermann observes:

"Goethe was silent, but I cherished his great and good words in my heart."

We can do no better.

From The Disinherited Mind

Professor Heller, in his remarkable book, "The Disinherited Mind,"[1] dealt with Goethe, Nietzsche, Burckhardt, Spengler, and Rilke, and made some reference to Hegel, Schopenhauer, Schiller and Hölderlin. His theme was briefly that they represented the "disinherited mind" of Europe, because they had deviated from the main Christian and humanist tradition. Mosley challenged the position of Professor Heller, in his review, extracts from which follow.

"Professor Heller, in opening his central theme, as I understand it, under the chapter title "Goethe and the avoidance of tragedy" writes: "It was the very kind of experience before which Goethe himself has always proved helpless: the exposure to the manifestations of evil and sin." I believe that Goethe's chief contribution to thought was to explain that phenomenon more adequately than any other mortal before or since.

All this talk of "the rule of the road" and "a generally valid spiritual mould" would doubtless have evoked from Goethe that great cry *Ich rufe, Natur, Natur,* which was the essence of his being. As Professor Heller justly observes elsewhere "unnatural" in the mouth of Goethe was one of the strongest invectives. *Diese verdammte Unnatur!* Such rules of the schoolmen were not for Goethe, whom Nietzsche described in a superb passage of *Götzen Dämmerung*: "He envisaged man as strong, highly civilised, skilled in all skills of the body, holding himself in check, having respect for himself as a creature who may be allowed to taste the whole width and wealth of naturalness, who is strong enough for this kind of freedom; who is tolerant, not from weakness but from strength, because he knows how to use to his advantage what would destroy an average character . . . ."

The *Ganzheit* of such a man could not be confined to the procrustean bed of any dogma which claimed to be divinely inspired but would be regarded by Goethe as very much man

1   *Bowes and Bowes.*

made. The limitations of clericalism of any kind were not for a man who believed "There must have been a time when the religious, aesthetic and moral perceptions were at one." A Nietschean quotation but a "Goethean thought."

I do not believe that these minds are "disinherited" because they have lost their way and fallen into a morass of confusion and contradiction. On the contrary I believe their philosophy to be profoundly antithetical to that of Professor Heller and of his friends, but nonetheless comprehensible and also logical. It is not until the antithesis between neo-Hellenism and "the Vicar of the Minster of Basle," between Goethe and the clerics is understood, that the possibility of some final synthesis between classic European and Christian values can be explored; and that work I believe not only to be interesting but necessary if the spiritual rift in Europe is to be bridged.

The first point to be grasped is that Goethe is not a lost sheep who has strayed, but a challenger as intense as Nietzsche, though more diplomatic, and, in many ways, more profound: in fact, he is the *fons et origo* of the movement of challenge within Europe. I shall at once be told that any such clear cut view is presumptuous, because so many commentators of the school of Professor Heller have found Goethe's thought such a mass of contradictions that his message, if any, is reduced to the meaningless. But it is precisely the impression of contradiction upon such minds which stamps the doctrine of Goethe; indeed the essence of Goethe is the concept of polarity which is also reflected in the mind of Nietzsche and of many of the great German thinkers. The duality which the clerics believe to be a contradiction is, in fact, the wholeness of the teaching. It is significant that in his considerable study of Faust, although he comments on the prologue in heaven, Professor Heller omits a quotation which in the light of the subsequent development of European thought might be regarded as some key:

Des Menschen Thätigkeit kann allzuleicht erschlaffen
Er liebt sich bald die unbedingte Ruh:
Drum geb' ich gern ihm den Gesellen zu
Der reizt und wirkt, und muss, als Teufel, schaffen.

(Man's active nature flagging, seeks too soon the level:
Unqualified repose he learns to crave
Whence, willingly, the comrade him I gave
Who works, excites, and must create, as Devil)

Why ignore these lines, why not permit Goethe to offer some
explanation of what he means in the part of his great work where
we should expect to find it? Is it ignored because the clear concept
of evil as an instrument of good is profoundly antithetical to
the particular set of Christian values which Professor Heller
seems to recommend? So we are permitted only the obscurity
and not the clarity of Goethe. Yet the idea of opposite poles
being complementary to each other, and even serving each other
is inherent in the German mind which is under discussion.

If we ask Professor Heller to interest himself with us in a possible
synthesis of these new antitheses, we might encounter that
prejudice, amounting to a complex, against Hegelian thought,
which he seems to share with most of the latter-day schoolmen
in our universities.

The concept of polarity in the Nietzschean sense seems at any
rate nearer to his comprehension than the thought of Goethe
which went further and deeper. For to regard evil as an instrument
of good is to be beyond even the idea of polarity, of energy or
progress between the opposing tensions; the whole concept is
more conscious, as was Goethe. It is at this point that Professor
Heller appears entirely baffled when he complains that "Goethe
has forestalled all dramatic tension in this respect by making in
the Prologue, the Lord himself a sure winner, as it were, party

to the wager." Yet, it may be at this very point Goethe observed something more of the drama of the universe than had yet been revealed to man. What else but a theory of evil in some degree evoking good is the concept of "challenge and response" in Professor Toynbee's *Study of History*, which is so rightly admired by Professor Heller? The fact that Professor Toynbee is a well known Christian encourages the belief that some synthesis between Goethe's thought and some aspects of Christian teaching need not be excluded. If this basis of Goethe's thought be in any way accepted, many an enigma is resolved. If, for instance, evil or suffering is believed to be an instrument of good, it is difficult to regard it entirely as tragedy. It is even conceivable that Goethe's "avoidance of tragedy" or "embarrassment in the face of tragedy" arose from the feeling that tragedy in the traditional sense does not exist. To an advanced neo-Hellenism there is no tragedy except disease and death, and perhaps they are only instruments in the hand of nature (or of God as revealed in nature) which models perfection from imperfect forms.

These conclusions seem to follow logically from such a premise. In this region Goethe moves far beyond the Greek sense of tragedy which contrasted the sunshine of life with the shadow of death in a mood of superb resignation achieved through beauty. It moves even beyond Schiller's dream of *Das zweite Hellas*.

Goethe moved beyond all other neo-Hellenists, except Nietzsche in his great conclusion to the *Birth of Tragedy* ... *Wie viel musste dies Volk leiden, um so schön werden zu können* .... and Nietzsche followed Goethe.

The "Olympian" faced the fact of suffering and the testing enchantment of pleasure, but regarded them both as formative instruments in the hand of God.

The essence of the doctrine is of course the "ewig Werdende." In this respect the German neo-Hellenists are all nearer to Heraklitus than to the "absolute" of Christian or even of Platonic teaching. The "ewig Werdende" must in turn be related to the "ewig Strebende"; it is impossible to become without effort. It is in this region that Professor Heller appears to fall into his most extraordinary misunderstanding of Goethe.

Professor Heller does not appear fully to understand the initial tensions and antitheses: still less is he likely to comprehend the great syntheses of Goethe. For this reason, perhaps, he scarcely mentions the vast theme of the "Helena"; he is not much concerned with the synthesis of the classic and romantic movements in the marriage of Helen and Faust and with all the profound symbolism contained in the birth and fate of Euphorion. He seems even more a stranger to the fundamentals of Goethe's thought; particularly to his at-oneness with nature. Our author announces: "Nature is fundamentally innocent" (is it the "red tooth and claw" that is innocent or only the Professor?) and "Goethe's genius is in communion with nature." He adds: "It is never with the spirit of a transcendent God or with the spirit of Man that Goethe's potentially tragic heroes are reunited after their dramatic crises. When the crisis is over, they are at one again with the spirit of nature. They are not purified in a tragic sense, not raised above their guilt through atonement, but enter, as it were, a biologically, not morally, new phase of life, healed by oblivion and restored to strength through the sleep of the just."

Exactly; after a long striving in search of a higher form they are entitled to the sleep of the just before fresh striving and the attainment of yet higher forms. Why not? These may not be the values of "The Vicar of the Minster of Basle"; but they are not far away from the values of Goethe. They may in the opinion of certain clerics be wicked, but they are not confused or embarrassed. They are profoundly different to the beliefs of Professor Heller and his friends. But that does not justify a charge of confusion; still less will it justify that charge of "maladjustment" with which the witch doctors of modern psychology pursue any thinkers who challenge established mumbo jumbo. Happily the scholarly work of Professor Heller never stoops to such a level in his study of Goethe. He has illumined the subject with a fine erudition, but I believe him in certain respects to be profoundly mistaken.

The case for Spengler seems even to be exaggerated. "For the history of the West since 1917 looks like the work of children clumsily filling in with lurid colours a design drawn in outlines by Oswald Spengler." True, "he has been utterly dead for the last fifteen years ..." "Yet his ill-tempered prophecies have completely come true." That is, of course, the best reason for his memory being dead in contemporary England; there is nothing the complacent dislike so much as being asked to learn from history. It is long since I read *Der Streit um Spengler* which is mentioned by Professor Heller; but I believe that in this book, or in some related publication, the names of some four hundred well qualified commentators of central Europe were mentioned who, on one side or the other, had been engaged in the controversy which surrounded Spengler's thesis. I recall, also, that the chief contribution to this discussion from academic circles in England at that time was a passing reference to the "preposterous Spengler" delivered in one of our leading intellectual weeklies by a delightful gentleman who is justly esteemed for his felicitous comments on the lighter aspects of French literature. But Professor Heller has read Spengler and studied him profoundly.

All this finger wagging and mediaeval moral prating appears simply a manifestation of the new schoolmen who seemed doomed to reduce yet another culture to sterility. Spengler would of course welcome such a phenomenon at this stage of affairs as proving his theory; he now expects the latter day schoolmen to petrify yet another civilisation of thought. When Professor Heller calls him "wicked" Spengler would smilingly dismiss, or serenely accept his outburst, as an example of the "second religiousness" which occurs in the Spenglerian chronology, "when money is celebrating its last victories and the Caesarism that is to succeed approaches with quiet, firm tread." So, do what he will to escape. Professor Heller becomes "Spenglerian *allzu* Spenglerian." How much more interesting if Professor Heller's fine mind accepted, as it does, that the Spenglerian premise has come true to date, and then went on to consider whether the Spenglerian conclusion might be amended on this occasion because modern science has introduced a new factor to the rhythm of civilisations, which Spengler was far from foreseeing. Then, we might, lift this debate from a mediaeval exorcism of those of whom we disapprove to the heights of this decisive age which may determine the fate of men; we might emerge from the childish to the adult. In the case of Goethe, too, we can conceive a more interesting discussion than patronising him as an "innocent" or denouncing him for a "confusion" which exists chiefly in the eye of the critics.

A serious discussion between Goethe who saw God revealed by his handiwork in nature and those who feel God revealed by some personal revelation in a private communication, would be interesting. But before the debate begins, the Professor must put away his old bell, book and candle. We must have a serious debate between the merits of observation and communication. It is even conceivable that both observation and communication are in some degree faulty and in some degree correct. Some observers of nature have undoubtedly been mistaken; the Churches, for instance, dealt severely with Galileo for refusing to believe that the earth was flat. On the other hand it must be admitted that the inspired recipients of personal messages from on high certainly obtain diverse impressions. The Dervish, for instance, believes that his personal communication from celestial spheres instructs him to slash himself with knives in the course of a whirling dance whose giddiness enhances his sense of spiritual exaltation; on the other hand an Anglican Bishop's private and personal message usually conveys a more sedate afflatus. May we not without wickedness discuss whether God reveals himself by his work in nature or by the diverse conceptions of him held by man? May we not even in these mystic spheres be scientific enough in spirit to believe that not all truth is inevitably contained in one vessel? When great minds and great spirits find themselves in antithesis, may we not seek truth in synthesis at a possibly higher level without being exorcised by the new academic dogmatism;

even if Hegel is the last taboo of the university witch doctors? Professor Heller has, at any rate, assisted in sweeping up the final dusty sterility of positivism. For that striving we may hope that someone, somewhere *kann ihn erlösen*. We can be grateful to him too for some stimulus to thought, for many agreeable moments and for a wealth of moving quotation. We can borrow again from the genius of Goethe, which Professor Heller so gracefully acknowledges, when we raise our eyes in conclusion to "disinherited" Olympus and say:

Der du, ohne fromm zu sein, selig bist!

Das wollen sie dir nicht zugestehen.

From Wagner And Shaw

How much I wish that in youth I had then had the wit to ask Shaw all the questions I would like to ask him now; how tragically often we feel that about old men we knew and loved when we were young. Above all, I would want to press him on the point of *Götterdämmerung*: whether, indeed, it was an irrelevant, redundant addition to *The Ring*, previously conceived and long subsequently executed; a grand opera, wantonly, almost carelessly attached to a supreme epic of the human mind and spirit: or whether Wagner was seeing once again a far vision, further even than Shaw could see; just as in *Parsifal* he saw beyond the reproaches of the suffering Nietzsche to something very near to the younger man's third metamorphosis - the unknown state beyond the superman - while Nietzsche felt only an intolerable loneliness at the seeming apostasy of the one other mortal who could sense the being beyond man.

"The Perfect Wagnerite" is happily very free of that strange clowning with which an over-sensitive nature protected itself from the laughter of clowns by the odd process of getting the laugh in first: entertaining as many of the jokes are, they always jar a little on any reader who is absorbed in the real profundities of Shaw's thought, which are sometimes almost entirely concealed by the mask of comedy.

The character of the Siegfried generation of heroes - the order of heroes which was subsequently to succeed for a period - created some disagreement, or misunderstanding, between Wagner and Shaw; this is our subject. It is clear that even in the view of Shaw the ring did not simply denote power through money; this is strange, because a realisation of the higher potentialities of the ring should have induced in him some reconsideration of his summary dismissal of *Götterdämmerung*. It is true, of course, that the ring in the hands of the usurious dwarf Alberich was simply the power of money, because money was all that he understood. At most, the only further use of the ring to him was power over his fellows - his craftsman brother Mime and the Niebelungen in general - by a satisfaction of the will-to-power in the narrow Adlerian sense of the desire to dominate. At its lowest, this is the will-to-power of the man who finds a crude delight in cracking the whip and compelling obedience, without purpose, except fulfilment of the lowest needs of lust, luxury, and the basest of all pleasures, bullying. But the ring, like all power in finer hands, could serve altogether different purposes; it could become the instrument of the will to the highest achievement, the most sublime and beautiful creation.

So Wotan turns from this dark, unknown care to the world of known and proved delight: "To me, Freia! Thou shalt be freed. Bought with the gold, bring us our youth once again! Ye giants, now take your ring." The old order, the highest type of man that society has yet evolved, fails before the supreme decision: he will not sacrifice beauty of life to live with the care which is the only personal gift of the instrument of destiny. He sets joy before mission. If Shaw had studied this passage a little more deeply, he might have spared his censure of *Göbtterdämmerung*.

The great remaining question is whether even the hero is capable of that high decision.

The young Wagner answered yes in *Siegfried,* and the old Wagner answered no in *Götterdämmerung:* that is the point which I believe Shaw missed.

After Siegmund who failed, came Siegfried who succeeded for a time; then must come the great third wave. But this triumph, this supreme achievement, the holy gift of creation, still, and always, demands the same price, imposes the iron condition of the last renunciation; all lesser love must pass that the greater love may be realised. So man reaches the Platonic apotheosis, from one fair form to all fair forms. Siegfried was to Shaw the highest idea, beyond whom he could not see.

Siegfried is the revolutionary hero of the northern sagas; Siegfried, too, is Hellenism: Goethe's dream union of the romantic and classic movements come true. To meet him is, indeed, a moment of rapture to sentient natures who live beneath contemporary civilisation: not only do they say, *"verweile doch, du bist so schön,"* but the exquisite memory of that moment, in a world which falls so far short of it, holds them forever. It is inconceivable, a thought too bitter, that, when he comes at last, even Siegfried fails. How great the effort of mind, will and spirit to realise there must even be a *jenseits Siegfried.* It is the eternal genius of Wagner which alone sees the end necessity and senses the final beauty in the enchanted land of mingling shadow and sunshine where art in music and poetry foresees thought.

To Shaw, the triumphant Siegfried - striding through the flames of convention and inhibition, after the overthrow of the old order, to his marriage with divine truth for the achievement of the new revolutionary world - was the dream which must come true, after the bitter failure of that movement of men he knew so well; the Siegmund generation, to whom the gods had given but one gift, the art of living without happiness. It was too soon to know and, certainly, too soon to face the necessity for that last effort which we now know and face; there is something even beyond Siegfried, and it must come.

Shaw had in him still much of the happy "exultation of the anarchist destroying only to clear the ground for creation," as he wrote of the singing Siegfried forging the sword. But after the clearing of the ground comes the creation, and it is the failure of Siegfried under this supreme test which Wagner dramatises in *Götterdämmerung*. That masterpiece was not an irrelevance but the supreme relevance, it poses the final question.

We may well ask too, why Wagner finds it necessary to begin *Götterdämmerung* and send the hero off in search of fresh "adventures", which lead to his downfall and the ruin of all order and beauty on earth: the only consolation being the final message that Shaw chiefly missed; the return of nature for yet another renewal after the rest and peace of oblivion, the presage of rebirth in the recurring motif of destiny proving, affirming and heralding another great upsurge of the life force.

Siegfried failed for the reason that even heroes fail; he was capable of human heroism but not of divine love. He failed to renounce joy for the sake of destiny. That was easier for the greedy dwarf whom the beauties of love had already spurned; it is, always, easier too for all the *verneiners,* for the life-deniers of the sad puritan tradition who can give up life so easily, because they have no life: it was more difficult for the hero, for Hellenism, with all nature, all life, all love, the sunshine and the flowers of heaven within them. It is easier for them to renounce what they never had: it is harder to renounce when you have all. Yet the great renunciation was to be not denial but the supreme affirmation: the hero renouncing even the delights of human love for the sake of the life force, in dedication to the winning of ever higher forms. All higher life must serve that purpose, and Siegfried was that life. He had to renounce the lower in order to achieve the greater. He had to set aside the human, even the superhuman, in service of the eternal; not because he lacked life but because he had so much, not to deny but to affirm, not for frustration but for a higher fulfilment. He was called to that high destiny and he failed; he was inadequate, he was not the final instrument of the life force. He had won the revolution and married divine truth with the ring of power; that was not the end but only the opportunity for supreme creation.

Now he sets out on "adventures"; he wastes his time having a good time, laughing and living as it is good to laugh and live till destiny smiles with the smile that ends laughter.

Until the moment of destiny when the ring brought him, through power, supreme opportunity, and the possibility of union with divine truth, Siegfried's life was the right preparation of the artist in action for the final achievement. To sing with the birds in the forest and savour experiences, "conflicts where one learns to interpret the meaning of nature a little," is a far better training and development for the coming mission than to creep about some dreary cloister; where man deludes himself in those dull, protecting, womb-assuring shades that he is combating instead of really serving the *"Geist der stets verneint."* Life is a better training than denial, but, in the moment of destiny, of fulfilment, all these creative impulses of life must be fused in the one decisive purpose.

The world awaited Siegfried as adult, but he was not there.

The message of *Götterdämmerung* was that if heroes fall short of that high demand they fail, and with them all their achievements; their whole world passes, while nature prepares another renewal of the life-force. Because the hero was not called to deny life but to fulfil it, he needed *Ganzheit;* the artist should not mutilate himself, but concentrate all his powers, all his acquired completeness of mind and body in his supreme work when the time comes. He must be a full man, but his *Ganzheit* must be applied, not dissipated. There comes a point where life must be entirely dedicated. The ring of power was won, the flames were surpassed, the union with the infinite possibility of divine truth achieved; yet Siegfried sought "adventures" instead of supreme creation. So Siegfried died, after being granted a last enlightenment. The divine truth born of the god enters again the flames; this time the fires of Siegfried's funeral pyre. The Valhalla of the old order perishes, also, in the holocaust of the world which the hero could not save, even after he had won it.

Nature, the Rhine, rises to take again the ring from the finger of the dead hero, whence no lesser power could wrest it.

Gödtterdämmerumg was written to show that the character of Siegfried was inadequate to this destiny, and must fail; the end-achieving hero had still to come: hence the final reversion to the great theme in the last message of divine truth to men in the completed cycle of the Ring. Wagner alone saw beyond - beyond the vision of both Nietzsche and Shaw - to a new form, shadowy, as yet obscure, visible in outline only, but still a higher form: the mysterious shape of Parsifal. Here is the beginning of the will to power and the will to beauty in the mystical union which is all-achieving: the man comes who weeps because he has killed a swan rather than exults because he can kill a dragon, who holds the all-powerful spear on condition that he does not use it.

In the vision of Wagner the new being was seen dimly, very darkly through the veil of a time that was not yet. But we can understand that these are men who will be ready to renounce the lesser in order to achieve the greater, who will yield joy to serve destiny because some are called to strive greatly that higher forms may come. Greater love hath no man than this; that he renounce the fullness of present life to serve the future life which shall thereby be brought to earth; this is "love that illumines, laughing at death." But to make that love perfect, he must first possess life and love in its full rhythm; he does not deny life but, through his final renunciation, fulfils life's creative purpose. He must have within him *"die ewigen Melodien"* and be "at one with all high things." Otherwise the synthesis of life and love would not be there. He would not be the final hero, the symbol of that generation of the higher men which is ready to give all that all may be won. That is what men must aim at becoming; this, I believe, is the message of the *Ring*.

Chapter 11

The Jewish Question

It was not until his Movement had been in existence for two years that Mosley first mentioned the Jewish question in a speech. Hitherto the Jews had meant no more to him than any of the other innumerable racial and religious minorities within the British Empire

The matter was forced on his attention when two things occurred: the first was that many Jews seemed to him to be determined to bring Britain into war against Germany, and the second was the high proportion of Jews among those who organised attacks on members of his Movement. The reason always given for the latter phenomenon was the treatment of their co-racialists in Germany under National Socialism, and their apprehension that British Union would develop on similar lines.

Mosley reacted strongly. He denounced any attempt to involve Britain in war with Germany in what appeared to him to be not a British but a Jewish quarrel, and also the violence, both physical and economic against members of British Union. Even at the height of this quarrel, however, he did not denounce Jews because they were Jews. He denounced *some* Jews, because of their actions. His attitude was political, not racial. He constantly stated that no man can be held responsible for his birth, but only for his behaviour.

After the war Mosley regarded the quarrel with the Jews as finished because the issues which created it were no longer present. The war with Germany was over; the question no longer existed of Jews involving Britain in a war which was not a British quarrel. Heavy losses had been inflicted on both sides in that quarrel, and no man in his senses would again desire to raise issues without purpose which were liable to lead to such terrible results. Mosley then determined not to reopen the question, and he held to that resolution in his speeches for many years despite considerable provocation. Mosley pursues his course without fear or favour, of the Jews or of anyone else.

The following quotations make plain his position with regard to the Jewish question before and since the war.

The first is from a pamphlet written by the East London leader of British Union and published before the war, stating that British Union was not against Jews because of their race, nor did it oppose them because of their religion; it concluded with these words:

"We do not attack them for what they are. We defend ourselves against them because of what they do."

Mosley himself first mentioned the question at a meeting in the Albert Hall on October 28th, 1934, which was two years after the founding of the Movement in October, 1932. In his speech he said:

"I have encountered things in this country which quite frankly I did not believe existed. And one of these is the power of organised Jewry, which is today mobilised against fascism.

And today we do not attack Jews on racial or religious grounds, we have taken up the challenge that they have thrown down.

I have been asked to enumerate the ways in which the Jews have assailed fascism and I will. In the first place they have physically assaulted us. And that can be proved. It is not a matter merely of our own observations. It is a matter of proof. Sixty-four people have been convicted in the courts of this country of attacks on fascists or fascist meetings since June last, and thirty-two -

exactly 50 per cent, are Jews. Now the Jews make up 0.6 per cent, of the whole population, yet they are guilty of 50 per cent, of the attacks upon fascists. And that we can prove from the law courts of this country.

Now the second point is this: we can prove, and we have publicly stated case after case of victimisation of fascists by Jewish employers - men and women dismissed for no better reason than that they were blackshirts."

He made a third point: The organised power of Jewry as a racial interest, has consistently striven for the last eighteen months and more to foster the policy of war. Markets have been lost to us. The German market has gone, on account of a Jewish boycott of their trade. Lancashire cotton goods cannot sell because the Jews prevented Germany buying abroad, because they will not let Germany sell abroad. And from every platform and paper which they control, directly or indirectly, they have striven for the past eighteen months to arouse in this country the feelings and the passions of war with a nation with whom we made peace in 1918.

But once more we tell them ... we fought Germany once in our British quarrel. We shall not fight Germany again in a Jewish quarrel (the meeting was held up at this point for several minutes by the cheering).

Four years later, in his book on British Union Policy entitled *Tomorrow We Live*, Mosley wrote as follows:

"We do not attack Jews on account of their religion; our principle is complete religious toleration, and we certainly do not wish to persecute them on account of their race, for we dedicate ourselves to service of an Empire which contains many different races and any suggestion of racial persecution would be detrimental to the Empire we serve. Our quarrel with the Jewish interests is that they have set the interests of their co-racialists at home and abroad above the interest of the British state.

An outstanding example of this conduct is the persistent attempt of many Jewish interests to provoke the world disaster of another war between Britain and Germany, not this time in any British quarrel, but purely in a Jewish quarrel."

(February, 1938)

In Mosley's post-war speeches references to the Jews are scarcely ever to be found, though he said recently, in a speech at Brixton, March 21st, 1956, that he had not spoken a word against the Jews at any of his meetings for several years.

"I used to do so before the war, when they were dragging us into a war with Germany, but that issue does not now exist."

(March, 1956)

In fact, the only occasion on which he has referred to the Jews in recent years was when the danger again occurred of Britain being dragged into a war not in a British but in a Jewish quarrel.

He dealt with the problem as follows in his book *The Alternative* (1947):

"...The constructive solutions of reason are seldom permitted to operate in real life. It is, so far, only rarely that the mind and will of mankind work in that way. Nevertheless, it is always our high duty and our wisest course to begin by offering the constructive solutions of reason. No one will accuse me of shrinking from the politics of passion when the unreason of men, or the overweening arrogance of an over-confident opponent, force them upon me; my record frees me from that suggestion. But, it has always been my way, in the first instance, to seek reason; if my opponents insist on passion, I am always ready. In this age-old problem I offer, once again, the solution of reason. For over two thousand years the Jews have asked for a national home, and sought again to become a nation. I adhere to the suggestion that they should be given a national home and the opportunity to become a nation.

The Jewish Question

To this end I propose the partition of Palestine and the placing of Jerusalem under a super-national authority which will afford Christian, Arab and Jew impartial access to their holy places. It is plain that even the whole of Palestine would not afford an adequate home to the Jewish population, even if it all were available without outrage of justice in the treatment of the Arabs. Such statesmanship would, therefore, in any case, be confronted with the problem of finding additional living room for the Jews. It is, naturally, desirable to provide such accommodation as near as possible to the home land of Palestine. But this consideration is not now so pressing in view of the rapid facilities for travel provided by modern transport. After all, the limbs of British Empire are a long way from the heart, and that was so even in the days when some of the journeys involved might occupy very long periods. Distance did not even then sever the ties or affection of relationship; still less should this happen in an age when science annihilates distance. No insuperable difficulty should be encountered, therefore, even if the main bulk of the Jewish population had to live at some distance from the traditional national home. Palestine would remain a home to them in the same sense that the Dominions regard England as home. But it should be possible to find an outlet for Jews in the constructive work of nationhood much nearer to the national home.

The national home is, and always has been, the final solution of the problem. We cannot blame nations for failing to solve the problem in that way, if they had no outside territory to their disposition: that charge, at least, cannot be laid at their door. But, in this great shake-up of the world, and the re-disposal of many lands which it must entail, it would be a tragedy for lack of energy and realist principles to miss so great an opportunity for the settlement of an age-old problem. It is a matter, too, which could be settled by consent if we accept as true and continuing the immemorial desire of the Jews to become a nation.

It is necessary to seek a solution which humanity, as a whole, will approve."

(1:10:1947)

In a statement reported in the *Hackney Gazette*, December 11th, 1953, Mosley said:

"I have never made any reference to Jews in speech or writing for nearly five years. If the Jews showed similar restraint, the future would look better. In the past faults have not only been on one side, but on both."

In a speech on November 12th, 1956, dealing with the British Government's intervention in Egypt, Mosley said: Arab fears that the British Government were in league with Israel had been reinforced by recent actions. We were bound by treaty in these regions to go to the aid of whoever was attacked. British Government had broken its pledged word by aiding the aggressor with an attack in the rear of the victim.

Britain had been dragged towards war for the second time in no British quarrel but a Jewish quarrel. For the second time we had been dragged towards war by international Jewish finance (At this point Mosley's speech was held up for several minutes by the cheering.) Mosley then said they were certainly not anti-Semites who were against all Jews just because they were Jews. No man, woman or child could help how they were born, and Jews were as much entitled to a fair deal as anyone else.

But he was resolutely opposed to Jewish financial interests which involved Britain in alien quarrels, and he would expose them always when they acted in a way contrary to the interests of his country. Union Movement was the only force in Britain which dared stand up to them. He opposed them not on the grounds of race but on grounds of what they did. And then only when they did something which injured Britain or Europe.

In a further speech on the same subject on November 18th, 1956, Mosley said: If it were true, as the Prime Minister had argued, that Suez was a "life and death" interest of England, he should have been impeached for leaving the Canal in 1954. In that case, too, he was greatly to blame for not being ready to strike back when Nasser grabbed the Canal. Why, too, when he did intervene, did he lose his nerve and stop before he had reached his objective which was the whole Canal?

Now he had put us in the position of fighting not in a British but in a Jewish quarrel. The tragedy was that this intervention of Eden in Egypt had certainly sacrificed Hungary, and given Russia an excuse to continue the massacre. Otherwise, at every bench and factory in Europe, any communist would have been met by his fellow-workers with the unanswerable question: "Why do you work and pay money in support of the vile tyranny which slaughters your fellow-workers in Hungary?"

Either the Russians would have been forced to free Hungary, or they would have lost the moral and political position of every Communist Party in Europe. And it was on their Communist Parties that they would depend for victory in the coming struggle of political ideas which would occur when military paralysis was caused by the new weapons of science. If communism outraged too far world opinion, communism was lost.

But Eden's diversion in Egypt had distracted attention and enabled Russia, albeit with great moral loss, to get away with murder in Hungary. The giant of Soviet Communism was rocking to his corner in defeat, when Eden let him out. But Hungary had shown that nothing on earth could in the end hold down the spirit of Europe which would rise again through a great idea to freedom, and a great life in European Union.

Chapter 12

Mosley's Electoral Record

Mosley's electoral record, which we publish below, will surprise those who have been told that he has been rejected by the British people. It shows, in fact, a record of electoral success without equal in our times. No one has been so successful in persuading the British public on so many diverse occasions to vote for him. In fact, it shows that Mosley enjoyed during much of his life an extraordinary popularity among our people. Even when he put himself outside the pale of the old parties and the establishment, they gave him support which no other isolated individual has received in modern time. The record indicates that his personal popularity and election winning capacity will return in overwhelming strength when the system of his opponents fails, his warnings and policies are proved right, and he emerges as the only man who had the courage to stand firm and tell the truth.

Harrow, 1918.

Ex-serviceman; served in Flanders both in trenches and as airman. Was elected as youngest M.P.; a Conservative supporting Lloyd George's Coalition Government. 13,959 to 3,007 votes, a majority of 10,952 votes.

Harrow, 1922.

Stood as Independent, after parting with the Conservative Party on their failure to fulfil their pledges to the war generation; also on account of the Irish question and the Versailles Treaty. Defeated the official Conservative candidate by 15,290 to 7,868 votes, a majority of 7,422 votes. In this election the whole weight of the Conservative machine was thrown against the young candidate, including speakers as well known as Lord Birkenhead.

Harrow, 1923.

The issue of the election was Protection and Harrow was an old Protectionist stronghold. Nevertheless, defeated Conservative candidate by 14,079 to 9,433 votes, a majority of 4,646 votes.

Ladywood, 1924.

Stood on behalf of Labour Party to challenge Neville Chamberlain in the Conservative stronghold which the Chamberlain family had held for sixty years. In six weeks' campaign Mosley reduced Chamberlain's majority to 77, after three recounts, on second of which Mosley was elected. Chamberlain left this constituency rather than face Mosley in a second fight. Figures: Chamberlain 13,374, Mosley 13,297. Chamberlain majority 77 votes.

Smethwick, 1926.

Mosley was returned for the neighbouring constituency Smethwick at a by-election in which he multiplied Labour majority by five in face of the bitter attacks of the whole Tory press. Figures: Mosley 16,077, Tory, 9,495, Liberal 2,600. A majority for Mosley of 6,582 votes.

Smethwick, 1929.

At the General Election Mosley retained his seat with an increased majority. Mosley 19,550, Tory 12,201, Liberal 3,900, a Mosley majority of 7,349 votes. In this same 1929 election, under Mosley's leadership and inspiration, Labour won six seats in the centre of Birmingham out of the total 12 seats in that City. Mosley thus broke decisively and finally the Chamberlain tradition and machine, which had held Birmingham in their grip for sixty years.[1] Before this 1929 election, which Labour won, Mosley had

---

1   An acknowledgement vide Daily Herald, 18th April, 1931: "The Prime Minister -

appeared as a speaker for the Labour Party all over the country and was usually asked to address the eve-of-poll meetings before important by-elections. He was also the speaker from the political side of the Labour movement elected to address great rallies at such events as the Durham Miners' Gala.

Labour won the 1929 election on a pledge to deal with the unemployment problem and Mosley was one of the ministers then charged with that task. Reference is made to this subject elsewhere in this volume. He resigned when the Labour Party betrayed all its pledges to the unemployed and refused either to adopt the policy which Mosley had proposed for the solution of the problem, or to adopt any alternative plan. At the Labour Party Conference in October 1930 he challenged the government on this issue and was narrowly defeated. For the Mosley resolution 1,046,000, against the resolution 1,251,000. In fact the government would have been defeated except for the late arrival of the miners' leader, A. J. Cook, who would have swung the miners' vote to Mosley.

As it was, the constituency organisations, who did all the work of the Labour Party at the General Election, voted some ten to one in Mosley's favour. It was only the block vote of the big trade unions led by Trade Union leaders like J. H. Thomas and Ernest Bevin who saved the Government.

March, 1931.

Mosley left the Labour Party and founded the New Party.

Stoke, 1931.

Mosley polled over 10,000 votes in face of the Coalition landslide, which was about twenty times the vote polled by any other candidate standing outside the old parties. Figures: Tory 19,913, Labour 13,264, Mosley 10,534.

(Ramsay MacDonald) - entered the Mosley stronghold - Birmingham - last night...."

October, 1932.

After the General Election the New Party was merged with other parties under Mosley's leadership in the fascist movement, which was founded in October 1932 and became known as British Union.

March, 1937.

British Union, owing to shortage of funds, made a habit of fighting local rather than national elections to build up and test its strength. The first big fight was in the London County Council elections of March 1937 where a very remarkable result was obtained. British Union candidates polled 23 percent in Bethnal Green, 19 percent in Limehouse and 14 percent in Shoreditch. The poll was the more remarkable because at that time only householders had the vote. Most of the young people had no vote, including the newly married, because, owing to the housing shortage, they were living with their parents or other people. But the young who had no vote were at that time almost solidly for Mosley and British Union. The vote took place within three years of the Olympia meeting when all East London was placarded with the words "March to Olympia and smash fascism." It was a striking proof that the mass of the people were rapidly swinging to Mosley and British Union when the war came.

After the war—Union Movement

After the war 51 organisations came together under Mosley's leadership to form Union Movement, February 8th, 1948.

L.C.C. *Elections* 1955

The same area was tested in East London, Bethnal Green, Shoreditch and Finsbury and Union Movement obtained an average of 6.2 percent of the vote which was slightly less than a third of the pre-war poll of British Union.

East London Borough Elections, May 1956

Elections were again fought in the same area which showed an increase of 50 percent in Shoreditch and Finsbury as the vote was raised from 6 percent, to 9 percent.

The Ratcliffe Ward of Limehouse was tested for the first time since the war and a vote of 11.7 percent was recorded as against the 19 percent pre-war in this area. So, at the time this book is published, despite all the adversity of the war years, Mosley and Union Movement have regained more than half the position they held in this working class stronghold before the war.

It is clear from the above figures that Mosley had an election winning record in the old parties without equal in our time, and after leaving the old parties secured extraordinary results in face of what was regarded as the impossible. Under the proportional system of the continent he would already have obtained a good parliamentary representation since the war.

Both the system of voting and the enormous expense of elections in Britain are great handicaps to new movements in this country, but for reasons well known to all who have closely studied politics these difficulties can disappear very quickly in a time of real crisis. It is remarkable that the election results just mentioned were obtained in the conditions least suitable for a new movement of a revolutionary programme; relative prosperity before the war, and great prosperity after the war. No great foresight is required to see what can happen if boom turns to crisis. In any case, those who think that test votes, varying between 9 and 11 percent, can safely be ignored, should read a little history before settling down to their customary complacency. In a continental election of modern times, a new movement polled less than a quarter of the votes polled by Mosley's Union Movement in these test votes; it polled 2 percent of the votes recorded. Four years later it was returned to power with a popular vote of 33 percent of the votes recorded; the economic situation had changed in the interval.

The situation can change rapidly in these days, either way. For instance, in January, 1957, a new movement previously regarded as an immediate challenger for power in a neighbouring country, also polled in a crucial bye-election only a fraction of the vote polled by Mosley's movement in these test votes. It had neither the constructive policy nor the solid basis of long and testing struggle which Mosley's movement possesses; consequently it lacked staying power.

The reason that much smaller votes on the Continent than those accorded to Mosley's Union Movement in Britain attract so much attention, is that the proportional system gives Parliamentary representation for these relatively small votes. This is clearly an advantage in the early days. But the British system is an advantage in the later stages; because it enables a new movement more rapidly to obtain a Parliamentary majority. The first rounds are harder, but the later rounds are more decisive. The change can come quicker when the people realise its necessity.

Chapter 13

The Press: Post-War

The press since the war presents an interesting contrast with the press of Mosley's early days. The boycott of the national press began before the war when he ceased to be their favourite and came to be regarded as the enemy of their system. The attitude of the great newspapers was as simple as that. Nothing was too good for him when they thought he was on their side, or too bad for him when they found he was not their man. Apart from occasional fair reports in the *Times* and *Daily Telegraph* the boycott was made complete after the war. For instance, no report appeared in the national press of the two great Trafalgar Square meetings, except some trivial references in the press of the Left which were as untrue as they were silly.

Mosley's best friends before the war were provincial newspapers, because they were in touch with the people and reflected what the people were feeling and thinking. After the war they were the only papers in Britain to give a fair report of his meetings. They are real newspapers, conducted by genuine journalists, who have a tradition of giving a fair account of anything that is news. If they falsify news of a local event, such as a large meeting, so many of their readers would know the facts that their reputation would be damaged. Local journalists are usually honourable people; and public opinion keeps them straight. They are remote from the private interest and vendettas of the press lords, which entirely control the news and opinions of the national press. Can it possibly be denied that Mosley's meetings are news, in a period when other politicians cannot get any meetings at all? News, after all, is the exceptional, and Mosley's meetings are exceptional; they have even more news value now than before the war, when other people could also get meetings, if not such large meetings.

An ex-Minister and television star writing for the largest daily circulation in Great Britain observed during July 1956 that a politician these days was lucky if he had an audience of 30. Can anyone look at the pictures in this book and then deny that Mosley is news? Why, then, is he subject to boycott? The answer is simple; the press lords believe him to be a danger to their interests. It is as simple as that, and as simple as that also for the British people to recognise the man who stands for their interests. This is the reason, and the sole reason, for the contrast in Mosley's treatment by the press when he was in the old parties and his treatment when he opposed the old parties. Readers may study the contrast in this volume, and also some samples of Mosley's speeches in all periods. Any balanced mind will surely feel there is a better reason to report him now than when he was the favourite of the press. The boycott is a matter of vested interest and not of news interest. Such is the present condition of the British national press.

The B.B.C. and television are in no better case; nor independent television. It would certainly appear at first sight, to anyone concerned with news, that a man who could draw Mosley's audiences would be more interesting to the television public than a politician who drew an average audience of 30. Yet it is those who draw the thirties and not the man who draws the thousands who are featured on B.B.C. and I.T.V. When Mosley appears on television it has to be in a country other than his own, where television features those who are news and not merely those who suit the interests of state and finance monopoly. For instance, not long ago a special film of Mosley was made for American television, and was shown over ninety stations, in contrast to the usual sixty which carry English personalities. Again, in August 1956 Mosley did a half hour recorded interview with Professor Milton Mayer for the American university programme, which offers an audience of some ten million people, a series equivalent to the B.B.C. Third Programme. But vested interest is more important than news interest in British television. Television had gone the way of the national press. The interests rule. How long they will rule is a question which this little volume may help the British public to decide.

It is only fair to record an exception to this rule as we go to press. I.T.V., in the Midlands, gave a very fair and full television programme of Mosley's great meeting in the Birmingham Town Hall on October 28, 1956. We hope these enterprising newcomers to television will give a lead to the rest in breaking a boycott which has become absurd to anyone with any sense of news value or of fair service to the public.

Press Reports Since The War
(Mostly local press)
Kilburn Times

"Porchester Hall, Paddington, was packed on Monday night when Sir Oswald Mosley outlined his plan for a 'better Britain.' There were no demonstrations, few interruptions and when Mosley sat down after 90 minutes loud cheers and handclaps came from every row of seats in the hall."

(20:4:1956)

Birmingham Evening Despatch

"...There was only one mild interruption from a packed audience during his 80-minute speech. Otherwise it was applause all the way ..."

(19:3:1956)

Hackney Gazette

"... Sir Oswald Mosley, leader of Union Movement ... made a 90 minute speech in Bethnal Green, on Tuesday night.

. . . people cheered Sir Oswald when he criticised Labour and

Tory M.P.s for putting up a sham in Parliament."

(20:1:1956)

Western Daily Press and Bristol Mirror

"The hall was crowded to the doors for the meeting. The audience included a group of university students who chanted: ' We want Mosley' . . ."

(12:3:1956)

Daily Telegraph

Reporting a meeting addressed by Sir Oswald Mosley at Finsbury Town Hall, the *Daily Telegraph's Man of the World* commented: "But after all these years I thought some of the fizz might have gone out of him. Not a bit of it. Alone, he held a packed proletarian audience - only a few velvet collars - for 75 minutes, pulverising each party in turn.

It may not be difficult these days to make the two main parties look silly; you don't have to have the gift of the gab. But Sir Oswald has it, today no less than in 1933.

It's the money lords, the Press lords who rule England today. King Bank and King Bunk.' Old stuff perhaps, but everyone seemed to enjoy it ."

(19:3:1956)

Birmingham Weekly Post

The *Birmingham Weekly Post* reported that the audience: "... stepped back out of the TV age ... on Sunday night into a heart-warming political meeting of the type thought to have been killed by the screens and channels that now afflict us. Many of them were young, and from their rapt demeanour many have found it a revelation that such entertainment could be possible without the medium of a TV screen. For Sir Oswald Mosley was making his first public speech in Birmingham since the war."

(23:3:1956)

South London Advertiser
(Describing a Mosley meeting at Brixton)

"The audience seemed hypnotised by his act . . . And there he sat, a strangely impressive man, flanked by a Union Jack and the movement's red flag with its black and white flash in the middle."

(31:3:1956)

Cambridge Daily News

The *Cambridge Daily News* reporting a debate referred to the: " ... very different atmosphere from the one that greeted Mosley when he came to speak in Cambridge about two years ago. Then it was trouble, trouble all the way.

"This time ... Sir Oswald ran into more cheers than jeers. Afterwards as Mosley and I talked, we were surrounded by a large crowd of undergraduates listening intently to every word he said."

(2:3:1956)

Western Mail

"... many were impressed, and indeed disturbed by his powers of oratory and the command which he is obviously capable of exercising over an audience."

(23:3:1956)

West London Observer

In reply to a correspondent who had previously complained in the *West London Observer* of political apathy another reader stated : " He should have attended one of Sir Oswald Mosley's

Union Movement meetings. He would have been confronted with undeniable evidence that apathy can be overcome with a forceful and eloquent speaker on the platform.

All of Mosley's meetings were held to packed houses, and the large audience displayed a keen and intelligent interest in the speaker's serious and constructive policy speech. The flood of questions which followed proved that the audiences were greatly impressed."

(11:5:1956)

Kensington News

"Sir Oswald Mosley . . . bitterly attacked the Government's decision to invite Marshal Bulganin and Mr. Kruschev to London, at a packed meeting in Kensington Town Hall on Tuesday. The hall started to fill half an hour before the meeting."

(23:3:1956)

Letter to the *Kensington News*

"The front page notice of Sir Oswald Mosley's meeting offered a welcome contrast to the conspiracy of silence observed by other organs of the Press. This Englishman who has the interest of his native land at heart receives little prominence from the nation's journalists, yet these same journalists, I warrant, will devote pages of eulogistic comments to the visit of the Soviet leaders who can by no stretch of the imagination be said to be concerned with the welfare of Britain."

(30:3:1956)

Kilburn Times

"Mosley Speaks" is the message appearing on hundreds of posters all over Paddington. But the announcement is not restricted to posters on main hoardings. It is also printed on hundreds of small stick-on-anywhere slips of paper. The propaganda campaign for this meeting - in Porchester Hall on Monday - has been noticeably successful.

So successful, in fact, that Sir Oswald Mosley has become the subject of heated argument in many of Paddington's pubs and clubs. It has sparked off a first-class row between Labour and Conservative groups on the borough council ...."

(13:4:1956)

St. Marylebone Record

"Paddington Council's Conservative majority was accused of *political trickery* by the Labour opposition at the council meeting on Thursday because Porchester Hall was let to Sir Oswald Mosley's Union Movement for a meeting on April 16th. Coun. R. W. Almand (Labour) led the complaint that *these filthy scum* should be allowed *to preach dissension*. The Conservative spokesman in reply condemned the attack of *spiteful criticism and a party move to catch a few Jewish votes in the coming election. . . .*"

(3:5:1956)

Letter to *Kilburn Times*

"I was disgusted with the vindictive narrowness of the views expressed by Paddington Labour councillors. To make such unfounded and scandalous charges against Sir Oswald Mosley in the council chamber is cowardly and unworthy of representatives of a democratic system."

(11:5:1956)

Birmingham Gazette

"A Conservative, Coun. A. T. Pugh, will tell Birmingham City Council tonight that it should stop a meeting being held in Corporation property by Sir Oswald Mosley, leader of the new Union Movement.

The Communist Party is also holding a meeting in Corporation property next Sunday, to be addressed by Mr. Harry Pollitt. This meeting is in the Town Hall. Coun. Pugh, however, will direct his attack at the letting to the Union Movement because, he said last night, *they are far more dangerous than the Communists.*"

(13:3:1956)

Letter to *Birmingham Gazette*

"As reported elsewhere in your columns, Mosley spoke to a crowded audience, and the 'applause all the way apart from one mild interruption' proved, at least to this large gathering, that the voice of Mosley was anything but 'forlorn.'"

(22:3:1956)

Trinity International Society, Cambridge.

"Sir Oswald Mosley has been invited to speak not because we believe in his Union Movement, but for two other reasons. We want to give undergraduates the chance to hear arguments against communism put by its most violent opponent, and because he is probably the finest public speaker in Britain."

G. Perry, Press Secretary,

(23:2:1956)

Varsity

Reporting the proposed visit of Sir Oswald Mosley to Cambridge University to oppose the motion "That this House welcomes Marshal Bulganin and Mr. Kruschev" the university newspaper, *Varsity*, in its issue of the 25th February, 1956, stated: "Nothing of this will be reported in the National Press. For some years all newspapers - save *The Times* - have kept a discreet silence about Sir Oswald's activities. Perhaps for the rest of the country, this is the right attitude.

But Cambridge should be able to think for itself. And just what DOES Cambridge think?"

Varsity then published the following comments: "I'm looking forward to debating against him ...I am expecting a powerful performance .... if we lose, it will probably be due to the emotional effect of Mosley's oratory." Gordon Slynn, *President* of *the University Law Society.*

"I welcome this visit . . . although I would rarely have agreed with him in the past and seldom do now, I respect Mosley's honesty and sincerity." Bob Parsons, Chairman of the University Conservative Association

Kensington News

"All who have ever listened to Sir Oswald Mosley are unanimous in agreement on his mastery of the art of oratory. Moreover, he impresses by his obvious sincerity and perfect grasp of all quotations.

Whenever he speaks, Mosley is assured of an enthusiastic full capacity meeting . . .

For 24 years, Mosley has fought for the small man. The political adventurers who are trying to steal the limelight on behalf of the overburdened ratepayer and small business man are mere opportunists hoping to make hay while the sun sinks.

Mosley's record on the other hand, shows that he has championed the cause of the small man consistently over many years. What is even more important, he has a definite and constructive policy for dealing with the situation."

(16:3:56)

Manchester City News

"Sir Oswald Mosley is not dead, nor is he lying down . . . In fact he is the leader of Union Movement, which sets itself up as an alternative to Labour and Tory faiths with a policy which can save Britain and the people."

"... Union Movement asked the middle class to come into a national revolution. Everyone associated with them became a serious person. They were not a bubble - they had been at it for years."

(2:3:1956)

Birmingham Gazette

"Sir Oswald, looking fit . . . was greeted by loud applause when he talked about his old days in Birmingham."

(19:1:1956)

Letter to West London Observer

"Opponents make use of the term 'dictatorship' in their efforts to discredit Mosley and his policy. His desire is to give to the people real liberty to enjoy the wealth that modern science has enabled them to produce, and to participate in the corporate structure of a resurgent and vital European nation."

(19:1:1956)

Portsmouth and Sunderland Newspapers Group

"This brilliant man, who could have played within the rules and become a famous statesman, now beats the air."

(10:7:1956)

The governing sentence is, of course, *played within the rules.*

From "Diary" by Ian Mackay
News Chronicle

"It was only a mile or two along this coast, a few years before the war, that I saw a mighty throng of cheering socialists leap to their feet in the Llandudno Pavilion with enchantment in their adoring eyes and almost worship a new revolutionary Messiah . . .. that was Mosley."

(23:5:1947)

Mosley kept faith with the people who trusted him. He fought through every adversity of fate, against every blow of his foes, to keep faith with the people of Britain. No man in modern times has ever endured a greater test of character. That proved character added to the universal acknowledgment of his abilities which these pages have shown, make him the man who can greatly serve Britain and Europe when our people too face the final test. We shall one day need a man.

Pre-War Publications

Mosley's Post-War Publications

My Answer	(August, 1946)
The Alternative	(October, 1947)
The Third Force	(March, 1950)
Mosley: Policy and Debate	(December, 1955)
Problem of Power: Government of Tomorrow	(December, 1955)
Automation: Problem & Solution	(January, 1956)
European Socialism	(August, 1956)
Wagner and Shaw	(August, 1956)

www.ingramcontent.com/pod-product-compliance
Lightning Source LLC
Chambersburg PA
CBHW070550270326
41926CB00013B/2262